INFINITE RESIGNATION

EUGENE THACKER

INFINITE RESIGNATION

EUGENE THACKER

Published by Repeater Books
An imprint of Watkins Media Ltd

19-21 Cecil Court
London
WC2N 4EZ
UK
www.repeaterbooks.com
A Repeater Books paperback original 2018
1

Distributed in the United States by Random House, Inc., New York.

Cover design: Prema Murthy
Typography and typesetting: Stuart Davies
Typefaces: Palatino

Printed and bound in the United Kingdom

ISBN: 9781912248193
Ebook ISBN: 9781912248209

Contents

A Sort of Preface. By definition, there can be no hope for a book like this – its very existence is dubious. If all is for naught, then why bother writing it down? Caught in a vicious circle, ensnared in the logical absurdities of awkward self-awareness.

It seems there are one of two options: either speak to this situation, or remain silent. The writer's failure is that they know they should choose the latter, but cannot help attempting the former. Writers (and readers... when there are readers...) console themselves by naming this failure: an apology, a confession, a testimony, a treatise, a history, a biography, a life. But the continual accumulation of that-which-cannot-be-put-into-words always points back to this one basic realization – that, when it comes to human beings, silence is the most adequate form of expression.

There are, then, two paths. Ultimately writers dream of taking neither path, leaving all paths for the forest. But it's just a dream.

ON PESSIMISM

~ * ~

A philosophy exists between the axiom and the sigh. Pessimism is the wavering, the hovering.

~ * ~

Whenever it occurs, however it occurs, pessimism has but one effect: it introduces humility into thought. It undermines the innumerable, self-aggrandizing postures that constitute the human being. Pessimism is the humility of the species that has named itself, thought furtively stumbling upon its own limitations on black wings of futility. (And is this helpful...?)

~ * ~

Pessimism is the night-side of thought, a melodrama of the futility of the brain, a lyricism written in the graveyard of philosophy. No one ever needs pessimism, in the way that one needs optimism, for instance, to inspire one to great heights and pick oneself up, in the way one needs constructive criticism, advice and feedback, inspirational books or just a pat on the back (though I like to imagine the idea of pessimism as self-help). Pessimism is a philosophically untenable position. No self-respecting philosopher would ever describe themselves as a pessimist – it's more of an indictment than a philosophy. Yet, without exception, everyone has, at

3

some point in their lives, had to confront pessimism, if not as a philosophy then as a grievance – against one's self or against others, against one's life or one's circumstances, against the state of affairs or against the world in general.

The closest pessimism comes to philosophical argument is the droll and sardonic, "We'll never make it," or simply: "We're doomed." Every effort doomed to failure, every project doomed to incompletion, every thought doomed to be unthought, every life doomed to be unlived.

~ * ~

When solutions produce problems, when thought flounders in the absence of order, unity, and purpose, when healthy skepticism turns into pathological sarcasm – this is usually when pessimism enters the fray. The problem is that when pessimism enters philosophical discussion, it is almost never helpful. In fact, it makes things worse. However, in its unending *miserere*, sometimes something interesting happens: it raises the stakes of the discussion, scaling things up beyond the self-interested level of human beings living in a human world, beyond our wants and desires, beyond our individual or collective self-importance. Besides, we didn't really think we could figure it out, did we? A strange philosophy, then – the most adequate, the least helpful.

~ * ~

Is there any philosophy that is not, in some way, built

up upon disenchantment – and that does not, ultimately, crumble beneath its weight? Disenchantment as
chanting, as a chant, a mantra, a solitary, monophonic
voice rendered insignificant by the intimate immensity
surrounding it.

~ * ~

No one has time for pessimism. After all, there are only
so many hours in the day. Whatever our temperament,
happy or sad, engaged or disengaged, we know pessimism when we hear it. The pessimist is usually understood to be the complainer, forever pointing out what is
wrong with the world without ever offering a solution.
But more often than not pessimists are the most sub-
dued of philosophers, submerging their sighs within
the lethargy of discontent. What little sound they make
is of interest to no one – "I've heard it all before," "tell
me something I don't know," sound and fury, signify-
ing nothing.

~ * ~

Things should be good, I tell myself, but they're, well,
not-so-good. Nothing seems to make sense – and it
should (shouldn't it?). Granted, things weren't exactly
perfect before, but now they're definitely worse (…or
so it seems). And this on top of the simplest of things:
having to live a life.

~ * ~

In presenting problems without solutions, in posing questions without answers, in retreating to the hermetic, cavernous abode of complaint, pessimism is guilty of that most inexcusable of Occidental crimes – the crime of not pretending it's all for a reason. Pessimism fails to live up to the most basic tenet of philosophy – the "as if." Think as if it will be helpful, act as if it will make a difference, speak as if there is something to say, live as if you are not, in fact, being lived by some murmuring non-entity both shadowy and muddied.

~ * ~

The luminous point at which logic becomes contemplation. Lost in thought. Adrift in deep space. Dreamless sleep.

~ * ~

Pessimism has a dubious status, both in everyday life and in the history of philosophy. Usually, pessimism is thought of as opposed to optimism – a negative to a positive, the worst versus the best, the glass half-empty or the glass half-full. In this understanding, the scales of optimism and pessimism are forever tipping back and forth, according to our attitudes, our circumstances, our fortunes and misfortunes. Look in any Dictionary of Philosophy and you will likely find a definition of pessimism, and, in addition to mentioning the nineteenth-century philosopher Arthur Schopenhauer, it will probably provide one of three definitions: "The view that this is the worst of all possible worlds," or "The view that life is not worth living," or even "The view that non-existence is preferable to existence" (usually with the addendum "See also: optimism"). But for me, the definition that best captures pessimism is given by the joke "I see the glass half full, but of poison."

~ * ~

Pessimism tries very hard to present itself in the low, sustained tones of a Requiem Mass, or the tectonic rumbling of a Tibetan chant. But more frequently it lets loose dissonant notes at once plaintive and pathetic. Often, its voice cracks, its weighty words abruptly reduced to mere shards of guttural sound.

~ * ~

If we know pessimism when we hear it, this is because we've heard it all before – and we didn't need to hear it in the first place. Life is hard enough. What you need is a change of attitude, a new outlook, a shift in perspective… a cup of coffee.

If we have no tolerance for pessimism, this is because it sees everything as brimming with negative possibility, the collision of a bad mood with an impassive world. If pessimism is so often dismissed, this is because it is often impossible to separate a "bad mood" from a philosophical proposition (and do not all philosophies stem from a bad mood?).

~ * ~

A Very Very Short History of Philosophy. I've always felt that there are basically two kinds of philosophies: those that begin in wonder and those that begin in despair. The philosophies of wonder marvel at the world; they are drawn to its shimmering presence, and are driven by curiosity, which euphorically leans towards knowledge. By contrast, the philosophies of despair recoil from the world; they are at once perplexed by and weary of its ephemeral and fragile contours. They are driven by a doubt that gives way to a still greater doubt, until almost nothing is left. The philosophies of wonder embrace the world; the philosophies of despair are suspicious of it.

It would be tempting to describe philosophies of wonder as "optimistic" and philosophies of despair as "pessimistic", were it not for the enthusiasm of the latter.

~ * ~

The very term "pessimism" suggests a school of thought, a movement, even a community. But pessimism always has a membership of one – maybe two (one of them imaginary). Ideally, of course, it would have a membership of none, with only a scribbled, illegible note left behind in some long-forgotten forest.

~ * ~

There are so many things that are possible, and so few things that are necessary. Sadly, the latter rarely overlap with the former.

~ * ~

People often presume that the saying "hope for the best and expect the worst" is pessimistic, but it's not. It's simply optimism through the back door. The best you can hope for is the worst.

~ * ~

Anatomy of Pessimism. Pessimism's two major keys are moral and metaphysical pessimism, its subjective and objective poles, an attitude towards the world and a claim about the world. For the moral pessimist, it is better not to have been born at all; for the metaphysical pessimist this is the worst of all possible worlds. For moral pessimism, the problem is the solipsism of human beings, the world made in our own suffocating image, a world-for-us. For metaphysical pessimism, the problem is the solipsism of the world, closed off and opaque, objected and projected as a world-in-itself. But both moral and metaphysical pessimism are compromised philosophically; they are cut short by their failure to locate human beings within a larger non-human world.

A stark musicality of thought, a headlong flight towards a horizon whose only promise is that all will be for naught, a generalized misanthropy without the *anthropos*. Pessimism crystallizes around this futility–

~ * ~

Kierkegaard once described the religious life as caught

between two states, which he characterized through the symbolic figures of the "knight of faith" and the "knight of infinite resignation." Faith is, for Kierkegaard, beyond all reason, and resignation our inability to accept or comprehend this. Though one may strive for faith, there is a sense that one is always destined for resignation (just as every "leap," no matter how high, must eventually fall).

Though he wasn't aware of it, Kierkegaard had outlined the arc of pessimist thinking. Between resignation and tranquility there is the smallest interval. Pessimism resides in that fissure.

~ * ~

Melancholy of Anatomy. The logic of pessimism moves through three refusals: saying no to the world as it is (or, Schopenhauer's tears); saying yes to the world as it is (or, Nietzsche's laughter); and refusing to say either "yes" or "no" (or, Cioran's sleep).

Crying, laughing, sleeping – what other responses are adequate to a world that seems so indifferent?

~ * ~

Cosmic Pessimism. Beyond moral pessimism and metaphysical pessimism this is another kind, a pessimism that is neither subjective nor objective, that is neither about the world-for-us nor about the world-in-itself. A pessimism of the world-without-us. I could call this a *cosmic pessimism*... but this sounds too majestic, too full of wonder, too much the bitter aftertaste of the

Great Beyond. Words falter. As does thought. And so we are left with a weakened pessimism, a pessimism that is first and last about *cosmos*, a suspicion towards the necessity and possibility of order. This pessimism entails a drastic scaling-up or scaling-down of the human point of view, the disorientation of deep space and deep time, all of this shadowed by an impasse, a primordial insignificance, the impossibility of ever adequately accounting for one's happenstance existence – all that remains is the desiderata of impersonal affects – agonistic, impassive, defiant, reclusive, filled with sorrow and flailing at that architectonic chess match called philosophy, a flailing that pessimism tries to raise to the level of an art (though what usually results is slapstick).

~ * ~

…how to avoid writing *about* pessimism…

~ * ~

Song of Futility. Failure is a breakage within the heart of relations, a fissure between cause and effect, a fissure hastily covered over by trying and trying again. With failure, there is always plenty of blame to go around; it's not my fault, it's a technical difficulty, it's a miscommunication.

For the pessimist, failure is a question of "when," not "if" – everything withers and passes into an obscurity blacker than night, everything from the melodramatic decline of a person's life to the banal flickering moments that constitute each day. Everything that is done undone, everything said or known destined for a kind of stellar oblivion.

When taken to its logical conclusion, failure becomes fatality. Fatality is the hermeticism of cause and effect. In fatality, everything you do, whatever you do, always leads to a certain end, and ultimately to *the* end – though that end, or the means to that end, remain shrouded in obscurity. By having a goal, planning ahead, and thinking things through carefully, we attempt, in a daily Prometheanism, to turn fatality to our advantage, to obtain a glimpse into an order that seems buried deeper and deeper within the fabric of the universe.

Futility is different from fatality, and different again from simple failure (though failure is never simple). The chain of cause and effect may be hidden from us, but that's just because disorder is the order we don't yet see; it's just complex, distributed, and requires advanced mathematics. Fatality still clings to the sufficiency of everything that exists… When fatality relinquishes even this idea, it becomes futility. Futility arises out of the grim suspicion that, behind the shroud of causality we drape over the world, there is only the indifference of what exists or what doesn't exist; sense and non-sense eclipse each other, and whatever you do ultimately leads to an irrevocable chasm between thought and world. Futility transforms the act of thinking into a zero-sum game.

~ * ~

Song of the Worst. At the center of pessimism lies the

term *pessimus*, "the worst," a term as relative as it is absolute. The worst is about as bad as it gets, the façade of "the best" shrouded by the passage of time or the twists and turns of fortune. For the pessimist, the worst is the propensity for suffering that gradually occludes each living moment, until it eclipses it entirely, overlapping perfectly in death (…which, for the pessimist, is no longer the worst).

"The worst" implies a value judgment, one made based on scant evidence and little experience. Perhaps this is why the true optimists are the most severe pessimists – they are optimists that have run out of options. They are almost ecstatically inundated by the worst. Nietzsche once called it a "pessimism of joy."

It seems that sooner or later we are all doomed to become optimists of this sort.

~ * ~

Song of Gloom, Song of Doom. Doom is not just the sense that all things will turn out badly, but that all things inevitably come to an end, irrespective of whether or not they really do come to an end. What emerges from doom is a sense of the non-human world as an attractor, a horizon towards which the human is fatally drawn. Doom is humanity given over to unhumanity in an act of self-abnegation.

Gloom is atmospheric, climate as much as impression, and if people are also gloomy, this is simply the by-product of an anodyne atmosphere that only incidentally involves human beings. Gloom is more climatological than psychological, the stuff of dim, hazy, overcast skies, of ruins and overgrown cemeteries, of a misty, lethargic fog that moves with the same languorousness as our own, crouched and sullen listening to a disinterested world.

Gloom is the counterpoint to doom – what futility is to the former, fatality is to the latter. Doom is marked by temporality – all things precariously drawn to their end – whereas gloom is the austerity of stillness, all things sad, static, and suspended, a meandering smoke hovering over cold lichen stones and damp fir trees.

Gloom and doom are the mortification of philosophy. I like to imagine that this realization alone is the thread that connects the charnel-ground Aghori with the poets of the Graveyard School.

~ * ~

Song of Spite. There is an intolerance in pessimism that knows no bounds. In pessimism, spite begins by fixing on a particular object – someone one hardly knows or someone one knows too well; a spite for this person or a spite for all of humanity; a spectacular or a banal spite; a spite for a noisy neighbor, a yapping dog, a battalion of strollers, the meandering idiot on their phone walking in front of you, large loud celebrations, traumatic injustices anywhere in the world regurgitated as media circus, spite for the self-absorbed and self-conscious people talking way too loud at the next table, technical difficulties and troubleshooting, the reduction of everything to vanity, spite of the refusal to admit one's own errors, of self-help books, of people who know absolutely everything and make sure to tell you, of all

14

people, all living beings, all things, the world, the spiteful planet, the inanity of existence…

Spite is the motor of pessimism because it is so egalitarian; it runs amok, stumbling across intuitions that can only half-heartedly be called philosophical. Spite lacks the confidence and the clarity of hatred, but it also lacks the almost cordial judgment of dislike. For the pessimist, the smallest detail can be an indication of a metaphysical futility so vast and funereal that it eclipses pessimism itself – a spite that pessimism carefully places beyond the horizon of intelligibility, like the experience of dusk, or like the phrase "it is raining jewels and daggers."

~ * ~

Song of Sorrow. Nietzsche once castigated Schopenhauer for not being pessimistic enough. He writes: "Schopenhauer, though a pessimist, *really* – played the flute. Every day, after dinner: one should read his biography on that. And incidentally: a pessimist, one who denies God and the world but *comes to a stop* before morality – who affirms morality and plays the flute… what? Is that really – a pessimist?"

We know that Schopenhauer did possess a collection of musical instruments, and we also know that Nietzsche himself composed music. But for the pessimist who says no to everything and yet finds comfort in music, the no-saying of pessimism can only be a weak way of saying yes – the weightiest accusation undercut by the flightiest of replies. The least that Schopenhauer could've done is to play the bass.

I'm not a big fan of the flute, or, for that matter, wind instruments generally. But what Nietzsche doesn't mention is the role that the flute has historically played in Greek tragedy. In tragedy, the flute (*aulos*) is not an instrument of levity and joy, but of solitude and sorrow. The Greek *aulos* not only expresses the grief of tragic loss, but it does so in a way that renders weeping and singing inseparable from each other. Scholars of Greek tragedy refer to this as the "mourning voice." Set apart from the more official civic rituals of funerary mourning, the mourning voice of Greek tragedy constantly threatens to dissolve song into wailing, music into moaning, and the voice into a primordial, disarticulate anti-music. The mourning voice delineates all the forms of suffering – tears, weeping, sobbing, wailing, moaning, and the convulsions of thought reduced to an elemental unintelligibility.

Have we rescued Schopenhauer from Nietzsche? Probably not. Perhaps Schopenhauer played the flute to remind himself of the real function of the mourning voice – sorrow and sighs rendered indistinguishable from music, the crumbling of the human into the unhuman.

~ * ~

Song of Horror. One of Kierkegaard's greatest intuitions was to comprehend the horror specific to religious experience. In his retelling of the Biblical parable of Abraham and Isaac, Kierkegaard focuses not on the heroic sacrifice Abraham is willing to make, but on everything that precedes this decision. In fact, the conclusion of the parable is the most uninteresting part –

a *deus ex machina* if ever there was one. What interests Kierkegaard is Abraham's inability to decide, to act, and to believe. Abraham is ordered to kill his son in the name of a cruel god, but there is no *reason* to do this, not even the reason of faith. Abraham is no tragic hero, sacrificing his son for the greater good of his people; he is bewildered, confused, and terrified of an unhuman, sovereign order utterly alien to the human world of family, community, and the habitual gestures that pass for religion. For Abraham, there is no decision to make, just as there is no meaning in his decision, no reward or punishment: "he suffers all the pain of the tragic hero, he brings to naught his joy in the world, he renounces everything…" For Kierkegaard this is the key moment, this dark night of distress and dereliction – not because it serves as the path to an affirmation of faith, but because it renders faith improbable, irrelevant, insignificant.

Kierkegaard arrives at this conclusion not by leaps and bounds, but, like any good philosopher, by steps. There is the horror of contradiction in Abraham's inability to decide and act (religious law forbids the killing of my son and yet God commands it); there is the horror of the irrelevance of any decision (whatever I do, I am doing harm and committing sacrilege); the horror of impassivity, feeling like a puppet ensnared within the labyrinths of political theology (any action I make is already ordained within a divine order hidden from me); and finally the horror of insignificance, on both a psychological and a cosmological level, the insignificance of human action vis-à-vis an essentially unknowable divine order.

None of this can be sustained by Abraham, or by any of us; we cannot live in this contradiction, this irrelevance, this cosmic insignificance. And so, in the end, God intervenes, Abraham is saved, and the story takes on the distasteful moral connotations it has had to this day. But Abraham's horror does not disappear. Thus Kierkegaard can say, "though Abraham arouses my admiration, he at the same time appalls me." That Abraham is irrevocably lost, inextricably enmired in this cosmic horror, gives his experience a religious quality, but one that refuses any religion: "One cannot weep over Abraham. One approaches him with a *horror religiosus*..."

~ * ~

Song of Nothing. In Buddhist thought, the First Noble Truth is encapsulated in the Pāli term *dukkha*, conventionally translated as "suffering," "sorrow," or "misery." The texts of the Pāli Canon also contain lists of the different types of happiness – including the "happiness of renunciation" and the strange "happiness of detachment." But Buddhism considers even the different types of happiness as part of *dukkha*, in that they themselves are fleeting and ephemeral.

It is likely that Schopenhauer, reading the Buddhist texts available to him, recognized some filiation with the concept of *dukkha*. But this is a multi-faceted term. There is, certainly, *dukkha* in the usual sense of the suffering and strife associated with living a life. But this is, in turn, dependent on finitude and temporality, existence as determined by impermanence and imper-

18

fection. Beyond what is worse to me, beyond a world ordered for the worst, there is a kind of impersonal suffering... the tears of the cosmos.

Perhaps Schopenhauer understood Buddhism better than even he was aware of. Though one thing for certain is that with Schopenhauer we do not find the enigmatic, "ever-smiling" countenance of the Buddha – or do we?

~ * ~

Emil Cioran once called music a "physics of tears." If this is true, then perhaps metaphysics is its commentary. Or its apology.

~ * ~

Black holes, dark matter, warped spacetime, strings and bosons... Ironically, metaphysics has been superseded by physics. The cosmos is even more indifferent than we initially thought (and more indifferent *to* thought as well).

~ * ~

We are mistaken if we think that the spite of someone or something necessarily implies the desire for its non-existence. Leopardi: "True misanthropes are not found in isolation but among people, for it is practical experience in life, not philosophy, that makes us hate." And so, strangely, the love of solitude entails the hatred of misanthropy. "And if such a person withdraws from society, in withdrawing he gives up his misanthropy."

~ * ~

Pessimism would be more lofty were it not for its defeatism. There is a sense in which pessimists are really failed mystics.

~ * ~

A Bad Mood (I). Pessimism always falls short of being philosophical. My back aches, my knees hurt, I couldn't sleep last night, I'm stressed out, and I think I'm finally coming down with something. Pessimism abjures all pretenses towards system – towards the purity of analysis and the dignity of critique. We didn't really think we could figure it out, did we? It was just passing time, something to do, a bold gesture put forth in all its fragility, according to rules that we have agreed to forget that we made up in the first place. Every thought marked by a shadowy incomprehension that precedes it, and a futility that undermines it. That pessimism speaks, in whatever voice, is the singing testimony to this futility and this incomprehension – "take a chance and step outside, lose some sleep and say you tried..."

~ * ~

You, the Night, and the Music. In a suggestive passage, Schopenhauer once noted that "music is the melody to which the world is the text."

Given Schopenhauer's view on life – that life is suffering, that human life is absurd, that the nothingness before my birth is equal to the nothingness after my death – given all this, I've always wondered what kind of music Schopenhauer had in mind when he described music as the melody to which the world is text – was it opera, a Requiem Mass, a madrigal, or perhaps a drinking song? Or something like *Eine kleine Nachtmusik*, a little night music for the twilight of thought, a sullen *nocturne* for the night-side of logic, an era of sad wings sung by a solitary banshee.

Perhaps the music Schopenhauer had in mind is music distilled to the point of non-music. A whisper would suffice. Perhaps a sigh of fatigue or resignation, perhaps a moan of despair or sorrow. Perhaps a sound just articulate enough that it could be heard to dissipate.

~ * ~

Teach me to laugh through tears.

~ * ~

There's a ghost that grows inside of me, damaged in the making. A hunt sprung from necessity, elliptical and drowned. Where the moving quiet of our insomnia offers up each thought, there's a luminous field of grey inertia, and obsidian dreams burnt all the way down.

~ * ~

After a long day, I lay down to sleep. Next to me, P

casually says, "The best thing about the day is that it ends…"

~ * ~

My favorite scenes from Voltaire's *Candide* come when the know-it-all Pangloss attempts to teach the naive – though increasingly suspicious – Candide, that this is the best of all possible worlds. After experiencing misfortune upon misfortune, Candide innocently asks: "If this is the best of all possible worlds, what must the others be like?"

~ * ~

Friday, 1:55pm. I am sitting at a corner table at Caffe Dante. It's cold and raining outside. In front of me are an espresso, a small glass of water, my phone, and this notebook in which I'm writing. The café is quiet and nearly empty, except for an old man reading the newspaper and a young couple, probably students. From time to time I overhear the clanking of cups and dishes, as well as the faint murmur of whatever the radio station is playing. The café has a "no laptop rule," which a faded, hand-written sign posted on the window announces to the sidewalk. People, bicycles, and cars casually pass on MacDougal Street outside. I've just eaten lunch at home, and the espresso is strangely good today. I wish I could just sit here with my notebook and coffee – a notebook that never runs out of paper and an espresso that is perpetually piping hot. But you know the rest. I've been so eager for these moments that it doesn't occur to me I might also *enjoy* them. I stop, I realize not only that I treasure this moment, but that this realization is such a cliché that I begin to be repulsed by it. Must write this down... and then what? The time passes – you can feel it without looking at a clock. The light outside changes, the lights inside brighten, people begin to hurry and honk, I remember I have to go to the grocery, the pharmacy, respond to emails, and so on. I think my back is starting to hurt again.

~ * ~

The Incorruptibles. Theologians often talk about the incorruptibility of the corpses of saints, corpses touched by divine intervention and miraculously impervious to the temporal processes of decay. The corpses of mystics such as Catherine of Genoa, John of the Cross, and Teresa of Avila are counted among the Incorruptibles of the Catholic Church. By contrast, I would like to be absolutely corruptible – nothing of my body would remain, not even hair or fingernails or the notebook in which I'm writing. Finally all words and memories would evaporate, leaving not even an echo or resonance. It's fantastical, I know – but no less fantastical than the Incorruptibles.

~ * ~

I never tire of re-reading *Notes from Underground*. It's one of the great anti-novels. In it Dostoevsky dispensed with the unending, nauseating, Byzantine entanglements of grotesque human vanity that seem to characterize many "big books" – in *Notes* he subtracted plot, character, even motive, and all that was left was the detritus of a confused observer failing to make sense of an even more confused cluster of events. I found – and find – that totally compelling.

I love the opening, the way Dostoevsky immediately sets a tone at once poetic and ridiculous, philosophical and mundane, melodrama and slapstick: "I am a sick man... I am a wicked man. An unattractive man. I think my liver hurts..." When I first read it as a student, I was instantly taken by the first part of the book, with its interior monologue, abstract ideas, and rigorous introspection. Now I have a greater fondness for the book's second part, which is almost entirely lacking in philosophical discussion and instead recounts mundane events that take on absurdly profound meanings – a simple walk in the park and the secret animosities that lay buried therein; social gatherings and the performative display of egos; a gesture of help that turns oneself into a hypocritical know-it-all.

Still, there are passages in the first, "philosophical" part of the book that still resonate with me: "...the pleasure here lay precisely in the too vivid consciousness of one's own humiliation; in feeling that one had reached the ultimate wall; that, bad as it is, it cannot be otherwise; that there is no way out for you, that you will never change into a different person; that even if you had enough time and faith left to change yourself into something different, you probably would not wish to change; and even if you did wish it, you would still not do anything, because in fact there is perhaps nothing to change into."

~ * ~

The weary balancing scales of optimism and pessimism – which requires reasons, which requires faith?

~ * ~

Two kinds of pessimism: "The end is near" and "Will this never end?"

~ * ~

Fernando Pessoa's *Book of Disquiet* is one of the most profoundly unfinished books I know of. It is a book that seems designed so as to ensure its failure to become a book. The manuscript was discovered posthumously in a trunk left in Pessoa's apartment, in which there were hundreds of papers, some bound and some loose-leaf, some typed and some hand-written, some dated and some not; Portuguese, French, English, and various translations; notebooks, stationary, envelopes, advertisements; prose, poetry, philosophy, literary criticism, manifestoes, plays, journalism, even astrology charts. The texts span a lifetime. (On top of it all, the entire book, we are told, is really the manuscript of a Bernardo Soares, an unknown assistant bookkeeper in Lisbon, whom Pessoa happened to meet one evening by chance.)

None of this is any surprise, given some of the themes that inhabit the *Book of Disquiet*: tedium, futility, refusal, sorrow, estrangement, weariness, doubt. There is no narrative per se, only a series of fragments, some of which intersect with each other, others which stand alone or apart from the others, all held together by a tenuous and nimble poetics that is neither quite literature nor quite philosophy.

One of the fragments nicely exemplifies both the logic and the pathos of pessimism: "Metaphysical theories can give us the momentary illusion that we've explained the unexplainable; moral theories that can fool us for an hour into thinking we finally know which of all the closed doors leads to virtue; political theories that convince us for a day that we've solved some problem, when there are no solvable problems except in mathematics... May our attitude towards life be summed up in this consciously futile activity, in this preoccupation that gives us no pleasure but at least keeps us from feeling the presence of pain."

The fragment concludes: "There's no better sign that a civilization has reached its height than the awareness, in its members, of the futility of all effort, given that we're ruled by implacable laws, which nothing can repeal or obstruct."

~ * ~

Pessimism is the introduction of humility into thought. But how to distinguish humility from futility?

~ * ~

The impact of music on a person compels them to put their experience into words. When this fails, the result is a faltering of thought that is itself a kind of music.

~ * ~

…luminescent arcs of confusion, hovering somewhere over the low aquatic floors of brittle stars…

~ * ~

If a thinker like Schopenhauer has any redeeming qualities, it is that he identified the great lie of Western culture – the preference for existence over non-existence. As he notes, "at the end of his life, no one, if he be sincere and at the same time in possession of his faculties, will ever wish to go through it again. Rather than this, he will much prefer to choose completely non-existence." And what goes for the living also goes for the dead: "If we knocked on the graves and asked the dead whether they would like to rise again, they would shake their heads."

In Western cultures it is commonly accepted that one celebrates birth and mourns death. But there must be a mistake here. Wouldn't it make more sense to mourn birth and celebrate death? Strange though, because the mourning of birth would, presumably, last the entirety of that person's life, so that mourning and living would be the same thing.

~ * ~

Pessimism's propositions have all the *gravitas* of a bad joke.

~ * ~

Most pessimists are pessimists not by philosophical training but by accident.

~ * ~

I often feel that "philosophy" is simply a long, tedious, testament of human hubris... I envy the philosopher who is able to confidently claim that philosophy is the pinnacle of human consciousness, or the height of human cognition, or that by which we ensure the nobility of critique. Not for me. Philosophy is always reducible to three things: a therapeutic function (to make us feel better, smarter, or wiser), an explanatory function (this is how the world works, its laws and variables), and a hermeneutic function (aha! so *that's* why things are the way they are). Philosophy as reducible to self-help, a guide to better living, and a map of the world made in our own image. Claustrophobia.

~ * ~

Voltaire once described optimism as "a cruel philosophy with a consoling name," which immediately suggests what pessimism might be: a consoling philosophy with a cruel name.

~ * ~

Cioran: "There is no limit-disappointment."

~ * ~

The Forgotten Histories of Pessimism. In the history of Western philosophy, the term "optimism" was the subject of debate far before the term "pessimism." This should give us pause, for it reflects as much on philosophy itself and the philosophical enterprise as it does on pessimism, that gloomy late-comer to the banquet of philosophy.

Nevertheless, in the late nineteenth century, pessimism suddenly became the subject of innumerable books, essays, and lectures, frequently reaching beyond the elite cloisters of the university. In 1877, the British psychologist James Sully published *Pessimism: A History and A Criticism*, a massive, six-hundred-page analysis of pessimism, in both its "reasoned" (that is, philosophical) and "unreasoned" (that is, poetic or artistic) manifestations. What made Sully's volume unique was not the stance he took on pessimism (he considered it an illness), but that he consciously placed pessimism within a historical context; instead of asking whether or not pessimism was right, he asked how one should place pessimism within the history of philosophy as a whole.

But how should one write a history of a philosophy that, at every turn, mitigates against philosophy itself? Sully takes great pains to resolve this dilemma, as in this, one of his many textbook-like definitions: "By optimism and pessimism we must mean, therefore, the hypotheses that the world is on the whole good, or conducive to happiness, and so better than non-existence, and that the world is on the whole bad, or productive of misery, and so worse than non-existence."

Such clear-cut distinctions allow Sully to erect a history of pessimism, stretching back to its "crude forms" in the Old Testament, in Greek and Roman antiquity, in Persian mythology, and in Indian philosophy. Sully also includes, in his cacophony of nay-sayers, Greek Skeptics, Epicureans, and Stoics; the Church Fathers and desert hermits; modern rationalists, empiricists, and idealists; Enlightenment thinkers and Romantic poets; Hume, Kant, and of course Schopenhauer. Eventually, his list includes nearly everyone – Sully ends up providing less of a history of pessimism and more a re-casting of world philosophy *en masse* as pessimistic. Perhaps this was intentional. Whatever the case, the ambitious scope of Sully's book is evident from early on, where he seems uncertain as to whether "pessimism" describes anything at all: "We do not think of them [pessimists] as a school adopting certain first principles in common, but rather as a peculiar make of person characterized by a kind of constituted leaning to a gloomy view of the world and its affairs."

Sully was not the first to attempt a history of pessimism. For instance, in 1855, the *Encyclopedia Britannica* included an entry on pessimism, written by William Wallace (also the author of *The Life of Schopenhauer*). Edmund Pfleideror's *Modern Pessimism* (1875), Agnes Taubert's *Pessimism and Its Opponents* (1873), and Olga Plümacher's *Pessimism in the Past and Present* (1883) each take pessimism to be a contemporary phenomenon, rooted in the legacy of German philosophy in the wake of Kant and German Romanticism. Others take a more expansive, European view, as in Elme-Marie Caro's study *Pessimism in the 19th Century* (1880), and Francis Bowman's overview *Modern Philosophy from*

Descartes to Schopenhauer and Hartmann (1877), giving us perspectives from France and England, respectively.

Caro introduces his book with a chapter on "Pessimism in History," tracing the pessimistic tendency back to ancient Greek tragedy, the Buddhist sutras, and the *Upanishads*. This was a strategy that would allow Caro to, later on in the book, describe Schopenhauer's philosophy as a "modern Buddhism." It also gave Caro the opportunity to tie pessimism back to its ancient cosmological roots, and to draw out the dark implications of a modern-day, "cosmic suicide." Similar approaches can be found in *The Philosophy of Disenchantment* (1885), by the American author Edgar Saltus, and in *Aspects of Pessimism* (1894), by the Scottish philosopher R.M. Wenley. Even Hartmann himself, who, for a brief moment, seemed to be the official spokesperson for pessimism, wrote *Towards a History and Foundation of Pessimism* (1880). All these works, however, seemed split on the question of pessimism's history: was it a brief experiment in morbid, melancholy, nineteenth-century German philosophy, or was it a universal tendency in *all* philosophy, ancient or modern, Eastern or Western?

In spite of their different approaches, what all these works agreed on was the dubious status of pessimism within the history of philosophy. Sully, for his part, minced no words, noting that "the metaphysical portico, so to speak, of this dark and gloomy edifice was found, after a slight inspection, to contain numerous cracks and flaws." Pessimism, he concludes, is "built of nothing but purely fanciful hypotheses which involve incoherent and self-contradictory conceptions." One tells the history of pessimist philosophy at the cost of discovering its quasi-philosophical status. Sully again: "...the psychology of pessimism, when its tangle of unexamined ideas is unraveled, shows itself to be radically erroneous."

"Radically erroneous." Perhaps even the pessimist would take this as a point of pride.

~ * ~

The ultimatum is the core of pessimist thinking. It is, for pessimism, a way of pushing thought to ultimately laughable conclusions. "When all is said and done, when it comes down to it, when push comes to shove, I mean really, basically"... These are the axioms of pessimism, axioms that reach their own ultimatum in reducing pessimism itself to nonsense. When I say that, basically, when all is said and done, philosophy is just people with degrees and professorships playing a Byzantine game of logic whose rules they've made up, and ceremoniously presenting it between the covers of large imposing tomes with titles of the type *X and Y* (*Being and Time, Process and Reality, Truth and Method, Difference and Repetition, Being and Event,* and so on) – when I say this, with little experience and less proof, with equal parts gaiety and gravity, it is made possible by the ultimatum, a purely phantasmic form of logic that pessimism covets, as one does the objects that make up a shrine – or as one covets a really good joke.

~ * ~

"Life is then given out as a gift, whereas it is evident

that anyone would have declined it with thanks, had he looked at it and tested it beforehand..." (Schopenhauer).

~ * ~

Nietzsche once noted that there were two types of pessimists – those that suffer from an impoverishment of life, and those that suffer from an excess of life. For the former, life outstrips my ability to embrace it; for the latter, the reverse is the case – my capacity to embrace life outstrips my ability to live it. In a sense, in neither situation do I actually live – instead, I suffer (too much life, not enough life). Thus suffering is the consolation for not having lived, and pessimism becomes a strange form of solace. A few, however, are more fortunate, wishing that they could leave the game of suffering altogether, for the more remote and perhaps more intelligible shores of stillness and silence.

~ * ~

Pessimism is the quietism of logic, a half-reasoned cry into a night space so vast and indifferent that no sound is made.

~ * ~

The Philosophy of Decomposition. Schopenhauer's two major works – *The World as Will and Representation* (1818) and *Parerga and Paralipomena* (1851) – are massive tomes of Germanic philosophy that go on for pages and pages about how it is preferable not to exist. Schopenhauer even added sections to *The World as Will and Representation*, doubling its size by the third edition in 1859. His omnivorous philosophy enlists the aid of idealism (the world as unreal, as representation, as the "veil of Maya"), atheism (the world as anonymous, indifferent "Will"), materialism ("my body and the Will are the same"), mysticism (self-abnegation and resignation as the path to "Willlessness"), nihilism (the ground of the world as groundless, without sufficient reason), and even pragmatism (the practices of ascetics and hermits). In the end, the work had to devour itself. Even autobiography is enlisted, allowing Schopenhauer to vent against academic philosophy, cultural fads, bad music, and noisy neighbors.

~ * ~

Divine Disbelief. For Nietzsche, the key to understanding Schopenhauer's grumpy attitude is that "he was the *first* admitted and inexorable atheist among us Germans..." For Schopenhauer, the "ungodliness of existence" was a given, from the lowest vermin to the heights of human self-aggrandizement. So strongly did Schopenhauer feel this conviction that, when challenged, he would lose his temper, the composure of the philosopher giving way to irritation, indignation, and disbelief.

~ * ~

In winter mornings, doubtful, viridescent shapes hover

noiselessly on the slightest sound. Subterranean, precipitous creepers ignore our pleas. Entire forests levitate.

~ * ~

Is Life An Affliction? This is the rhetorical question posed near the end of Edgar Saltus' 1885 book *The Philosophy of Disenchantment*. For Saltus, there was an unbroken line of efflorescent grumpiness that stretched from Buddhism and Greek tragedy to Schopenhauer and his now-forgotten followers. But in his narrative Saltus is careful to note the varieties of pessimism. He cites melancholic pessimists, "who from dyspepsia, torpidity of the liver, or general crankiness of disposition, are inclined to take a gloomy view of things." Then there is temperamental pessimism, which "displays itself in outbursts of indignation against the sorrows of life." Contrasted to this is a pessimism of resignation, "the quiet folding of hands... that with tearless eyes awaits death without complaint." There are the miserable pessimists, "who complain and sulk, who torment themselves and others." An accidental pessimism, "which asserts itself on a rainy day, or when the stocks are down." The list goes on. Saltus closes with a final type: "...finally, there is hypochondria, which belongs solely to pathology."

What all these have in common is the assumption that pessimism originates in a thinking, feeling, human subject – and for Saltus, this assumption is the pinnacle of human hubris. "In none of these categories do the victims have any suspicion that a philosophical significance is attached to their suffering." I am an effect of pessimism, and not its cause. This prompts Saltus to argue, a little awkwardly, for a "scientific pessimism," an approach that "rests on a denial that happiness in any form ever has been or ever will be obtained, either by the individual as a unit or by the world as a whole..."

Perhaps this is the insight of "scientific" or philosophical pessimism – that it evokes a profound enchantment of the impersonal that can neither be verified nor assuaged. Even its being stated is a failure.

Yet the idea of a scientific pessimism seems almost comical, something out of the tales of Kafka, Jarry, or Roussel. What kind of measurements, what type of scientific method, what sorts of lab equipment would be involved?

~ * ~

Optimism, pessimism – simply a matter of scale.

~ * ~

Good luck is bad luck because nothing lasts. Bad luck is bad luck because it's worse than what came before.

~ * ~

Being born as the greatest failure. Living as its alibi.

~ * ~

A Very Brief Epiphany. Philosophers ancient and modern

have carried on lengthy debates about what makes human beings unique from other living beings. A whole arsenal of exalted qualities have been mobilized in this project, assuring humanity its dominion: reason, consciousness, language, memory, emotion, labor, play, even boredom. But it's a project which is both as old and as brief as the human species itself.

On most days I feel with great certitude that there is nothing unique or noteworthy about human beings – much less human culture. At the end of the inquiry all that remains is this looming abyss of indifference between one being and another, between one principle and another, between one judgment and another.

But then, in a frustrated euphoria, I realize that this too fails, and it's all an elaborate trick I've played on myself, that what makes human beings unique is their capacity for disenchantment. I feel a minor sense of contentment. (And then I look over at our cat, curled up on the chair.)

~ * ~

The claim that it is better not to have been born is only effective if it is spoken to no one in particular – otherwise, someone is liable to take it personally.

~ * ~

The Silent World. "There is but one truly philosophical problem, and that is suicide." So begins Camus' *The Myth of Sisyphus*, with a statement as weighty as it was when his book was published in 1942. To Camus'

37

question we might add another: "Can one live, and be against life?" To live in this way – let alone to pose the question – would seem to be at once tragic and comical; such a life would also be an absurdity, a product of a world almost helplessly cast in our own solipsistic image. Camus again: "The absurd is born of this confrontation between the human need and the unreasonable silence of the world."

~ * ~

Pessimism is the most indefensible of philosophies. It speaks, but has no right to an audience. In the court of philosophy, it has committed perjury simply by taking the stand.

~ * ~

An Inventory of Affects (I). There are currently some 7 billion people on the planet, a figure that could double by the end of the century. Scientists tell us that the planet is presently capable of adequately sustaining a population of 1.5 billion people.

Bleakness on such a scale is hard to believe, even for a pessimist.

~ * ~

One of the most remarkable achievements of Schopenhauer's philosophy is the way he pulls enthusiasm apart from optimism. The pages upon pages of aphorisms, fragments, and notes in the late works attest to an almost beatific form of pessimism.

~ * ~

The only philosophy worth pursuing is the one that poses questions without answers. Anything less is hubris. But this can never be proved – by definition.

~ * ~

Pessimism is a form of nihilism insofar as it confuses two claims: the world is that which does not exist, and the world is that which should not exist.

~ * ~

Tuesday, late morning. Editing this book on the computer. It's tiring and tedious. Taking a break, I look over, and open my notebook at random. A line I copied jumps out (though I didn't bother to write down who said it): "The more one writes, the less one thinks." Is the reverse also true?

~ * ~

Many of Dostoevsky's characters are damned with an acute awareness of their own hypocrisy – even as they are acting it out. A character in *The Brothers Karamazov* confesses: "I am very often passionately determined to serve humanity, and I might quite likely have sacrificed my life for my fellow-creatures, if for some reason it had been suddenly demanded of me, and yet I'm quite incapable of living with anyone in one room for two days together… I love humanity, but I can't help being surprised at myself: the more I love humanity in general, the less I love men in particular…"

What's more, magnanimity and misanthropy seem to go hand in hand: "I'm capable of hating the best men in twenty-four hours: one because he sits too long over his dinner, another because he has a cold in the head and keeps on blowing his nose…"

~ * ~

Schopenhauer once described comedy as "seriousness concealed within a joke." The inverse is philosophy.

~ * ~

I have to admit my pessimism is provisional – all things turn out for the worst (until they don't); it's better not to have been born (until it isn't)…

~ * ~

Supernatural Slumber. What most readers of Pascal's *Pensées* know, but few admit, is that Pascal is only interesting when his faith is shaky. His portrayal of religious crisis is unparalleled in philosophy. Without faith, he notes, there is only an "impenetrable darkness"… those "frightful spaces of the universe"… "I know not who put me in the world, nor what the world is, nor what I myself am"… I am nothing but "a shadow which endures only for an instance and returns no more"…

and so on. Without faith, says, Pascal, all that remains is the abyss of my finitude and the "supernatural slumber" that is life.

That said, what is equally clear in the *Pensées* is that while Pascal's pessimism is provisional, his faith is absolute. One can only call Pascal a pessimist with great caution.

Nevertheless, I keep coming back to the *Pensées*, secretly hoping to discover a provisional faith that would open onto an absolute pessimism.

~ * ~

Askesis. A paraphrase of Schopenhauer: what death is for the organism, sleep is for the individual. Contrary to what many may think, pessimists sleep not because they are depressed, but because for them sleep is a form of training.

~ * ~

World-weary chrysalids hurl themselves upon us at a depth no human eye can see, and around us this night a thousand million firefly anatomies breathe in and out in their slow-burning liturgical glow.

~ * ~

I feel a sense of awe – wonder, even – at the stupidity of suffering.

~ * ~

Optimism as an expression of anxiety.

~ * ~

Kierkegaard: "Hang yourself, you will regret it; do not hang yourself, and you will also regret that; hang yourself or do not hang yourself, you will regret both. This is the sum and existence of all philosophy."

~ * ~

The Best of All Possible Worlds. "Optimism is the doctrine which justifies the existence of evil in the world by assuming that there is an infinitely perfect, benevolent, and omnipotent original Being. This justification is furnished by establishing that, in spite of all the apparent contradictions, that which is chosen by this infinitely perfect Being must nonetheless be the best of all that is possible. The presence of evil is attributed, not to the choice of God's positive approval, but to the inescapable necessity that finite beings will have essential defects."

Thus did Kant summarize the position of philosophical optimism, exemplified in his time by Leibniz's *Theodicy* (1710). Kant was also critical of such positions, noting that "not every extravagance of opinion deserves the trouble of a careful refutation." Nevertheless, in his lecture notes from the 1750s, he did plan to devote one of his courses to the question of optimism. And, foremost among his criticisms was, quite simply, the *unlikelihood* of what Leibniz called "the best of all possible worlds." As Kant notes, "the concept of the

most perfect of all worlds is a self-contradictory concept." A generation later, Schopenhauer would go a
step further: "…against the palpably sophistical proofs
of Leibniz that this is the best of all possible worlds, we
may even oppose seriously and honestly the proof that
it is the *worst* of all possible worlds." A step too far?

~ * ~

On Contempt. A brief word from Nicholas Chamfort
(1741-1794), aphorist and failed suicide: "In order to
view things correctly, one must give words the opposite
sense to the one the world gives them. Misanthrope, for
instance, means philanthrope…"

~ * ~

A Litany of Pessimists. I've been undergoing treatments
for chronic pain – everything from acupuncture to science fictional sounding things like Myofascial Active
Release Technique and Extracorporeal Pulse Activation
Therapy. During a session the other day I realized that
there is not one but many types of pessimism, form-
ing an entire classification system, a typology, an etiology: moral pessimism (La Rochefoucauld, Chamfort,
Vauvenargues.), metaphysical pessimism, historical
pessimism, political pessimism, literary pessimism
(Huysmans, Kafka, Pessoa), romantic pessimism
(Baudelaire), Buddhist pessimism (Schopenhauer and
his followers), practical pessimism, Dionysian pessimism (Nietzsche), religious pessimism (Pascal, Kierkegaard), dialectical pessimism (Adorno), existential

pessimism (Dostoevsky, Camus, Unamuno), redemptive pessimism (Christianity), heroic pessimism (also see: skepticism), healthy pessimism (positive psychology), and so on.

In the process of enumerating such symptoms, the philosopher and the physician trade places.

~ * ~

From Miguel de Unamuno's *The Tragic Sense of Life*: "… from feeling compassion for other people, for those akin to you, beginning with those most akin to you, for those you live among, you go on to feel compassion for everyone alive, and perhaps even for that which does not live but merely exists. That distant star shining up there in the night will one day be extinguished and turn to dust and cease shining and existing. And as with the one star, so it will be with the whole of the starry sky. Poor sky!" The confinement of being human.

~ * ~

It has become a truism in philosophy that the unexamined life is not worth living. On the other hand, nothing ensures continual confusion, uncertainty, and doubt like the sustained examination of life – let alone "my" life.

~ * ~

Logical Pessimism I. Traditionally, paradox is understood to be a problem for philosophy, especially those philosophies that make some claim to being systematic. But in pessimism paradox is (paradoxically) a foundation. Pessimism – the philosophy that demonstrates that all philosophy is destined to fail (its first and final proof).

~ * ~

Logical Pessimism II. Paradox has long been understood to undermine the coherence of philosophy. And yet, in the history of philosophy paradox is an essential part of philosophical thinking. Historians have even christened them with names, names of philosophers long since dead, whose puzzles continue to animate philosophical thinking. There is, for example, Epimenides's paradox. Epimenides, a Cretan, stated that all Cretans were liars... Then there is Eubulides's paradox, which simply has the form "I am lying" or "What I am saying is false." This continues into the modern era – witness Russell's paradox: Suppose a library is compiling a list of all its books, and that this list is to be compiled in a book as well – is this book itself to be included in the list?

No doubt one could continue with such examples – Schopenhauer's paradox, Nietzsche's paradox, Kafka's paradox, Bernhard's paradox... A philosophy that states that all philosophy is destined to fail – would this not constitute the paradox specific to pessimism?

~ * ~

Logical Pessimism III. What separates pessimism as a

philosophy from pessimism as a bad attitude is that the former attempts to use inductive reasoning, always moving from the particular to the general. It's not just that my life has no meaning, it's that all life is void of meaning. But this distinction doesn't really hold. At the end of the day, pessimism's bad attitude is its most refined aspect.

~ * ~

Logical Pessimism IV. A distinction is often made in philosophy between deductive and inductive logic. The latter involves making a truth claim by moving from the particular to the general ("The two or three books of philosophy I've read are ridiculous, therefore all books of philosophy are ridiculous"). By contrast, the former involves moving in the opposite direction ("All human beings are mortal; a philosopher is a human being; therefore, philosophers are mortal").

Optimism and pessimism, humanism and antihumanism, natalism and antinatalism – all these pairings rely on presenting inductive logic as if it is deductive logic. A *fiat* by way of confusion.

~ * ~

Logical Pessimism V. Too often we simply align optimism and pessimism with affirmation and negation, respectively. We should distinguish, to begin with, the affirmation *of* optimism from the affirmation *in* optimism, just as we should distinguish negation *in* pessimism from the negation *of* pessimism itself.

A number of combinations result from this. For instance, the negation *in* pessimism – that is, the many things the pessimist says "no" to – is contradicted by the pessimist's affirmation *of* pessimism itself (whether as a philosophy or a bad mood).

It seems that, at the level of logical consistency, optimism ultimately wins out, since even the most hardened pessimist must, at the very least, affirm pessimism itself.

We have left out another alternative – the double negative. But who would have any interest in saying "no" to many things, to everything, including pessimism itself?

~ * ~

Logical Pessimism VI. The pessimist dreams of a negation without affirmation. What usually results is a negativity that is not negative.

~ * ~

Logical Pessimism VII. Writing about the character of the know-it-all, Theodor Adorno notes: "Nothing is more unfitting for an intellectual resolved on practicing what was earlier called philosophy, than to wish, in discussion, and one might almost say in argumentation, to be right." I completely agree. But he had to have been aware of the hypocrisy of making such a statement. I say this because, a few sentences later, he adds: "When philosophers, who are well known to have difficulty in keeping silent, engage in conversation, they should try

47

always to lose the argument, but in such a way as to convict their opponent of untruth."

~ * ~

Logical Pessimism VIII. Analysis is the horizon between comprehension and confusion.

~ * ~

Logical Pessimism IX. I've been intrigued by philosophical logic recently, mostly because of Frege's insight – that logic has little to do with the features of human thought... Frege's insight...

~ * ~

Logical Pessimism X. Wittgenstein once remarked that a serious and robust philosophy could be written entirely as jokes. Pessimist philosophers discover this only too late.

~ * ~

Logical Pessimism XI. Accuracy at the cost of clarity.

~ * ~

Logical Pessimism XII. "Of the silence and darkness that surround the laws" (Joubert).

~ * ~

The pessimist can never be political – or, to be more precise, the pessimist can never live up to the political. (Still, one imagines pessimist slogans – "Drop All Causes!" or "Not To Be!") Resistance, rebellion, revolt, protest, and intervention all fall outside the scope of the pessimist worldview. The pessimist is the most despised of nay-sayers, a stranger even to abstention, refusal, and precious forms of Bartleby-ism. Above all, the pessimist is incapable of suicide, that solution of solutions that constitutes a horizon for even the most dyed-in-the-wool existentialist. Ironically, it is the pessimist's deep-seated misanthropy that keeps them alive. Weary of the all-too-human drama of life and the living, the pessimist is also aware that suicide solves nothing – that suicide is *insoluble*. One discovers oneself detached from the world (a world in which one is ensnared, like prey) all the while participating in it. Death becomes simply another, more covert, form of human drama (tragedy, eulogy, and the funerary cosmetics of memorialism). Both Schopenhauer and Cioran understood this – but so also did Beckett, and many stand-up comedians. One commits suicide not because one wants to die, but because one is already dead… in which case suicide is not worth the trouble.

~ * ~

The people who constantly complain are never helpful – this is a platitude. But if this is true, then it is also true that the people who are always helpful never complain, and this is just as disturbing.

~ * ~

Cioran. It's hard to think of another writer so confident in their uncertainty. Pascal's despair, Kierkegaard's melancholy, both assuaged by their faith. And Schopenhauer held tight to his philosophy, though it lay in ruins, just as Nietzsche held tight to his determined enthusiasms for life, though they stemmed from a body in ruins. What was there left for a writer like Cioran to do, but abdicate everything?

~ * ~

That Joke Isn't Funny Anymore. The only thing worse than a young pessimist is an old optimist; the pessimist is a well-informed optimist; the pessimist is the person who looks both ways when crossing a one-way street; the pessimist, when faced with the choice between two evils, chooses both; the pessimist fears we live in the best of all possible worlds; if everything is going well, you've obviously overlooked something...

Jokes that aren't funny are sometimes renamed philosophical arguments (though deep down pessimism rarely makes such distinctions).

~ * ~

Bad Utility. In so far as it considers itself "philosophical," pessimism fancies itself as impervious to the demands of utility. But no philosophy, however much it tries, ever fully escapes the lures of utility. Thus it is possible that pessimism is actually quite useful, if not intellectually noble. It can have a critical function, in which the utility of pessimism lies in its capacity for critique of the *status quo* (the pessimism of Adorno, Camus, Unamuno); it can have a moral function, in which pessimism serves as the mirror of hypocritical humanity (the pessimism of Pascal, Voltaire, Leopardi); and it can even serve a higher purpose, in which pessimism's negativity serves as an affirmative prelude to something else, a philosophy beyond philosophy that cannot be named (the pessimism of Nietzsche, Lev Shestov, Keiji Nishitani).

In these three recuperations, pessimism becomes accidentally helpful.

~ * ~

The problem with contemporary philosophy is that it begins in helplessness, when it should end with it. We lack even the most rudimentary theory of "giving up."

~ * ~

"The nullity of all existence." This was how Japanese philosopher Keiji Nishitani once summarized Schopenhauer's pessimism. Nishitani was one of the earliest non-Western thinkers to take Schopenhauer's engagement with Buddhism seriously. He understood that Schopenhauer's insight is to have provided – or to have attempted to provide – a philosophical basis for this "nullity." For Schopenhauer, a blind, impersonal, cosmic Will manifests itself ceaselessly in a myriad of ways, suspending one within the interminable pendu-

lum swing of striving and disappointment. As Nishitani notes, "as long as the will to life is operative,
dissatisfaction arises ceaselessly from within." Suffering is the unavoidable result. On the other hand, "when
the desired is attained and dissatisfaction is momen-
tarily held in check, what has been attained becomes a
burden." Boredom sets in. "Boredom is insight into the
essentially void nature of our existence and the existence of all things."

But Nishitani also understood that one can only
make such claims by resorting to less-than-philosophi-
cal arguments. It takes very little to doubt the validity of
one's existence. Yes, it can happen as the result of a long
and arduous process of philosophical reflection, but it
can also happen quite spontaneously. It is a thought
that can be well-formed, but also a thought that occurs
incidentally, haphazardly, only partially-acknowl-
edged. Self-reflection as the result of a traumatic life
event. Or as the result of tedium, banality, listlessness,
boredom. For a reason, or for no reason at all.

"But," Nishitani notes, "when this horizon does open
up at the bottom of those engagements that keep life
moving continually on and on, something seems to halt
and linger before us… the meaninglessness that lies in
wait at the bottom of those very engagements that bring
meaning to life." Little doubts that easily give way to
the "Great Doubt." In such moments, "our very existence has turned into a question mark."

~ * ~

The Rigor of Futility. That pessimism is often thought

of as a philosophy strikes me as at once apt and unusual. Why should a philosophy about the futility of everything require a method? Still, philosophers of pessimism such as Hartmann, Mainländer, Saltus, and even Schopenhauer have imagined a "scientific pessimism" (Saltus's phrase) – but it would have to be a scientific pessimism that would go all the way, a science that works *too well*, shoring up all the pretenses of human civilization, engulfed by an indifferent universe of emergent properties, complex patterns, and a hyper-chaos of singularities. Unamuno once referred to this as the "rationalist dissolution." Such a scientific pessimism would, I imagine, bear some relation to the idea of philosophical rigor. But if such rigor only leads to the realization of its own absurdity, then it seems that the scientific pessimism of which Saltus dreamed can only have one method: the stark and arresting claim that it is better not to have been born is often preceded by a much lengthier exegesis... that is, in the end, undercut by its own conclusion.

~ * ~

On Physical Pessimism. At the doctor's office. During our conversation, the tail end of a sentence jumps out: myofascial morbidity factors. What a fantastic phrase. I'm reminded of how much pessimism is taken to be a highly intellectual affair, whether one is a moral pessimist (the glass half empty) or a metaphysical pessimist (emptiness as the property of all glass).

But what about physical pessimism? It's surprising that there aren't more physical pessimists in philosophy. What is more inevitable than the breakdown of the body, than illness and aches and pains, than the crumbling, aleatory sigh of every joint and muscle and organ, of all matter? Is not the corpse the ultimate expression of this type of pessimism? A physicalism pushed to the point where it becomes aching and blissful nothingness. Is this physical optimism?

~ * ~

Only human beings have the gall to conceive of something like "bad luck" or a "well-lived" life. How *dare* this happen to *me*? Lichtenberg writes: "It is a good thing that lack of thought does not produce the same effect as lack of air…"

~ * ~

Magnum Opus. It is no accident that philosophical pessimism is often allied with the short form in writing – the aphorism, the maxim, the parable, the fragment, the journal entry… But if this is so, it is *not* because the pessimist has attained such heights of philosophical wisdom that only a few carefully-chosen words suffice. No, the secret of the short form is not endless toil – it is laziness, listlessness. The pessimist harbors no ideals concerning literary craft or "finding one's voice" as a writer. There is only what suffices, what is finished enough, what can be left off, cast away, abandoned, when it physically hurts too much to write so much and to sit for so long. This is the secret of the short form in Nietzsche (style as illness) and also in Schopenhauer (style as intolerance).

~ ✳ ~

Pessimism and Prayer. Schopenhauer once noted that religions should be classified based on whether they are pessimistic or optimistic, and not in terms of whether they are monotheistic or polytheistic. In these terms Schopenhauer finds family resemblances between Christianity and Buddhism (their conviction that existence is equal to suffering, their preference for a mystical state anterior or posterior to existence). Setting aside Schopenhauer's understanding (or misunderstanding) of world religions, I can see how seductive this approach is. In fact, it is hard not to regard every religion as inherently pessimistic, in that the very idea of religion is bound up with a profound devaluation of the world as it is.

This, of course, was Nietzsche's critique, of religion and of Schopenhauer. But if Schopenhauer scoffed at the idea of a better world up there, out there, or beyond, he certainly saw this as no reason to reevaluate and reaffirm the world as it is. This is part of what makes Schopenhauer frustrating as a philosopher (Nietzsche eventually had enough of Schopenhauer – it was time once and for all to get out of bed). One senses that for Schopenhauer, the world does exist, *and* it's horrible, *and* there's not much one can do about it. As far as philosophies go, this hardly requires the erudition of a philosopher. But that is, perhaps, the key to understanding pessimism and its peculiar fascination with religion. What Schopenhauer was really after was not only a religion without God, but a religion without hope – something that, apparently, philosophy could not provide.

~ * ~

Scientists have long noted the ephemeral, arbitrary appearance of life on the earth, especially when set against the rise and fall of planets and galaxies. Philosophers, for their part, have added a caveat – that it is the unique provenance of we human beings to worry about the brevity and arbitrariness of life, to concern ourselves with what Nietzsche once called "the outbreak of life." Surely, Nietzsche notes, this must be some sort of practical joke. "Our uniqueness in the world! alas, it is too improbable a thing!"

However, in the face of such crises human beings have also developed coping techniques, one of which is human culture, often expanded to such a degree that "the human" eclipses the world, even the entire universe, all there for our interstellar gaze, self-centered dreams, and prophetic inquiries. We have managed to render even the cosmos banal.

Going to sleep and getting up, going to work and coming home, making plans, having goals, checking off items on the to-do list of everyday life – the modesty of being human. Nietzsche again: "How little pleasure suffices for most people to find life to be good…"

~ * ~

Lev Shestov once noted, with some exasperation, how

philosophy seems to be able to argue anything, from any possible angle. "The business of philosophy," he contests, "is to teach mankind to live in uncertainty – mankind who is supremely afraid of uncertainty, and who is forever hiding behind this or the other dogma… the business of philosophy is not to reassure people, but to upset them."

On the other hand, Shestov also notes how loquacious, how chatty philosophers become the nearer they are to their own death – Socrates, for instance, was known to have whiled away the hours in incessant conversation with pupils, colleagues, and friends. "The days, even the hours of the old man are numbered, and yet he talks, talks, talks…"

~ * ~

Every outing I make, every trip I go on, I can't help but to think of all the things that can possibly go wrong. Sometimes it's mere superstition – if I imagine all the things that can go wrong beforehand, then they won't happen. But before anything has happened, I am euphorically overwhelmed with myriad possibilities. The world of the worst seems wide open, a world overflowing in all its misanthropic splendor. For a brief, furtive moment, I forget that "the worst" is what happens to *me*.

~ * ~

In some remote region there are organisms that dare not live, composed as they are of all the impassivity of stellar dust and strange geometries.

~ * ~

The Will-to-Die. For Camus, the problem of suicide is *the* philosophical problem. In a world in which neither God nor science serves as the guarantee of a meaningful life, suicide presents itself as the last gasp of the individual's increasingly precarious hold on the order of things.

Camus ultimately came down on suicide – it failed to find something that never existed to begin with. For Camus, suicide is something to be heroically overcome, and overcome by embracing the contradictions and the absurdity of existence. But what he never considered was suicide on a species-wide level. This was the intuition of the nineteenth-century German philosopher Philipp Mainländer, for whom human beings – and all their self-ascribed virtues – were but an evolutionary accident. Like Schopenhauer before him, and like Miguel de Unamuno after him, Mainländer realized that the pinnacle of the human species was the realization of the meaninglessness of the human species. Mainländer even went beyond Schopenhauer; in contrast to what Schopenhauer referred to as the blind Will-to-Live, Mainländer argued for a pervasive Will-to-Die inhabiting not only all living beings, but all beings, living or non-living, animate or inanimate. As such, Mainländer offers a bizarre ethical response – since human life is essentially meaningless, and since a general Will-to-Die courses through all that exists, the human species should simply allow itself to die out –

perhaps just as arbitrarily as it came into being.

For Mainländer there is no apocalyptic cataclysm, just unfortunate and angst-ridden anomalies running themselves out in an absurd drama to which the world as such is indifferent. Thomas Ligotti provides a concise paraphrase of Mainländer's position: "… the knowledge that life is worthless as the value of all human wisdom…"

And herein lies the greatest horror of Mainländer's philosophy – that even the meaninglessness of the species has some meaning. A species-horror that can only be assuaged by a species-wide, unintentional suicide. That is, one simply goes on living.

~ * ~

How am I to live? What should be done? There is a sense in which all philosophy is obliged optimism.

~ * ~

A nocturnal robe of obsidian draped over our most precious, most anonymous thoughts.

~ * ~

That pessimism – especially "philosophical" pessimism – may be reduced to a sigh is given in Kafka's rendition of the myth of Prometheus:

> There are four legends concerning Prometheus:
>   According to the first, he was clamped to a rock

in the Caucasus for betraying the secrets of the gods to men, and the gods sent eagles to feed on his liver, which was perpetually renewed.

According to the second, Prometheus, goaded by the pain of the tearing beaks, pressed himself deeper and deeper into the rock until he became one with it.

According to the third, his treachery was forgotten in the course of thousands of years, the gods forgotten, the eagles, he himself forgotten.

According to the fourth, every one grew weary of the meaningless affair. The gods grew weary, the eagles grew weary, the wound closed wearily.

There remains the inexplicable mass of rock. – The legend tried to explain the inexplicable. As it came out of a substratum of truth it had in turn to end in the inexplicable.

That weariness (*müde*) – that is pessimism – too tired to think... matter too tired to persist...

~ * ~

Spiritual Abattoir. No one has articulated existential doubt like Pascal; in him doubt is pervasive and shadowy, hemming one into a kind of cosmic claustrophobia. In spite of his earnest attempt to provide an apology for religion, it is Pascal's morose doubt that spoke to later thinkers like Nietzsche and Cioran, and that still resonates today. No one else has meditated at such length on the horrific conjunction of spirit and flesh that is the human creature: "Imagine a number of men in chains, all under sentence of death, some of whom are each day butchered in the sight of the others; those remaining see their own condition in that of their fellows, and looking at each other with grief and despair await their turn." The brutalist imagery sounds like a passage from Edgar Allan Poe or H.P. Lovecraft. Pascal concludes: "This is the image of the human condition."

The image is all the starker when we realize that it can be taken literally or figuratively.

~ * ~

There is no better occasion for pessimism than optimism.

~ * ~

The rift between the "as is" and the "as if."

~ * ~

The very possibility of the worst – without experience – a *naive* pessimism…

~ * ~

It has become a truism in human cultures that the questions without answers are the most profound questions, just as the problems without solutions are the most thought-provoking problems. We may never know what the meaning of life is, or what separates humans from animals – and the forests in which trees might possibly fall in our absence have long since vanished, having been transformed into books containing opaque philosophical statements.

The wager made by human culture – by philosophy, by the arts, by music – the wager is that for every limit that human knowledge comes up against, there is a secret reserve, in which the problems without solutions and questions without answers are safeguarded as the essence of what it means to be a human being living in a human world. The effect of this is to produce a kind of consolation, the comfort of there always being something more, or at least something more than myself. I don't know the answer and I certainly don't have any solutions, but perhaps someone, somewhere does, or perhaps future generations will pose the questions-without-answers in new ways, making it possible to continue the Great Conversation, etc.

But it is also from this attitude that human culture grows and spreads, like some jargon-filled, Panglossian amoeba. There is always something more to say, or to say differently, or to say in a high falsetto, or in the register of birds and bats, or, ultimately, in a cacophony outside the range of hearing altogether. Human culture: a kind of incessant ringing in the ears.

~ * ~

False Modesty. Nietzsche once wrote: "The aphorism is a form of eternity; my ambition is to say in ten sentences what everyone else says in a book – what everyone else does not say in a book." Decades later, Karl Kraus would write: "There are writers who can express in a

mere twenty pages things I sometimes need two whole
lines for."

~ * ~

For the pessimist, good days are few and far between...
and almost never worth the trouble. The simplest of
requests – to not be bothered, to have quiet, a decent
cup of coffee – is asking too much.

~ * ~

The mortality of even the most opulent ideas, patiently
withering with all the indifference of our dissipating
flesh and nerve and bone.

~ * ~

Optimism of Pessimism. For the pessimist, nothing is
more horrific – or enviable – than happy people, people
who seem to go about their lives, blissfully ignorant
of all the varieties of doom that inhabit each living
moment. Every breath an expiration, every gesture for
naught, every birth a crime. Pessimists falsely comfort
themselves with the assurance that this awareness is
the price one must pay for a higher form of consciousness.

~ * ~

Cold Rationalism. Lunch with R and N, under the vaulted
arch of constellations. Our talk turns to developments

in the sciences. I realize that, for the pessimist, the only real significance of the sciences is their ability to reveal the insignificance of being human. (I think they would agree with me, but neither of them would ever use the term "pessimism.") Beyond this, the pessimist secretly dreams of a science *devoted* to demonstrating the insignificance of everything that exists. (And would not such a science then take on a religious quality?)

~ * ~

It is *we* who suffer, it is we who suffer each other, it is we who suffer the world into which we are thrown. That the world is against us is incidental.

~ * ~

An Inventory of Affects (II). D sends me an article from *Scientific American.* By a process I do not understand, scientists have been tallying the number of stars in different galaxies as well as the rate of their creation. Their survey is breathtaking, absurd even. It seems that most of the stars that currently exist were created "roughly" 8 to 11 billion years ago. What's more, the rate of the creation of new stars is not even 3% of what it was "back then." The result? A perpetual *fin-de-siècle*, in which we as human beings again find a covert way of placing ourselves at the center of the cosmos – even if it means that the price of this existential solipsism is the long and languorous decline of that same cosmos itself.

~ * ~

Peripatetic Wisdom. Lyricism and laughter, sorrow and spite, the bittersweet smile of futility, all intermingled in the sullen suspicion of all life (and above all human life) as a weary cosmic joke. The same effect is gained by tripping on a flat sidewalk, or missing the last step on the stairs.

~ * ~

Pessimist writing often adopts one of two strategies – the literary or the philosophical. Each has specific forms available to it. For literary pessimism, there is the diary, the confession, the parable, the monologue – Goethe's *The Sorrows of Young Werther*, Dostoevsky's *Notes from Underground*, Hamsun's *Hunger*, Kafka's diaries, Hartwig's *Am I A Redundant Human Being?*, Klíma's *The Sufferings of Prince Sternenhoch*, Lagerkvist's *The Dwarf*, Dazai's *No Longer Human*, Hrabal's *Too Loud a Solitude*, Bernhard's *Extinction*, Jang Eun-jin's *No One Writes Back*, and Pessoa's *Book of Disquiet* (a book for which I have too much fondness).

For philosophical pessimism, there is the essay, the meditation, the fragment, and above all, the aphorism – the stray *Pensées* of Pascal, Lichtenberg's "waste books," the journals of Kierkegaard, the notebooks of Joubert and Leopardi and Camus, the essays of Montaigne and Shestov, Schopenhauer's aphorisms, the fragments of Nietzsche, Adorno, and Cioran.

In the literary strategy, thought expands, cataloging and accounting for a horizonless panoply of events, experiences, ideas, and affects, whereas in the philosophical strategy, thought contracts, condensed into epiphanies, maxims, and glimpses into the horizon of thought itself. Both, however, dovetail on an incompleteness central to pessimism, a fundamental disenchantment about having ever begun the pessimistic discourse at all.

Through the act of writing, pessimism resigns itself to the speculative debris of clear and coherent ideas – philosophy as driftwood.

~ * ~

Psycho-Somatic and Cosmo-Somatic. Research into the mind-body connection tells us that the body can manifest physical correlates of mental and psychological states. We know this much in an everyday way based on our experiences of stress and sickness. But what such research doesn't tell us is how this extends beyond the body to the self-world relationship. If my body suffers in tandem with my mind, then why wouldn't the world suffer in tandem with my self? A solipsism that is also the ultimate form of empathy with the unhuman. The one fantasy pessimism allows itself – the sadness of the cosmos.

~ * ~

We sing to the subterranean, precipitous creepers and ask them which path to take. Rosary of stars, seaweed skin, the once-hushed sleep that begins to form our shadow.

~ * ~

"My life is miserable. All life is miserable." "My existence is disappointing. All existence is disappointing." There is a logic that is precious to pessimism, more precious than the most oblique and finely-shaped crystal. It is predicated on the ability – the willingness – to jump from the contingent to the absolute… a leap of the least noticeable effort. No one has analyzed this leap to the extent that Nietzsche has. A fragment from a posthumously-published essay contains this opening:

> In some remote corner of the universe, poured out and glittering in innumerable solar systems, there once was a star on which clever animals invented knowledge. That was the haughtiest and most mendacious minute of "world history" – yet only a minute. After nature had drawn a few breaths the star grew cold, and the clever animals had to die.

In passages like these Nietzsche invokes a stellar pessimism, the allure of a "no-saying" scaled-up to the level of stars, nebulae, and black holes. He also makes tactical use of this pessimism to question the greatest presumption of all, the presumption of being human: "One might invent such a fable and still not have illustrated sufficiently how wretched, how shadowy and flighty, how aimless and arbitrary, the human intellect appears in nature."

Nietzsche remained not only a "joyful" pessimist but also a venomous pessimist, the philosophical equivalent of spitting: "There have been eternities when human consciousness did not exist; and when it is done for again, nothing will have happened."

How far this all seems from Nietzsche's concerns with ulcers, poor eyesight, aches and pains...

~ * ~

Kant, author of the massive, systematic *Critique of Pure Reason*, once noted: "Making plans is often a luxuriant, boastful occupation of the mind by which one gives oneself the airs of creative genius, demanding what one cannot perform oneself, censuring what one cannot do better, and proposing what one oneself does not know where to look for..." Was he speaking about philosophy, or about life?

~ * ~

We ask the whole mass of our tectonic sorrow, the most fragile part of our bodies, the most tenuous aspect of our spectral limbs, the least reversible, the least recognizable part of ourselves... everything that is not the nocturnal sky, the hush of the nameless, gem-covered seafloor... greedily assigning attributes towards which the sky and the fireflies and the jewels are indifferent.

~ * ~

Literary studies of Dostoevsky often note his keen ability to peer into the mysterious depths of the human psyche. I disagree. After finishing *The Brothers Karamazov*, my only epiphany was that it was, in a way, a waste of time. But I meant it as a compliment. There are no redeeming qualities to his characters, no real rationale for their motives, no real consequence of their actions – there is no secret heart of the human soul, and the human being is the most worthless and insignificant thing in the world: a waste of time. This is Dostoevsky's real gift as a writer. But one has to read him to appreciate this.

~ * ~

The pessimist is a logician with an aptitude for disappointment.

~ * ~

The link between pessimism and mysticism is suggested by the anonymously-authored, fourteenth-century text *The Cloud of Unknowing*: "No human being can think of God. Therefore, it is my wish to leave everything that I can think of and choose for my love the thing that I cannot think." *I love what I cannot think.* Though pessimists are rarely so generous with their feelings.

~ * ~

"I can't go on, I'll go on." Resignation is the hypocrite's suicide. In resignation I don't die, but neither do I stop living. If I am resigned to life, I have accepted not just fatality but futility as well – including the futility of dying. What remains is an interminable, haunting choreography of gestures and glances, the morose pleasures of sleep and listless time. To really end things, to really cease to exist, one would have to *resign* from life, not end it.

~ * ~

A Bad Mood (II). In the dimly-lit corners of contemporary academic philosophy, one debates the question of whether it is better not to have been born. On the one side, "natalists" argue for the intrinsic value of human life – indeed, of all life (the latter claim conflicts with the former). On the other side, "anti-natalists" argue that it is not only harmful to reproduce and bring more human lives into the world, but that it is irresponsible to do so. The debates go on interminably in scholarly journals and on public radio talk shows.

The elevation of "life" beyond all other phenomena; what both the natalist and the anti-natalist positions presume is the division between the living and the non-living – itself a product of human knowledge and vested interests.

But shouldn't the real anti-natalist be against existence itself as well as life? A pessimism of this sort would not take sides in tepid debates among philosophers over survival and extinction, natalism and anti-natalism, life and death. Instead, it would highlight the arbitrariness of those very divisions. At its limit would be a subharmonic "no" without any object of negation. One would think that this would lead to silence... or at least to quiet.

~ * ~

I hadn't heard from T for a while, and was about to contact him when I get his email. He tells me that a friend of his had recently committed suicide. He had hanged himself, and had placed black tape in an "X" over his eyes and mouth.

I send my condolences; but the harrowing image of blackened out eyes and mouth sticks in my mind. I cannot think of a more devastating expression of the refusal of pessimistic thinking – one's own death is not even enough.

~ * ~

Apparently we are comically arranged (I almost said "cosmically," not "comically").

~ * ~

The indifference of the clouds, when seen from above, strikes me as solemn and melancholy. We fail to really comprehend such strange affects of the impersonal (and this failure suffices).

~ * ~

Pessimism – a defeatist optimism.

~ * ~

Garden of Delights. Nietzsche, in his criticism of religion, describes the feeling of resentment specific to the species, the yearning to be someone else, to be somewhere else, to be something else: "In this swamp-soil of self-contempt, every poisonous weed flourishes, and all so small, so secret, so dishonest, and so sweetly rotten. Here swarm the worms of sensitiveness and resentment…" That is, a garden.

~ * ~

I no longer want to hear about how your revolution failed. Again.

~ * ~

Whatever I'm thinking seems pretentious and naive. Whatever I feel seems cliché and scripted. Whatever I see around me seems a tireless pantomime of tedious significance. Tragedy turns to farce, and life-affirming life becomes grotesque, filling me with revulsion.

To be aware of all this is to experience estrangement to such a degree that it almost becomes tranquility.

~ * ~

The Vesicles of Death. There are moments in Freud's writing where one suspects that the human being itself is simply a symptom of some deeper, more nebulous, cosmic pathology, the play-thing of drives, instincts, and other obscure forces that precede the human being's emergence into an illusory or even delusory self-consciousness. "If we are to take it as a truth that knows no exception that everything living dies for *internal* reasons – becomes inorganic once again – then

72

we shall be compelled to say that 'the aim of all life is death' and, looking backwards, that 'inanimate things existed before living ones.'"

For instance, in *Beyond the Pleasure Principle*, Freud picks apart the presumption that human life is governed by the search for pleasure over pain, and happiness over unhappiness. "It must be pointed out," he notes, "that strictly speaking it is incorrect to talk of the dominance of the pleasure principle over the course of mental processes. If such a dominance existed, the immense majority of our mental processes would have to be accompanied by pleasure or lead to pleasure, whereas universal experience completely contradicts any such conclusion." The search for happiness at the core of the pleasure principle is, in Freud's words, "at loggerheads with the whole world, with the macrocosm as much as with the microcosm." After all, he asks, "what good to us is a long life if it is difficult and barren of joys, and if it is so full of misery that we can only welcome death as a deliverer?"

Then what keeps us going? What keeps us going is certainly not "us," not anything inherent in our psyche or our convoluted rationalizations for our motives and actions, but something more nebulous, "an urge inherent in organic life to restore an earlier state of things which the living entity had been obliged to abandon under the pressure of external disturbing forces." The so-called death drive. Freud also defines it as "the expression of the inertia inherent in organic life," and underscores its primordial nature: "...it must be an *old* state of things, an initial state from which the living entity has at one time or another departed and to which it is striving to return…" The pull of the organic towards the inorganic, of the animate towards the inanimate, of the living towards the unliving – the pull towards something "old."

In these moments, the human being is turned inside-out, revealing the entirety of human civilization as a big-brain neurosis, beneath which a deeper, multi-layered geo-trauma manifests itself in a myriad of ways, from frenetic protozoa to the torpid, stumbling forth of human self-awareness.

In his essay Freud seems acutely, even anxiously aware of the pessimistic tone of his theory: "It may be difficult, too, for many of us, to abandon the belief that there is an instinct towards perfection at work in human beings, which has brought them to their present high level of intellectual achievement and ethical sublimation and which may be expected to watch over their development into supermen. I have no faith, however, in the existence of any such internal instinct and I cannot see how this benevolent illusion is to be preserved." (Adding: "The present development of human beings requires, as it seems to me, no different explanation from that of animals.")

~ * ~

A contemporary novelist – I forget who – once said "I write in order to indict humanity." But to fill pages upon pages of characters, motives, plot devices, and descriptions of inner states seems as banal and ineffectual as the legal process itself. It seems like such a waste of time – even for a pessimist.

~ * ~

In 1904 the Czech writer and vagrant Ladislav Klíma published one of his few works of philosophy, a slim but imposing book titled *The World as Consciousness and Nothing*. Taking his cue from Schopenhauer, Klíma's pessimism refused even the German philosopher's solace of music and mysticism. For Klíma there was only an unhuman, blind "Will" driving every existing thing, living or not, towards a state of non-being. So overcome is Klíma with this thought that, after the publication of his book he renounces it, rarely mentioning it to anyone. Later, he writes, "to this day I don't know if even a dog barked at it."

~ * ~

A Floating Gravesite of Humanity. Astronauts frequently refer to their first view of the earth from space as a life-changing experience. Often dubbed "the overview effect," this experience has been evoked as a lesson for us non-astronauts about the wondrous unity of all life on the planet.

Nietzsche, however, had already given us a different version of the overview effect, long before the first primates had tenuously crept their way into outer space: "The astronomers, who sometimes really are granted a field of vision detached from the earth, intimate that the drop of *life* in the world is without significance..."

Not only that, but human beings are unique in having achieved a literal incarnation of the overview effect in philosophy – known as "critical distance." The further we are from it, the closer the world becomes, and the closer it becomes, the easier it is to engineer the miracle of self-control. For Nietzsche, this is the more far-reaching significance of the overview effect – to efface the world by gazing upon it, we astronauts of *Angst*: "The most dispassionate astronomer can himself scarcely feel the earth without life in any other way than as the gleaming and floating gravesite of humanity."

~ * ~

Leopardi: "There is no clearer sign of not being very philosophical or wise than wishing all life to be wise and philosophical." Pessimism and idealism become uneasy bedfellows.

~ * ~

On Mortification. Spending an October weekend at H and D's place upstate. The dense, crisp foliage of the trees is awash in a muted glimmer of oranges, yellows, and reds. Inebriated, P and I drift off to sleep with music softly playing. In the middle of the night we suddenly awake to see the ghostly silhouettes of deer outside, silently grazing in the cold near-dawn. In the early morning, Hildegard von Bingen plays on the stereo, as I sit on the large worn carpet on the concrete floor, stretching achy limbs. P and I decide to go down to swim in the anodyne chill of the spring-fed pond, populated at its fringes by tentacular, wavering lily pads. We swim until we can no longer feel our feet.

~ * ~

The Grand Hotel Abyss. In the late 1930s, Theodor Adorno, forced into exile by the Nazi regime, made his way to New York, before eventually settling in California. There, the philosopher most associated with the Frankfurt School wrote, with his colleague Max Horkheimer, *The Dialectic of Enlightenment,* which contains some of the century's most caustic, sarcastic indictments of Western culture. The irony of the fact that Adorno was living a stone's throw away from Walt Disney Studios could not have been lost on him. It was not lost on the Hungarian Marxist philosopher Georg Lukács, who in turn indicted Adorno for having "taken up residence in the Grand Hotel Abyss... a beautiful hotel, equipped with every comfort, on the edge of the abyss, of nothingness, of absurdity. And the daily contemplation of the abyss between excellent meals or artistic entertainments, can only heighten the enjoyment of the subtle comforts offered."

If only all hotels were so profound; if only all philosophers were so resigned.

~ * ~

A *Manual of Style*: the bad joke, the memo, the epitaph.

~ * ~

A line from one of Thomas Bernhard's novels: "I could

actually say he was unhappy in his unhappiness but he would have been even more unhappy had he lost his unhappiness overnight, had it been taken away from him one moment to the next, which is again proof that basically he wasn't unhappy at all but happy, and by virtue of and with his unhappiness, I thought."

~ * ~

It appears there is a science to pessimism after all. I've just read an article about a group of psychiatrists – in Germany – whose research shows that people with a "dark," pessimistic outlook live longer and lead more well-adjusted lives. They even go so far as to suggest that people with optimistic attitudes are more at risk for disease, depression, and early death. I've been on a health regimen without knowing it.

~ * ~

An argument against procreation: "...the species needs itself as a species..."

~ * ~

We are mottled with unearthly growths, serene stone and graphite assemblies hidden deep in the overgrowth of our contempt for the world.

~ * ~

Nietzsche was arguably the first philosopher to push

pessimism to its breaking point: "Pessimism is proved only by the self-refutation of our dear pessimists…" But how to distinguish refutation from fulfillment?

~ * ~

The Sickness of Thought. In his essays, aphorisms, and notebooks Schopenhauer is straightforward – even axiomatic – about his pessimism. "Human life must be some kind of error," he notes, without further explanation, argument, or reason. Almost as if he dares you to argue the contrary… and then live out your life.

Not content with such truisms, Schopenhauer presses on. Even supposing life is meaningful – by virtue of this realization that life is meaningless – even this would only amount to an ephemeral, insignificant flutter of existence between the non-existence before my life and the non-existence after it: "For the infinity *a parte post* without me cannot be any more fearful than the infinity *a parte ante* without me, since the two are not distinguished by anything except by the intervention of an ephemeral life-dream."

But something still remains. We're still aware of this. The Spanish philosopher Miguel de Unamuno would strive to abolish even the awareness of our insignificance. "If consciousness is no more – as some inhuman thinker said – than a flash of lightning between two eternities of darkness, then there is nothing more execrable than existence." Unamuno's book *The Tragic Sense of Life* is an extended attempt to render insignificant not just life itself, but our consciousness of life – inclusive of its purported insignificance.

And yet, something is always left over, a nagging shadow of the thought of the vacuousness of all thought, the sticky, sickly residue of existence, of life, of meaning. "But there is more to it than that: man, because he is man, because he possesses consciousness, is already in comparison to the jackass or the crab, a sick animal. Consciousness is a disease."

~ * ~

...that most American of replies, "don't create problems if you don't have a solution"...

~ * ~

Published in 1948, Osamu Dazai's *No Longer Human* is a unique kind of novel – an anti-novel, really. Presented as a series of "notebooks" written by its protagonist, Ōba Yōzō, the novel provides a taxonomy of failure, as we witness the strange, pervasive sense of estrangement that Yōzō senses at home, at school, at work, among friends and lovers and strangers, even in moments of solitude. He tries wearing masks, playing the class clown, the angst-ridden artist, the upstart careerist. He tries art, politics, religion. He tries being a sensualist, an ascetic, a loafer. But the result is always the same – not "getting" what it means to be human. Resigned, he observes, "I have never been able to meet anyone without an accompaniment of painful smiles, the buffoonery of defeat."

Dazai's novel does not provide any happy endings, eulogies for a nation or a people, or elegies for the human spirit; there are no grand epiphanies, no heroic struggles, no sufferings stoically endured, no wrongs righted or lovers reunited. Dazai's protagonists take on the task of living only to find themselves more confused and bewildered than before. It's as if there were some guide book – *How To Be Human, And Why* – that seems to have been given to everyone else, except you. Dazai's recurring phrase for this is "the dread of human beings."

Such an estrangement is almost metaphysical – a perplexity about incessantly finding one's self ensnared in a human world of human beings; as if "being human" were something that happens accidentally, or incidentally.

~ * ~

With pessimism, there is a certitude that no amount of reason or faith can overcome. Humor at once deflates and strengthens it.

~ * ~

Shestov once noted that we only think with any integrity when we realize there is nothing to be done – when our hands are tied. "Artists and philosophers like to imagine the thinker with a stern face, a profound look which penetrates into the unseen, and a noble bearing – an eagle preparing for flight. Not at all. A thinking person is one who has lost their balance..." Shestov adds: "...in the vulgar, not in the tragic sense."

~ * ~

Only beings can dream of the impossibility of non-being.

~ * ~

There is no better time for pessimism than the present – whenever that is. Still, for the philosopher the question remains: is the world in which we find ourselves a tragedy, a comedy, or both? "The life of every individual," Schopenhauer writes, "viewed as a whole and in general, and when only its most significant features are emphasized, is really a tragedy; but gone through in detail, it has the character of a comedy." And, to make things worse, "our life must contain all the woes of tragedy, and yet we cannot even assert the dignity of tragic characters, but, in the broad detail of life, are inevitably the foolish characters of a comedy." In its stumbling thought, pessimism magnifies what Japanese philosopher Keiji Nishitani once called "the tendency towards the loss of the human."

But this is ridiculous, for what would be left after a philosophy without the human at its center? All that would remain is something strange and impersonal, pointing to the horizon of our ability to understand both ourselves and the world into which we are thrown. Comedian George Carlin puts it more succinctly: "Save the planet? We don't even know how to take care of ourselves yet... besides, there is nothing wrong with the planet. The planet will be fine. The *people* are fucked..."

~ * ~

Evening. Listening to R's lecture. Afterwards, the usual tedious questions are asked. Talk about "ontology," "foundationalism," "contingency," "finitude," "realism," and so on. Suddenly a phrase jumps out: "...I would say be very wary of anyone telling you you're suffering for a reason..." I forget the question that this was the response to.

~ * ~

In his 1710 treatise *Theodicy*, Leibniz noted that this is the best of all possible worlds. But he made the mistake of *arguing* this. Only disappointment can follow.

~ * ~

Sperno Ergo Sum (I). In modern philosophy, Descartes's formulation *Cogito ergo sum* represents the pinnacle of humanist thinking, the elevation of the human via the machinations of reason.

Pessimism has its own version: that the pinnacle of humanity lies in its ability to be disgusted with itself. What really separates us from other forms of life is our ability to detest our kind, to recognize the stupidity of being human.

I spite, therefore I am.

~ * ~

Sperno Ergo Sum (II). In the history of philosophy, faith

is continually subject to reason, even though philosophy was once said to be the handmaiden to theology. In the eleventh century, Anselm of Canterbury formulated what would come to be known as the "ontological argument" for the existence of God: God is that beyond which nothing greater can be conceived. (The failure to prove the existence of God itself serves as a proof, grounded as human beings are in finitude and temporality.)

From the austere negations of the ancient Indian materialists, to the funereal perambulations of Schopenhauer, pessimism also has its own ontological argument: existence is that beyond which nothing worse can be conceived.

~ * ~

Sperno Ergo Sum (III). Though an individual animal may express hostility towards members of its own species, human beings are unique in that we may feel hostility towards the species as a whole; that is, human beings feel *disgust*. Disgust doesn't quite have the active character of hatred, nor the passive character of repulsion – it is a kind of shriveling of being, a contracted, condensed, withering of life. One feels disgust only indirectly – a floating plastic bottle in a pond, discarded food strewn along a forest trail, a half-empty bag of seaweed-flavored chips cast along the beach. Disgust is always disgust at what is left behind.

~ * ~

Sperno Ergo Sum (IV). A park, a beach, a city street, an outdoor market, a concert, a restaurant, bar, café… There is no better display of existential squalor than human beings performing their own enjoyment before each other.

~ * ~

Sperno Ergo Sum (V). Misanthropy as the highest form of anthropocentrism.

~ * ~

Sperno Ergo Sum (VI). Pessimism is the logical extension of humanism.

~ * ~

Sperno Ergo Sum (VII). "You can spit on yourself without opening your mouth" (Stanisław Lec).

~ * ~

Sperno Ergo Sum (VIII). I long to write a masterpiece of ugliness, a grand treatise of misanthropy, a magnum opus of vitriol and disgust – an indictment of a species whose greatest achievement is the realization of its own extinction. (And I will surely fail even in that.)

~ * ~

Sperno Ergo Sum (IX). There are times when I feel that

the only real aptitude of our species is that we can ruin *anything*. Nothing escapes our tainted and gloaming fingers.

"It's like we're all worms in the dirt," P says to me. "Our function is to decompose things, to break them down."

Like maggots.

~ * ~

Nietzsche provides the most astute critique of pessimism. Like religion, pessimism also says "no" to life and to the world as it is. For Nietzsche, "the futility, fallacy, absurdity, deceitfulness" of such a refusal is that it always finds itself in a double-bind: "A condemnation of life on the part of the living is, in the end, only the symptom of a certain type of life..." Hence the criteria for any pessimist philosophy is compromise. Nietzsche again: "...to raise the problem of the *value* of life, you would need to be both *outside* of life and as familiar with life as someone, anyone, everyone who has ever lived."

Perhaps what Nietzsche is grappling with in passages like these is a suspicion concerning the arbitrariness of life. To be alive and to refuse life: "...this is enough to tell us that the problem is inaccessible to us."

~ * ~

The quiet vertigo in our ears is the slumbering turning of diffident dripping black moons.

~ * ~

...hearing instructions on the subway platform so distorted it sounds like moaning; seeing the news on TV without sound; sitting on the toilet; standing in an elevator alone; waiting at a crosswalk at an abandoned street; walking through the park and seeing a squirrel steal food from a child...

~ * ~

"We can tell whether we are happy by the sound of the wind. It warns the unhappy man of the fragility of his house, hounding him from shallow sleep and violent dreams. To the happy man it is the song of his protectedness: its furious howling concedes that it has power over him no longer" (Adorno).

~ * ~

The point at which writing *about* pessimism must become pessimist writing.

~ * ~

An Inventory of Affects (III). Over breakfast one morning, P tells me about something she read. A leaked UN report connects food shortage to climate change. Its conclusions are not uplifting. While food demand will increase 14% globally over the next decade, global food supply will decrease 2%. As plant and animal species run the risk of extinction due to changes in climate, the development of new land for agriculture and farming could also intensify climate change through the emission of large amounts of CO_2. The result is a large-scale reduction in the global human population, especially in high-poverty, tropical regions. A slow starving of the species. The coming global conflicts will not be over wealth, power, or energy, but over the elements – H_2O, O_2, CO_2… a conflict of breath… an elemental war…

~ * ~

Our bodies are shimmering, honeydew cadavers, and our cadavers are powdered black onyx, and every limb and tendon and nerve the humility of small crepuscular plants.

~ * ~

While listening to an interview with a neuroscientist, I hear the following: "No philosopher has been able to distance themselves from their pain." Pessimism as *anterior* to philosophy.

~ * ~

Written in a diary form, Mela Hartwig's *Am I A Redundant Human Being?* is less a novel and more a treatise on resignation. It recounts a life that is, by every turn, nullified in its being lived. Not exactly a life of failure, but neither – for this reason – a "successful" life. A life continually estranged – from relations with others, from a job, from the city, from one's own body and thoughts.

Everything falls flat. "This is the story that I want to write," the diary proclaims, "though, it's so laughably mundane, so incontestably banal, that it's really no story at all."

Greater or less effort in acclimating herself seems to have no effect. All that remains is a lassitude born of the nullification of all effort. "My laziness became stronger than I was. It was like a sickness. It was like narcosis. Yet it was accompanied by an inexplicable restlessness."

~ * ~

Alibi for the Brain. A character in one of Dostoevsky's novels states: "You still can't find the right answer to this question and you're very worried about it… You, too, in your despair, are for the time being amusing yourself with magazine articles and discussions in society without believing in your arguments and smiling bitterly at them with an ache in your heart…"

~ * ~

Low-grade, chronic pain for weeks, months. I'm trying to listen to my body, but I don't know what language it's speaking.

~ * ~

The Silence of God. In his 1909 book *La Réligion de la musique*, Camille Mauclair contrasts two types of silence: an everyday silence, and silence as the absence of all sound. The first type of silence we hear in contrast to the sounds that precede it – and even then we continue to hear this contrast as "quiet". The second type of silence is, strictly speaking, inaudible. "Only the silence of God is silence, and ours is by contrast filled with noise."

Still, Mauclair insists that even in this divine silence there is a kind of musicality. "I imagine," he notes, "a music that would express nothing of our own language of passion… but instead an *ideal cessation of all sound…* that which is voiced in the realm of spirit when life expires."

~ * ~

A Haven. A café, a cold, clear, winter late-afternoon – it's warm inside, music muffled in the background, an espresso in front of me, an open notebook in which I'm trying to sort out the variants in Pessoa's *Book of Disquiet*. Gradually, I become distracted by the annoying young couple near the front of the café – the very tone of their over-excited voices betrays a knowing self-absorption that is all too familiar. They are annoying by their very existence, everything about them, their mannerisms, every expression… but it's especially their voices that concern me. They're so loud, so quirky, so hyperactive – I feel that I've never heard so many words crammed into a single breath, an unending commentary on virtually every thinkable topic, soaked in banality and cliché. Such irritation is contagious. The person next to me, pretending to be too busy doing nothing, refuses to move their huge bag and laptop to make a little room. With disbelief, I overhear someone else order a pint of beer with an espresso shot. Two parents with cantankerous strollers stumble in...

All antipathy eventually becomes auto-antipathy. (And what am I, a sullen and shadowy lump, grumbling in the corner?) I spend so much time writing in cafés in order to fuel my misanthropy. At the end of my writing this I realize how I've just wasted my time, crossing it out with a big "X".

~ * ~

A Taxonomy of Failure.
- Trying, then failing. Failing to appreciate this. (Dostoevsky's *The Idiot*)
- Trying and trying again. Failing and failing again. (Bernhard's *The Loser*)
- Failing better. Each time. (Beckett's trilogy)
- Not bothering to try in the first place. (Ajita Kesakambali, Diogenes, Zhuangzi)
- Failing, unaware that one had been trying. (Kafka's *The Trial*)
- Failing, unaware that one has failed. (Krasznahorkai's *Satantango*)
- Trying awkwardly, failing awkwardly. (Dazai's *No Longer Human*)
- Bewildering failure. (Lispector's *The Passion According to GH*)
- Clinical failure. (Carrington's *Down Below*)
- Certain effort, uncertain failure. (Gogol's *Dead Souls*)
- The mind is willing, the body unable; the body

is willing, the mind unable. (Artaud's letters)
- Failure to fail. (applies to all writers)
- Successful failure. (applies to all authors)

~ * ~

A Master Class in the Aphorism. Around 1879, as he is forced to retire from his teaching position due to ill health, Nietzsche ceases writing in the style of the essay, and begins composing the dense aphorisms that he would continue to produce until his final productive year in 1888. In the first published work of this type – *Human, All Too Human* – one can see Nietzsche deploying several techniques for writing "antiphilosophically."

One such technique is the swerve, in which Nietzsche avoids direct attacks on a topic, preferring instead an indirect approach of twists and turns, with a tone that is now ironic, now sardonic, now spiteful, but never direct. In *Human, All Too Human*, Nietzsche does not attack Christianity directly, but notes that the problem with Christianity is Christians – too comfortable to get out of bed, not even worthy of the suffering that is really their greatest reward.

Another technique Nietzsche uses is that of the "low thought," in which the highest, loftiest ideas are suddenly re-interpreted according to the basest, most rudimentary explanations. Nietzsche's favorite ruses are biology and psychology, carefully deployed in a way that takes the highest human notions – the soul, morality, consciousness – and brings these down to earth, made "low" through the cold reductive lens of science.

Our highest moral ideals are nothing but decisions made on empty stomachs.

Finally, there is Nietzsche's overwhelming spells of enthusiasm, which can suddenly burst through the layers of irony and sarcasm he has so carefully constructed. At the end of a long and weighty section in which he has dismantled the pretenses of morality, Nietzsche suddenly jumps in with this: "And with that, forward on the track of wisdom with a firm step and a steady confidence! Whatever you are, serve as your own source of experience! Throw off the dissatisfaction with your nature, pardon yourself for your own self, for in every case you have in yourself a ladder with a hundred rungs on which you can climb to knowledge..." These are passages that contain such enthusiasm it almost seems inappropriate. The philosopher suddenly breaks into song.

As a student, when I first read passages like these, I wanted to jump up with Nietzsche in affirmation. Now, re-reading them, I almost look down in embarrassment. How should one balance the stark, cynical critique of the human condition with such explosions of sincerity? The fault is mine, not Nietzsche's. I have, it seems, become *immune* to his enthusiasm.

~ * ~

Everything does work out in the end, one way or another.

~ * ~

Shestov: "To be irremediably unhappy – this is shameful... And since, sooner or later, every individual is doomed to irremediable unhappiness, the last word of philosophy is loneliness."

~ * ~

The pessimist's shortcoming: an enthusiasm for non-being.

~ * ~

In a sepulchral light the color of growth and of death, starfish majestically descend from the air in swirling, anodyne arabesques. Prisms float in their stillness and dream, crouching to leap even in their sleep, gathering gloom from uneven fathoms in their unhuman spines.

~ * ~

Threnody for a Damaged Life. Theodor Adorno's *Minima Moralia* is one of the most absorbing indictments of human culture that I know of. Written in exile during the 1940s, it is a collection of fragments in which each part is a whole. Never has so much care been given to the fragmentary; in form and content it embodies the challenges confronting philosophical thinking in the modern era.

"Estrangement shows itself precisely in the elimination of distance between people." When we are closest we are the farthest apart. We treasure our precious, unique, individual "experience" at the very moment it is revealed to be illusory: "To speak immediately of the immediate is to behave much as those novelists who drape their marionettes in imitated bygone passions like cheap jewelry, and make people who are no more than component parts of machinery act as if they still had the capacity to act as subjects, and as if something depended on their actions." The vanity of reflection. The pretentiousness of thought.

Negativity rules the day in *Minima Moralia*. Nothing is immune to Adorno's critical vitriol, above all the practice of thinking itself, which has, he bitterly notes, become reduced to self-help: "Ready-made enlightenment turns not only spontaneous reflection but also analytical insights – whose power equals the energy and suffering that it cost to gain them – into mass-produced articles, and the painful secrets of the individual history, which the orthodox method is already inclined to reduce to formulae, into commonplace conventions." Crises are identified, classified, and tethered to an entire diorama of therapeutic modalities, from algorithmic personality tests to the menu-option of anxiety disorders that increasingly seem inseparable from the media-saturated culture from which they emerge. Top-down approaches to cognition become directly correlated to advanced pharmacological design. A glitch in the code. You just need a top-up. "Terror before the abyss of the self is removed by the consciousness of being concerned with nothing so very different from arthritis or sinus trouble."

In the end, it is the rigor of *Minima Moralia* that I find compelling. But it is also its Achilles heel. There is a fascinating tension at work in nearly every fragment of the book. Adorno is constantly bemoaning the loss of humanity in and by humanity itself. And yet he hesitates, on principle, to state that things were better before. Adorno holds on dearly to his negativity (his "determinate negation" to the nth degree); it is the one thing he will not relinquish. This puts him in the position of stating that things are worse now, and they were bad before. In one of his last entries, Adorno himself admits that anything resembling "philosophy" is only possible within the framework of redemption. But a redemption from what? – from existence itself?

~ * ~

All the trees whose names we have forgotten have long since embraced our entwined limbs.

~ * ~

For the pessimist, sadness is pre-philosophical.

~ * ~

There are those philosophers who walk, those who sit, and those who lay down.

~ * ~

The profound failure.

~ * ~

Pessoa distinguishes tedium from boredom. Whereas boredom is the result of constraints, tedium is the result of a lack of all constraint, the wan and anonymous equivalence of all things, whether the world brimming with significance or emptied of all meaning. With tedium one is perpetually "imprisoned in the worthless freedom of an infinite cell." For Pessoa, all that remains is "the discomfort of having to keep living."

~ * ~

The claustrophobia of having to ceaselessly observe one's surroundings.

~ * ~

Nietzsche on philosophers: "...sometimes they even wallow in books, as in their own dung..."

~ * ~

Winter. Cold, wind, snow storms. A blizzard shuts down the city for days. After the storm, P and I witness the devastation to the physical surroundings of the New York area – loss of power, flooding, toppled trees, networks down. Reports pour in through all channels – apocalyptic images of burnt-out buildings, flooded streets, incidents of tragic deaths.

With great discomfort I watch as everyone – including myself – engages in the determined, even aggressive act of recuperating the event so that it has meaning. Images of heroism, stories of loss, idyllic expressions of cooperation and neighborliness, and a pervasive rhetorical blanketing of the world again made in our own image. This happened to us and for us.

The human species – omnivores of profundity.

~ * ~

During one of our many conversations at work, B says to me, "I think Schopenhauer liked music *before* he liked philosophy…" On my way home I kept wondering whether this made Schopenhauer a better pessimist, or a worse musician.

~ * ~

Misanthropology. While all pessimists are misanthropes, not all misanthropes are pessimists. Misanthropes share with pessimists the venomous spite towards the *anthropos*, whether it be derived from concrete experience or from abstractions and generalities (method matters little in misanthropy). But the misanthrope still holds out the hope for a life apart from human beings – a hope that, by definition, can never be fulfilled, since a misanthrope without others is no misanthrope.

Misanthropy has something else in common with pessimism: a refusal to overcome misanthropy. Certainly there are means for doing so. One can abandon society and one's fellow beings for desert caves, as did Saint Antony. One can abandon civilization and the modern world, as did Thoreau. One can even abandon one's craft and finally one's self, as did Rimbaud. But even here the ridiculous details of the everyday –

of living – tend to get in the way, ruining everything. Eventually other people come to visit you at your desert cave, asking for advice; or you find that you need a new pair of boots, more paper to write on, supplies and a blanket, or you realize you've simply exchanged one banal life for another, and you end up writing abbreviated, plaintive letters home as an illness eats away at your cadaverous body.

Contrary to expectation, the misanthrope does not seek a paradise of life without others. This is why misanthropes are frequently found in populated areas. Molière understood this well, portraying it in his 1666 play *Le Misanthrope*:

> All are corrupt; there's nothing to be seen
> In court or town but aggravates my spleen.
> I fall into deep gloom and melancholy
> When I survey the scene of human folly,
> Finding on every hand base flattery,
> Injustice, fraud, self-interest, treachery…
> Ah, it's too much; mankind has grown so base,
> I mean to break with the whole human race.

But beneath this there is a further austerity to the misanthrope – the strange comfort in knowing that, even in the absence of all people, there would still remain a final misanthropy, against oneself. Misanthropy, like pessimism, is an *a priori* state, apart from any experience. Leopardi: "Men are wretched by necessity, and determined to believe themselves wretched by accident."

~ * ~

If hope is a virtue, is futility salvation?

~ * ~

The Forsaken Philosopher. Philosophers rarely disown their works. I find this odd, since there are many examples of artists and writers either disowning or destroying their work… though even here nothing is for certain. Consider the case of Kafka, who left instructions that his work should be destroyed after his death, only to have his wishes promptly ignored by his editor. Likewise, when Thomas Bernhard died in 1989, his will explicitly forbid the future publication of his remaining writings, a wish that was obediently ignored by his heir.

Still, considering the frequency with which philosophers change their positions, it's curious there aren't more philosophical disownings. How fascinating it would be to encounter a thinker who would not only undertake an ambitious philosophical project, but who, after finishing it, would disown it entirely. Imagine writing a massive tome like *The Critique of Pure Reason*, or *The Phenomenology of Spirit*, or *Being and Time*, or *Logics of Worlds*, and then, without explanation or warning, promptly disowning it… What strange euphoria would follow?… The act of disowning might feel effortless, weightless…

~ * ~

To be reduced to the status of soil and worms and silted matter.

~ * ~

I Think, Therefore I Am Not. Are there philosophical diseases? (And if so, are there treatments for them?) Consider Unamuno's stark claim that consciousness is a disease, a sentiment Cioran would extend to existence itself.

More often than not, philosophers are dumbfounded by illness, rendered mute or superfluous before the withering away of the most basic gestures – eating, walking, sleeping. Nietzsche's persistent digestive problems are perhaps the most well-known example. Why has no one ever thought of a "divine stomach," he asks.

If there is a philosophical disease, it would have to be Cotard's syndrome. In the nineteenth century, the Parisian neurologist Jules Cotard delivered a lecture, "On Hypochondriacal Delusions in a Severe Form of Anxious Melancholia," in which he identified a unique form of delusion in which individuals refuse to believe in their own existence. Variants include the belief that one is dead, or that one's body is a putrefying corpse (hence the phrase "Walking Corpse Syndrome"). Cotard was no philosopher. But he did have the wherewithal to describe the condition as *le délire de négation*. It would be difficult to find a more apt definition for pessimism. Pessimism: the delirium of negation.

Cotard's many case studies read like biographies of pessimist thinkers. For instance, one case concerns a

"Mademoiselle X." She not only denied the existence of God and the soul, like any good philosopher, but she also denied the existence of her body, of her mind, and claimed that she no longer needed to eat. She died of starvation.

~ * ~

Feral Humanism. In one of his notebooks Jean Baudrillard writes: "If we consider the superiority of the human species, the size of its brain, its powers of thinking, language, and organization, we can say this: were there the slightest possibility that another rival or superior species might appear, on earth or elsewhere, man would use every means at his disposal to destroy it."

So great is our monopoly on species-superiority that we are willing to take it to its logical conclusion. Nothing can come after us – we will ensure it. Extinction proves the superiority of the species.

Baudrillard calls this "feral humanism."

~ * ~

Thursday, 8:50pm, late summer. Walking, standing, sitting, waiting, talking, looking, not looking... The suffocation of egos everywhere, a miasma of selfhood... (Must write this down, must get going, things to do...)

~ * ~

We do not live – we are lived.

~ * ~

Told in the form of an extended interior monologue, Clarice Lispector's *The Passion According to GH* is a book that returns again and again to the theme of the nullification of the human, to the zero-point at the core of the human being, a "prayer of the neutral" – but a prayer without religion, without God, without humanity, without hope, only "plankton struggling" towards "the great living neutrality"... "a murmur without any human meaning." At one point, the text announces, "more than a star, today I want the thick and black root of the stars, I want the source that always seems dirty, and is dirty, and that is always incomprehensible." (The entirety of the book's "plot" consists of a solitary woman confronting – and communing with – a large insect.) And yet, behind all prayers "the continual breathing of the world is what we hear and call silence." In another passage Lispector is more concise: "I had humanized life too much."

~ * ~

A Bad Mood (III). It is well known that Schopenhauer was little read during his lifetime. That began to change as he reached old age, and was discovered by a generation of young followers, eager to take up the stark insights of *The World as Will and Representation*. Julius Bahnsen, Philipp Mainländer, Julius Frauenstädt, Stephan Gätschenberger, Edouard von Hartmann, Edmund Pfleiderer, Olga Plümacher, Johannes Volkelt... thinkers even less read than Schopenhauer, their pessimism at once darker, starker, more scientific, more ambitious...

The reverse is happening today, as a kind of Schopenhauer revival seems to be taking place among public intellectuals. But today's Schopenhauerians are different – they're more tame, more predictable, more popular. Their careers and their book sales are at stake.

Really, I'm just resentful that I spent time reading these books when I could've been reading other books... or not reading at all, or drinking coffee, or staring at the sky. But how to distinguish a waste of time from simply passing time? Maybe that's what pessimism really is: the inability to separate "a waste of time" from "passing the time."

~ * ~

To think is to condescend to exist. The least offensive act.

~ * ~

"What can be usefully postponed can be even more usefully abandoned" (Epictetus).

~ * ~

Lest it be indicted for a lack of levity, pessimism is not without its own form of inebriation, a drunkenness imbibed on misanthropy and the intoxication of futility. The witches' scene from *Faust* gives us an example of a pessimist drinking song:

The world and ball
Both rise and fall
And roll and wallow;
It sounds like glass,
It bursts, alas,
The inside's hollow.

In the play Goethe has the song sung by the witch's familiars – a pack of monkeys.

~ * ~

Between 1250 and 1360 Grams. This past month I've had conversations with a young priest, an old professor, and a very old shaman. I've come away a little disappointed from all of them. Is the fault mine? Have I not listened carefully enough, or said the right things? Why do we all *know* so much? And why do we feel the unbearable urge to tell each other that we know so much? It's as if we are burdened by the question of what to do with thought, by our brains, by the very weight of the organ...

~ * ~

Two kinds of philosophers: those who say profound things about obvious topics, and those who say obvious things about profound topics.

~ * ~

Ad nauseum. Nothing inspires spite for humanity like

nature documentaries – even those that imagine the extinction of the human species. I used to find these fascinating, with a twinge of moral righteousness. There was a TV series called *Life After People*, which imagined what would happen to the planet if all human beings suddenly disappeared (one can always dream). Infrastructure collapses, "nature" takes over, animals run wild. But the truly depressing moments were those in which the *remnants* of humanity persist, long after the disappearance of the last human beings – steel structures, oil rigs, mines, and the cores of nuclear reactors, continuing to mark the planet with the indelible stain of humanity – the horror of humanity still there. All this is rendered the more insidious in the documentary *Human Planet* – a title as nauseating as its content. An exercise in spectator cruelty, each episode introduces us to the immensity of an indifferent, inhuman world – ocean, mountain, desert, jungle, forest, grassland – only to witness the pathetic and inconsequential "journey" of humanity towards its confrontation with and control over the world. Though it presents a heroic narrative of humans in relation to their surroundings, all it really does is evoke in me a deep-seeded hatred of humanity in its learned stupidity. I had to stop by the time I got to the "Grasslands" and "Desert" episodes; against the majestic backdrop of sandstorms the size of a continent, we see human beings stealing the kill from lions, burning down entire grasslands to make hunting for antelope easier, using dynamite to blow up tree ranges housing flocks of birds that feed on crops, using helicopters to herd cattle. It matters little to me whether they're on the Mongolian steppe, the deserts of

West Africa, the Australian Outback, the marshlands of Southeast Asia... I can't escape the feeling of nausea...

And this is just the tip of the iceberg – the ongoing spectacle of humans blissfully ignorant, boisterous, over-confident, scheming, and talking big about their dominion over the world – a suffocating, self-absorbed, vacuous place called the world-for-us – to say nothing of how human culture has legitimized the most horrific actions against itself, a sickening and banal drama of the exchange of bodies, the breeding of species, the struggle for power, prosperity, and prestige. It just keeps going on and on, no matter how many films or TV shows imagine – like a myth – the disappearance of the human. If I had the patience, I would write my own existentialist novel, my own version of Sartre's *Nausea*, except I would call it *Ad nauseum* and it wouldn't have any human characters in it... for that matter no living beings, no thoughts or emotions, just an extended threnody of species-specific self-loathing.

Our uniqueness. The next day I'm walking on the street and I see a poster on a passing bus announcing a new documentary: *Mankind – The Story Of Us All*. I laugh, but feel like to spit.

~ * ~

The pessimist: a lonely hermit.

~ * ~

Only optimists have truly suffered. The pessimist is deprived even of this.

~ * ~

Across our tranquil, tenebrous skulls pass apparitions
retrieved from the dimly-lit dusts of oblivion.

~ * ~

*I've Seen This Happen In Other People's Lives, Now It's
Happening In Mine.* There are moments when I feel
that living in cities is constituted entirely of pedantic
little conflicts, micro-confrontations that can suddenly
tip your attitude and ruin your day. That woman who
nonchalantly cuts into the front of the lunch line. That
suited man who shoulders you on the sidewalk while
rushing by. That student too self-conscious to give
up their seat to an elderly man on the subway. The
barista who blames you for the fact that they forgot
your coffee. Ridiculous, all of it. Each day a litany of
these types of banal confrontations. It makes me want
to opt out, not only of urban living, but of the entire
species. You would think that after all these years I'd be
used to it. I know that, as a thick-skinned city dweller,
I should learn not to take things so personally, to brush
it off and not let it get to me. But I fail. I end up awake
at night, half-consciously imagining a whole repertoire
of revenge fantasies, of instances in which I know just
the right thing to say or do which will have the most
devastating effect. It's always, of course, after the fact,
when it's too late and serves no purpose (other than to
deprive me of sleep).

Contrary to what the great works of literature tell us,
living in the modern city is neither heroic nor tragic –

nor even comedic. It's simply pedantic. The ancients didn't have a genre for this kind of experience. These micro-confrontations neither cathartically explode into full-blown conflict nor do they mercifully disappear after one has tolerated them enough and "paid their dues." Living in a city like New York is barely worth the hassle. But it is *always* barely worth the hassle – a kind of urban purgatory. I don't think we appreciate this enough; we are occluded by the over-confident provinciality that keeps a person in such a city. Jean Baudrillard once observed that people in New York are always smiling – to themselves.

~ * ~

I am a pessimist because I believe in disbelief.

~ * ~

Resignation – consolation prize for a life of studied defeatism. Pessoa: "A cup of coffee, a cigarette, and my dreams can substitute quite well for the universe and its stars…"

~ * ~

Over lunch, S helps me clarify the antagonism that is at the core of pessimism. To be against the world is actually to express two different kinds of antagonism: an antagonism against the world made in our own image (anthropomorphism) and an antagonism against the world made for our purpose (anthropocentrism). I realize that philosophical pessimism is defined by its inability to get beyond these antagonisms; what results is sorrow, despair, world-weariness, and... Pessimism resides in the weight of those ellipses, "and so on..."

~ * ~

From Lichtenberg's *Waste Books*: "First there is a time when we believe everything without reason. Then, for a short time, we believe discriminatingly. Then we believe nothing at all. And then we believe everything again and, indeed, cite reasons why we believe everything."

~ * ~

Sorrow and Laughter. The connection between pessimism and mysticism seems to be part of pessimism's history itself. However, while Schopenhauer made reference to the *Upanishads*, the Buddhist sutras, and Meister Eckhart, he did not explicitly tie the mystical impulse to pessimism. Decades after Schopenhauer's death, the Scottish philosopher R.M. Wenley published *Aspects of Pessimism* (1894), which contains one of the first attempts to draw out the correspondences between pessimism and mysticism. As he notes, both pessimism and mysticism harbor within themselves a deep suspicion of the world as it is: "The idea of development leads us to regard man as the highest result of the cosmic process, and so we try to read the universe in the light of an intelligence analogous to our own."

Wenley concludes with what remains one of the most

eloquent descriptions of pessimism: "Pessimism is the final resort of the Saint, of one who would turn his back upon man's estate like most Mystics; of the knave, who knows just enough about life to deem himself able to laugh at it; of the coward, who is overwhelmed by his surroundings, and would beg, or rather whine off; or of the thinker, whose thought, in his own self-delusion, turns upon a negation."

~ * ~

Pessimism is the most *generous* of thoughts; it includes everyone, if only by virtue of their existing.

~ * ~

"A good supply of resignation is of the first importance in providing for the journey of life" (Schopenhauer).

~ * ~

Wrapped in Stone. Jung once wrote of how he was taken with the philosophy of Schopenhauer above all other thinkers: "He was the first to speak of the suffering of the world... these things which the others hardly seemed to notice and always tried to resolve with all-embracing harmony and comprehensibility." For Jung, student of science that he was, Schopenhauer's pessimism seemed to be confirmed even in "the pitiless tragedies concealed in a flowery meadow."

But even prior to his discovery of Schopenhauer, Jung wrote of the profound depression he experienced on walking into a gothic cathedral: "...there the infinity and the cosmos, the chaos of meaning and meaninglessness, of impersonal purpose and mechanical law, were wrapped in stone..."

~ * ~

An Inventory of Affects (IV). I read a news item about a young Chinese man who attempted to commit suicide by offering himself to a pair of Bengal tigers at the zoo. After a few haphazard tugs, the tigers refused to eat him. Taken into custody, the man was subsequently treated for depression.

~ * ~

From Dostoevsky's prison memoir, *Notes From A Dead House*: "Towards morning, when the fleas themselves finally calm down, as if in a swoon, and you really do seem to fall into a sweet sleep in the morning coolness – the pitiless rat-a-tat of the drum suddenly resounds by the prison gate, and reveille begins. Cursing, you listen, wrapping your sheepskin around you, to the loud, distinct sounds, as if counting them, and meanwhile, through sleep, the unbearable thought enters your head that it will be the same tomorrow, and the day after tomorrow, and for several years on end, all the way till freedom. But when will you be free, you think, and where is this freedom? And meanwhile you've got to wake up; the everyday walking and jostling begins... People get dressed, hurry to work. True, you can catch another hour of sleep at noon."

~ * ~

Why are people so loud and irritating? *Homo sapiens* – the species that thinks aloud.

~ * ~

Theologians like Aquinas wrote extensive, elaborate treatises on the destiny of the soul after death. I've always found it disappointing he didn't expend the same energy investigating the greatest mystery of all – what happens to the body after death (a problem left to the physicians).

~ * ~

Sometime around 1650, Pascal begins to tell his acquaintances of a proposed scientific work, a "treatise on the void." At the root of the work – which Pascal would never finish – is the notion, borrowed from Aristotle, that "nature abhors a vacuum." For Aristotle, this meant that nature was inherently fecund and inventive. Pascal didn't necessarily agree with Aristotle. But his main dispute is with the tendency to anthropomorphize the natural, physical world. In a fragment from the *Pensées*, Pascal writes: "Nothing is more absurd than to say that inanimate objects have passions, beliefs, horrors, that unfeeling objects, without life and even incapable of life, have passions, and presuppose a soul sensitive enough to receive them…" That a vacuum exists is one question, but that it is a source of horror is for Pascal quite another. The void doesn't care. Pascal's tone turns into a mocking incredulity: "Besides, what is there in the void to make things afraid? Does the void have arms, legs, muscles, nerves?"

~ * ~

As Impersonal and Anonymous as Music Itself. Like many pessimist authors, J.K. Huysmans gives music a privileged status among the arts. And music is, for Huysmans, most effective in its primordial forms: The plainchant, for him, surpasses the most complex orchestral music in its ability to move mass, sound, and air. In his novel *À Rebours*, Huysmans reveals an almost devout reverence for chant: "The traditional melody was the only one which, with its powerful unison, its harmonies as massive and imposing as blocks of free-stone, could tone in with the old basilicas and fill their Romanesque vaults, of which it seemed to be the ema-nation, the very voice." The impossibly high, vaulted cathedrals, the levitating and amorphous clouds of incense, the *De profundis* "bewailing its moral destiny" like an invisible, liturgical whirlpool of dark matter – for Huysmans all this serves no other purpose than as support for music.

Huysmans' eulogy to plainchant reminds me of an oft-repeated myth concerning a group of Tibetan monks who were able, with only the sound of their chanting, to levitate and move massive stone blocks. Compared to this, the rest of us just *sing*, and badly at that.

~ * ~

The most devastating thing about suffering is that it is relative. There is always someone who hurts more, someone who hurts less.

~ * ~

In this tenebrous hall of mosses there is a wind-blown hush, distilled to nothing, except our own damp and disoriented nocturnal gaze. Forms of negation borne of the fecund and fruiting bodies of our most secret austerities.

~ * ~

It is no accident that the great pessimists of modernity – Huysmans, Kafka, Pessoa, Walser – were also life-long bureaucrats. They reveal to us the devastating possibility that "wasting time" and "passing time" amount to the same thing. (I recall a large faculty meeting trying to decide how to decide – there was eventually a vote on how to vote – which turned out inconclusive.) The more I think on it the more amazed I am that Beckett didn't spend all his spare time in committee meetings.

~ * ~

All events reach us instantaneously. So on the lookout are we for the tragic that bad news almost reaches us before it happens. A *speculative* pessimism.

~ * ~

Shipwreck of Life. Schopenhauer was a pessimist from the start. There is no key life experience that converts him to pessimism. As a student, he wrote the following in one of his notebooks: "Life itself is a sea full of rocks and whirlpools which man avoids with the greatest caution and care, although he knows that at every step he comes nearer to the greatest, the total, the inevitable and irremediable shipwreck, indeed even steers right into it, namely death…"

A few years prior to his death, Schopenhauer encapsulated the same sentiment in a notebook he titled *Senilia*: "This world exists as we can see for ourselves, only I would like to know who has got anything out of it."

That Schopenhauer bothers to write down such thoughts makes him a philosopher. But what he says is so unconditional that it makes him less than a philosopher (which he may have preferred).

~ * ~

The planet a grave mound. All the ages reduced to one.

~ * ~

The optimism of no longer having to live. How many times have I allowed myself this thought?

~ * ~

With pessimism the most basic distinctions quickly fade. From Bernhard's *The Loser*: "It's possible we have to assume that the so-called unhappy person doesn't exist, I thought, for we first make most of them unhappy by taking their *unhappiness* away from them."

~ * ~

All We Ever Wanted Was Everything. For the past eighteen months I've been struggling with chronic pain in my arms. I've had to stay off the computer almost entirely and can manage to write only a phrase or two in my notebook. Sometimes even holding open a book to read is difficult. So I just sit there. And ache. I watch the clouds – indifferent, impassive, impersonal. The doctors and therapists tell me it will get better, eventually. But "eventually" is so dubious a word.

If I'm lucky, eventually I'll have less and less to say, which means less to write down, until I stop writing altogether.

~ * ~

Cioran once noted that the function of the eyes is not to see but to weep.

~ * ~

Whereas the philosopher says "the world is morally neutral," the pessimist says "the world is morally indifferent."

~ * ~

In the winter of 1903, the author Ishikawa Takuboku began to show symptoms of the tuberculosis that would take his life a few years later, at the age of twenty-six. Initially, he kept a journal to chronicle his struggle with the illness, but the entries soon give way to confused resignation and embittered missives against his family, his colleagues, his country, and ultimately humanity in general. Continually beset by poverty, unemployment, and a failing career as a journalist, he writes, "I don't think that anything a human being does, whatever it is, has any worth. I'd thought literature was more noble, more valuable, than anything else, but I didn't know then what noble meant. Can anything human beings do be noble? Humanity itself is neither noble nor valuable."

The one consolation Takuboku allows himself is that he can write *tanka* (the short, thirty-one syllable poem) of a fair quality. One of his poems, from a collection titled *Fistful of Sand*, reads: "Somehow, / I feel there are more people than I expect, / who think the way I do." But even these only seem to add insult to injury. In his diary he asks, "Is there anything I can do besides read and write? I don't know. At any rate, I do feel as if I must always be doing something. Even when I'm indulging in idle carefree thought, I always feel as if I am being dogged by that 'something'."

~ * ~

To have lived a life of no consequence, the duration of each day brimming with meaning.

~ * ~

Schopenhauer, quoting Petrarch in the third, 1859 edition of *World as Will and Representation*: "If anyone who wanders all day arrives towards evening, it is enough."

~ * ~

It is just as impossible to hate everyone as it is to love everyone. Sometimes one motivates the other.

~ * ~

Kierkegaard: life is a tightrope.

Nietzsche: life is a jump rope.

Kafka: life is a trip rope.

Schopenhauer: life is a noose.

Cioran: life is a noose, improperly tied.

~ * ~

I like to imagine a philosophy without mastery, without system, without the human, without this… without that… without… without… just debris…

~ * ~

Birth is metaphysical injury. Healing takes time – the

span of one's life.

~ * ~

The best one can hope for is that others will also feel depressed – the only form of inspiration the pessimist writer can give the pessimist reader. The Russian decadent authors of the 1890s excelled at this. Leonid Andreyev, having attempted suicide several times, declared that he hoped his works would inspire readers to end their own lives, and legend has it that he kept suicide notes sent to him by (former) readers. The same can be said of Valery Briusov and Fyodor Sologub. Sologub, who once wrote of one of his characters – "And he, too, will enter into life and give life to yet more beings, who will be as ghostly and unnecessary as a dream" – Sologub was, as a child, made to walk to school barefoot in order to teach him humility.

~ * ~

Adorno commenting on the way people use language at work: "…they greet each other with the hallos of familiar indifference… instead of letters they send each other inter-office communications without address or signature… random symptoms of a sickness of contact." Later on he notes, "no thought is immune against communication…"

~ * ~

One always laughs at oneself – especially when laughing at others. One is always spiteful of others – especially when spiteful of oneself.

~ * ~

A paraphrase of Voltaire: The gods made human beings in their image. To add insult to injury, human beings returned the favor.

~ * ~

Futility and euphoria. Muteness and loquaciousness.

~ * ~

A Bad Mood (IV). For a time I had the luxury of being able to walk to work. But the luxury could quickly become a burden, depending on who I encountered along the way. There is someone walking in front of me, chain-smoking, and the wind is, of course, blowing back in my direction. There is someone out walking their miniature, shivering, and completely untrained dog-rat, who wanders out directly in front of me on their expensive leather leash, leaving a raisin-sized turd behind. There is someone who is walking – no, skipping – while listening to their headphones, singing aloud for everyone else to hear – completely out of tune and off-pitch (but no one can keep them down because they're really feeling the music). There is someone (either naive or just out of college) who I can feel is going to try to get my signature for whatever futile cause they say they're supporting, even though they're simply doing it to put it on their C.V. when they apply to law school. There is someone either going to or returning from the gym, aggressively pushing a huge, military-issue, two-lane stroller with formless, whining protoplasm buried inside. There are overweight people who won't move out of the way (this has to be intentional). There are roving groups of jittery, insecure teens talking ten times louder than humanly required. There are clusters of inertial, self-aware people grazing all day long at the café, leaving open not a single chair or table, all of them droopily tethered to their laptops (no doubt pretending to work). There is someone. There is always someone. How is it possible to feel nothing but unmitigated spite for so many different kinds of people?

The list goes on – new additions are added each day. I try hard to simply enjoy the clear, sunny day, the (not-so-fresh) air, and so on. But I'm secretly waiting for the day when I come across a chain-smoking, dog-walking, overweight, pack of freelancers, pushing huge strollers while asking you if you have a second to save the planet. If I did, I would most likely embrace them.

~ * ~

The problem with the world is that one must always speak from within it.

~ * ~

"...the supreme triumph of reason, which is analytical, that is, destructive and dissolvent, is to cast doubt upon its own validity" (Unamuno). The pessimist looks forward to this.

~ * ~

"Do you laugh?"
"Only when it hurts."
We sit in silence.

~ * ~

How diffuse, how ambient the sense of estrangement is – and yet it seems to have an etiology. From Camus' diary of 1942: "What does this sudden awakening mean, in this dark room, with the sounds of a city that has suddenly become foreign to me? And everything is foreign to me, everything, without a single person who belongs to me, with no hiding place to heal this wound. What am I doing here, what is the point of these smiles and gestures?"

~ * ~

One myth concerning Lao Tzu tells us that he was born with a long white beard and when he first walked, he walked with a cane. Maybe we are all like this, born too old.

~ * ~

The German term *Schadenfreude* refers to those moments when we feel a secret (or not so secret) pleasure at the misfortunes of others. Better them than me. As

Nietzsche notes, "it is only since humans have learned to see in other humans their equals that *Schadenfreude* has existed."

~ * ~

Medieval mystics often make reference to the importance of silence in leading the ascetic life. Practical manuals such as *The Perfection of Monks*, *The Rule for Solitaries*, and of course *The Rule of Benedict*, all stress the centrality of silence as part of the monk's relation to the divine.

Such texts also distinguish between several kinds of silence. There is the silence of the external world when one is alone, there is the silence of one's inner thoughts in prayer, and there is the enigmatic silence of the presence of God, withdrawn from every possible human silence.

When all this fails, we arrive at a last type of silence – the silence of bewilderment, the silence of the dumbfounded… the silence of pessimism.

~ * ~

Pessimism cannot do without hypocrisy.

~ * ~

Syllogisms, propositions, axioms, diagrams and sets – the more complex and Byzantine a philosophy is, the more it displays a fidelity to system bordering on belief.

~ * ~

Centuries prior to the nineteenth-century vogue for Schopenhauer, Buddhist thinkers understood pessimism better than the so-called pessimists themselves. For instance, the second-century logician Nagarjuna speaks of the "nectar of vacuity" at the core of everything that exists...

~ * ~

The aphorism: a voluptuous immobility.

~ * ~

"How old are you?"
"Old enough to have regrets. Young enough to write it down."

~ * ~

The ellipsis is the punctuation mark of pessimism. It undermines whatever precedes it...

~ * ~

I have a great admiration for Dostoevsky, but I never had the patience to read six-hundred-page novels. I still don't. That said, I've made some exceptions in my inability to read big books. And I can now say that *The Idiot* is one of my favorites. Though it lacks the scope and philosophical profundity of *The Brothers Karamazov*, it is the austerity of the novel that I admire. Everything centers around the Prince Myshkin character, at once the most noble and the most ridiculous – everything becomes even more complicated than it was prior to his arrival, relationships become more ramified, motives are double and triple-layered, everything crumbles and falls around him – and gradually even he becomes suspicious he is helpless to do anything about it. It's as if every gesture – every action, every sign, every word offered – only makes things more messy. With *The Idiot* Dostoevsky has written an extended parable of the saying "the road to hell is paved with good intentions."

It took Dostoevsky some time to crystallize the novel around this central character. He made eight separate plans for the novel, and it wasn't until midway through that the character of the Idiot takes center stage. In his notebooks, he begins by describing the Idiot in almost romantic terms: "The Idiot's passions are violent, he has a burning need of love, a boundless pride..." But then Dostoevsky will also note: "He takes delight in humiliation" and "He is ashamed of everything and everyone." In subsequent plans the Idiot is more con-niving, playing people's self-interest against each other, inciting conflict and suspicion, even described at one point as an Iago-type character. It is in the fourth and fifth plans for the novel that Dostoevsky seems to give in and let the Idiot's contradictions stand as they are: "...he is filled with morbid pride to such a degree that he cannot help considering himself a god, and yet *at the same time* he has so little esteem for himself (he analyzes himself with great clarity) that he cannot help despising himself intensely, infinitely, and unjustifiably." Dostoevsky adds this is "the chief and paramount idea of the novel."

By the fourth plan the Idiot has become the central character of the novel. In his notebook Dostoevsky writes: "The Idiot is waiting expectantly and anxiously, as if there were something he had to do. He bestirs himself energetically and thus drives his sadness away by deluding himself" (to which he adds, "N.B. As if he had a goal, though he has none"). In the later notebooks the Idiot is described only in single, plain phrases: "Characterization. Magnanimous principles, childhood. Envy. Indignation." In another notebook: "The Idiot's personality. A bizarre creature. His oddities. Gentle. At times he says not a word." In another: "Downtroddenness. Timorousness. Self-abasement. Humility. He is fully aware he is an Idiot." This continues until the final notebook, where Dostoevsky writes: "Let us bring to an end the story of a person who has perhaps not been worthy of so much of the reader's attention – we agree as to that."

From Dostoevsky's earliest notes, however, one characteristic of the Idiot did not change: "He is an epileptic and has nervous seizures."

~ * ~

There is a euphoria in pessimism that eclipses every optimism.

~ * ~

"You don't even live once" (Karl Kraus).

~ * ~

Living: a body in search of a corpse.

~ * ~

Pessimism – a sorrowful logician, dutifully at work.

~ * ~

We investigate the axioms of black moons, measure liturgies of ash and dust, predict how and why our mud-laden bodies hang in heavy space. Every stumbling thought of purgation a halo of bones. Cold celestial limbs.

~ * ~

Self-Help. The moment you think you're a pessimist is the moment you cease to be one.

~ * ~

Nietzsche's insight is that we need not wait for God to will our suffering, so that we may then affirm it.

~ * ~

The world illuminated in its inconsequentiality.

~ * ~

The Life Almost Worth Living. "A thousand different kinds of troubles assailed me in single file; I would have suffered them more cheerfully in a single pile" (Montaigne).

~ * ~

An Inventory of Affects (V). Scientists estimate the Earth is approximately 4.5 billion years old, the result of solar nebulae and the subsequent gravitational accretions of matter in space. The earliest life forms on the planet are estimated to have evolved 3.5 billion years ago, with Photosynthetic life forms appearing 2 billion years ago. The first complex (multicellular) life forms evolved approximately 580 million years ago, the first vertebrate mammals 380 million years ago, the era of the dinosaurs 230 to 265 million years ago, and the first hominids approximately 200,000 years ago.

When arranged on the clock, with a full hour representing the history of the planet, the appearance of the earliest human beings would occupy the final seconds of that hour. It is the misfortune of our species to regard these final few moments as a culmination point.

~ * ~

Pessimism – like music – always takes itself too seriously.

~ * ~

The Linguistic Turn in Pessimism. Every word uttered a

complaint. Every word written a confession.

~ * ~

My optimism: that pessimism be unconditional.

~ * ~

To be so enamored of that which is not human that it is pathological. Lacking a term for this "spiritual sickness," the theologian Rudolf Otto uses the term *theopathy* – the devoutness towards that which is unhuman.

~ * ~

An axiom is a short logical statement of a self-evident truth. A theorem is a truth proposition that can be demonstrably proven using mathematics or logic. An epigram is a short statement, often of a literary character, expressing a general truth.

What then of the aphorism? It is short, and makes pretenses to a truth claim, or at least to saying something significant. Unlike the axiom, it lacks the predilection for self-evident truths. It also lacks the logical rigor of the theorem. It lacks even the imagination of the epigram.

What does the aphorism do? It is *aphorizein*, that which marks off, divides, sets apart–

No doubt pessimists cherish the aphorism due to this setting-apart. It is the dream of a self-sufficient negation, a lull in the abyss, the tranquility of a barely heard murmur. It is a disappointing dream, too, because the aphorism is also *aphorismus* – concise, encapsulated, definitive. The dream of saying something that would dissolve – or absolve – itself, with all the ease of giving up.

~ * ~

It is said that the ancient philosopher Empedocles threw himself into the crater of Mt. Etna in order to seek truth in the only place it existed: the bowels of the earth. (He died.)

~ * ~

Aches and Pains. To the indifference of the cosmos corresponds the indifference of the body – the latter less spectacular, but no less grandiose.

~ * ~

"Only the living may be dead, the waking sleep, the young be old" (Heraclitus).

~ * ~

Too Much Coffee. Nietzsche once described the pessimist as a clever person who has ruined their stomach so as to complain about the food, also an apt description of how the pessimist writes...

~ * ~

The eighteenth-century French aphorist Chamfort relates a comment made by an acquaintance, whom he refers to as a "pleasant misanthrope": "It is only the futility of a first flood that prevents God from sending another."

~ * ~

When you're alone, your voice sounds different. Vaster. More empty.

~ * ~

Wrong Decision. D sends me one of his catches of the day. This one is from a children's book, one of those "choose your own adventure" stories (even though no adventure is really worth choosing):

> #292 – The last thing you experience in this life is the feeling of being sucked into the void of darkness. No trace of you remains in this world, for you have passed into a realm of timeless existence. You have become a slave of an ancient evil. Your adventure ends here.

An entire exegesis could be written about this passage, which, I assume, is one of the endings of this particular choose-your-own-adventure book. I'm fascinated by the possibility of unexpectedly coming across this passage in a book – for an adult as well as for a twelve-year-old. It's too bad these techniques aren't employed in all books. How thrilling it would be to read philosophical books, knowing that the next page could be the end of the book. Ideally, after reading such a passage, the book itself would spontaneously combust and disintegrate into weightless ashes.

~ * ~

Pascal once referred to human beings as nothing more than thinking reeds: "There is no need for the whole universe to take up arms to crush him; a vapor, a drop of water, is enough to kill him…" And yet, even in the throes of death, human beings are capable of being conscious of their own state, and thus, for Pascal, the human being wins a small victory.

And the universe? "The universe knows nothing of this."

~ * ~

Schopenhauer: The world is tragic…
Nietzsche: The world is tragic!

~ * ~

The farce of human culture – reluctance, resentment…

~ * ~

Dostoevsky's *The Idiot* has one theme: human beings drowning each other in their humanity. For six hundred pages.

~ * ~

For optimists, the most perplexing question is how one becomes a pessimist – if one is not born one. For the pessimist, the question is how each person, by virtue of being born, is not already a pessimist.

~ * ~

The longer we suffer, the more we dwell on suffering – eventually suffering and the thought of suffering eclipse each other entirely...

~ * ~

Afraid to be content. Content to be sad.

~ * ~

"Without music, life would be an error" (Nietzsche). With music, life is still an error. Why then do so many pessimists – Pascal, Schopenhauer, Nietzsche, Kierkegaard, Adorno, Cioran – praise music? As proof or consolation?

~ * ~

If enthusiasm is the weakness of pessimists, then procrastination is the weakness of optimists. Stanisław Lec: "Optimists and pessimists differ only on the date of the end of the world."

~ * ~

The body withers away and dies. The science of anatomy is our only solace.

~ * ~

"Society is made up of two great classes: those who have more dinners than appetite, and those who have more appetite than dinners" (Chamfort).

~ * ~

I'm reading Wittgenstein's *On Certainty*. I read aloud some of the sections to P, feeling like an amateur stand-up comedian: "What reason have I, now, when I cannot see my toes, to assume that I have five toes on each foot?" "If you tried to doubt everything you would not get as far as doubting anything. The game of doubting itself presupposes certainty." "A doubt without an end is not even a doubt." And so on.

We make the sound for this type of thinking – that of tires spinning in the mud. It's become one of our jokes, used for the most everyday situations in which we find our thoughts spinning out of control, maddeningly turning in on themselves. We simply indicate it to each other by making that sound. An old car, a winter night, the inertia of mud or snow, the comedic futility of trying and trying again, as if in a clumsy dance…

~ * ~

A Bad Mood (V). "The Road Less Traveled," "Stumbling on Happiness," "Learned Optimism," "The How of Happiness"… a nauseating list of ineffectual ideas whose odorous pages seems to pour forth year after year like some kind of psycho-pharmaceutical hemorrhage of the American psyche. Where are all the "unhappiness gurus"? And yet we do have books like "The Uses of Pessimism," "The Power of Pessimism," and a host of condescending, blathering articles in the likes of *Psychology Today*… The entire discourse is so unbelievably vapid and imbecilic that I cannot help but make sweeping, general indictments against all over-educated, vain, and cretinous self-help gurus while refusing to read a single page of their so-called books. This enthusiasm lasts for as long as it takes to read the titles.

~ * ~

There are those rare moments when I'm grateful for words. "Egregious." No other word so effectively describes what it means to be human.

~ * ~

Forewords, Prefaces, Introductions, Appendices, Endnotes… M reminds me of the absurdity of all these quasi-textual texts. "If it's that important to read, why don't they just call it 'Chapter One'?" I laugh along with her, and suggest an alternative: that the whole book be called an Afterword, since none of it is important.

~ * ~

What the astronomer accepts, the philosopher still struggles with: whenever I look out upon the stars, infinite in every direction, I am at the center of it all. Cosmic horizon, cosmic solipsism.

~ * ~

Sometimes I'm asked if I'm a pessimist. I need to find a clever answer to this question. Or make up a good joke. But the truth is that I am a pessimist... except when writing about pessimism. I've managed to make pessimism a form of therapy.

~ * ~

Tears of the Cosmos. When I cry, I cry out of fear, anxiety, or regret. For its part, Christian mysticism outlines a theology of tears, which encompasses tears of purgation, tears of love, and tears of passion.

The first two kinds of tears are still with us today – we cry out of frustration or fear, and we cry out of feelings for others. But what of the third kind of tears, the tears of passion? Is there no secular equivalent? We are much too cynical to regard this as anything but a dress rehearsal. And yet suffering is everywhere – we are inured with it daily. The whole world suffers. If you are naive enough, you go further: *the universe suffers*. That suffering is universal is a commonplace. But that the universe suffers – even, that the cosmos has the structure of suffering – this is a reminder that our suffering is never simply "ours."

But how can there be a passion of the universe, when the universe remains so starkly indifferent?

~ * ~

Is it just as possible that "the worst" is, on the larger scale of things, so insignificant that it is self-deprecating? In one of his notebooks Joubert writes: "...the most terrible, the most horrible of catastrophes imaginable, the conflagration of the universe, can it be anything more than the crackling, the burst, and the evaporation of a grain of powder on a candle?"

~ * ~

I read somewhere that the Japanese author Haruo Satō wrote more unfinished stories than finished ones. I imagine the author of *Gloom in the Country* and *Gloom in the City* – masterpieces of introspective, opulent dreariness – must have found it difficult to begin writing, let alone to finish. As if the first line written is actually the result of a prolonged period of resignation.

~ * ~

The Tears of Kant. Cioran once wrote, "I turned away from philosophy when it became impossible to discover in Kant any human weakness, any authentic accent of melancholy, in Kant and in all the philosophers." I keep returning to Kant, but for the opposite reason. Each time I read, and witness the scintillating and austere construction of a system, I cannot help but to feel a certain sadness – the edifice itself is somehow depressing.

~ * ~

The Dullness of the Worst. There is a pessimism that consists entirely of passing the time. I think of the great non-novels of the past century – Kafka's *The Castle*, Pessoa's *The Book of Disquiet*, Walser's *The Assistant*, Bernhard's *The Loser*, back to Dostoevsky and forward to Krasznahorkai. A droll and dour and laconic pessimism of "whatever" – a listless life indistinguishable from merely existing, a merely existing indistinguishable from not existing at all…

~ * ~

Montaigne, Pascal, Leopardi, Kierkegaard, Nietzsche… I admit it's inaccurate to call them pessimists. They themselves never used the term (the same goes even for Schopenhauer). They were, perhaps, too *interested* in life. Isn't that the pessimist's frailty?

~ * ~

The lie of philosophy is given in the analogy of travel. When one returns from visiting a faraway place, one enjoys, for a while, a renewed sense of confidence, effortlessly undertaking tasks that would have previously been too intimidating.

Something similar happens to me, but in terms of

thought. After exploring another discipline, genre, or field, the myopia of traditional ways of thinking is made all the more evident, as is the arbitrariness with which we demarcate one discipline from another. I feel ready, even eager, to question everything.

But – as with travel – it doesn't last. The old habits return. In this sense philosophers – who have something to say about everything – are the worst kind of tourists.

~ * ~

Pessimism – a useless revelation.

~ * ~

In one of his last works Samuel Beckett writes: "Fail better." How disappointing. The therapeutic function soon gets the better of us all.

~ * ~

On Enthusiasm. "The world is so contemptible that the few decent persons who are to be found in it respect those who despise it and are influenced by the contempt itself" (Chamfort).

~ * ~

To "go through the motions" takes real courage – the somnambulist's courage.

~ * ~

"...the more I studied, the more I realized that I was ridiculous. For me, in the final analysis, higher learning amounted to explaining and proving my ridiculousness" (Dostoevsky).

~ * ~

The aphorism – the only thing the pessimist covets more than a gloomy outlook. As exact and rehearsed as a joke.

~ * ~

I've been emailing with T about various things, including our shared interest in the concepts of refusal, renunciation, and resignation. I mention I'm finishing a book called *Infinite Resignation*. He replies that there is surprisingly little on resignation as a philosophical concept. The only thing he finds is a book evocatively titled *The Art of Resignation* – only to find that it's a book about how to quit your job.

I laugh, but secretly wonder if I should read it.

~ * ~

We need fewer wise men these days. Lichtenberg: "It would be a good idea if some child would write a book for an old man, now that everyone is writing for children."

~ * ~

Human culture *inspires* hatred in me.

~ * ~

If there is one thing to learn from Nietzsche, it's the virtue of being wrong.

~ * ~

In the Library. An hour of contemplation is preferable to a lifetime of ambition, though neither produces tangible results.

~ * ~

Every faith should have as its aim *disbelief*.

~ * ~

Like Nietzsche, Keiji Nishitani was convinced that the way to move beyond pessimism was to move through it, and for the Kyoto School thinker this was the case more than ever, as modern science and technology were rapidly revealing an impersonal and indifferent order of things uncannily reminiscent of Schopenhauer and his acolytes. He writes: "The anthropomorphic view of the world, according to which the intention or will of someone lies behind events in the external world, was totally refuted by science." This was Schopenhauer's contribution. Nietzsche would take the next step. "Nietzsche wanted to erase the last vestiges of this anthropomorphism by applying the critique to the inner world as well."

So concerned is Nishitani about the problem of pessimism that he states: "the overcoming of this pessimistic nihilism represents the single greatest issue facing philosophy and religion in our times." Elsewhere, however, Nishitani confesses, "even we in the present age remain pious and show traces of a negative attitude to this life."

~ * ~

An Inventory of Affects (VI). We now consider suicide a medical, and not a philosophical, problem. And yet, we are told, suicide rates worldwide have only increased – one million people per year in the US alone. Research continues, new medicines are developed, no sure pattern can be detected. Perhaps the next stage is to consider suicide a mathematical problem, a stochastic problem, a game of chance.

~ * ~

To be continually dumbfounded by the insignificance of thought – of human thought…

~ * ~

We are invisible like our crystalline joints and our fibrous limbs and as tangible as the shadow play of thought itself.

~ * ~

Nietzsche once defined "not being able to wait" as one of our most typically human qualities. In culture as in history, all tragedies and comedies are simply the result of someone not being able to wait. If Medea had simply taken the day off? If Hamlet had put things off for even longer? If Arjuna has called the whole thing off? But not being able to wait is regarded as too much of a virtue to be sidelined like this – "not being able to wait" itself cannot wait.

How, then, should we understand an instantaneous, on-demand, twenty-first-century, "global" culture such as ours, constituted almost exclusively by waiting? Waiting for the subway, waiting for lunch, waiting for a friend, waiting at the airport, waiting to be called, waiting to not hurt, waiting to heal, waiting to be noticed or to be left in peace, waiting for a sign...

~ * ~

Over coffee, A gives me his book manuscript for my feedback. I am eager to read it, and, while I admire his work, I don't seem to be able to provide any illuminating feedback. I begin by underlining passages, writing marginalia, dog-earring pages – but towards the end of the manuscript I begin to draw images on the pages, spurred on by a particular sentence or turn of phrase. The last chapters contain images of black crystals, a flock of birds or bats, a gnarled hand, a smoking cauldron, and webs of lines draped between words – all, of course, poorly drawn. I hope he takes it as a compliment, if not as feedback.

~ * ~

Futility of the Brain. We imagine ourselves at once reducible to our brains and yet irreducible to any part of our being. The brain – that grotesque symbol that at once qualifies us as human beings and yet draws us down into a sullen and abject world of corpses and grey matter. In a way, the brain is simply our ability to authorize ourselves to take the brain for granted – each time we say "I think…", "I know…", "I don't know…", "I am…", "I was…"

Wittgenstein: "'I know that I am a human being.' In order to see how unclear the sense of this proposition is, consider its negation. At most it might be taken to mean 'I know I have the organs of a human.' (E.g. a brain which, after all, no one has ever yet seen.) But what about such a proposition as 'I know I have a brain?' Can I doubt it? Grounds for *doubt* are lacking! Everything speaks in its favor, nothing against it. Nevertheless it is imaginable that my skull should turn out empty when it was operated on."

The empty skull – the brain at its most useful.

~ * ~

Schopenhauer, Buddhism, Christianity, romanticism, decadence, nihilism, aestheticism, art for art's sake… For Nietzsche, all these are merely avatars of the pessimist viewpoint. What they all have in common is that they say "no" to life as it is; they preach resignation, refusal, sometimes even redemption. Where they differ from each other is *how* they say "no" – a question of style.

~ * ~

Why do I feel threatened by overly-gregarious people?

~ * ~

When a person recovers from a serious illness, our typical response is to immediately attribute some sort of cause to the recovery. A return from the brink of death cannot be insignificant. Someone or something must be thanked; there must be a reason this has happened. "Thanks to the doctors, you pulled through." "It must be God's will."

But we also know how tricky it is to attribute a miracle exclusively to science or religion. A doctor says, "We've done all we can, God willing, he'll pull through." A family member says, "Thank God the doctors were able to save him."

For centuries, philosophers have taught us how unreliable causality is, capable of being shaped and molded to fit whatever we already believe, and need to prove. What we are less able to do is to consider the arbitrariness of life, especially when it miraculously recedes from death. Do we ever really have the wisdom – the detachment – to see that the miracle of life *is* this arbitrariness?

In the meantime, a part of me mourns the person who has come back to life; nothing is more selfish, or more tragic.

~ * ~

Woven from sea moss, the slow swaying of time. In marrow-soaked dark and birchbark, we watch over what we fail to notice. The forests are not so closed, and our eyes not so open, where we sorrowfully graze on luminous garlands hung high.

~ * ~

Kierkegaard famously wrote "my sorrow is my castle." Unfortunately not all of us have as much space.

~ * ~

Birth: the originary trauma.

~ * ~

Tenebrism. To the obscurity of the world corresponds the obscurity of our understanding about the world. The philosopher argues that clarity in one area will lead to clarity in the other. The pessimist is unable to achieve even this level of clarity. On this, Nietzsche wrote: "The essential element in the black art of obscuritanism is not that it wants to darken individual understanding but that it wants to blacken our picture of the world, and darken our idea of existence."

Reading this, I realize that I've betrayed Nietzsche as frequently as I've read him.

~ * ~

I Refrain. When Montaigne's *Essays* are discussed, they are usually discussed within the context of skepticism, not pessimism. Montaigne was, perhaps, too *intrigued* by life. Nevertheless, the two overlap in several ways. Skeptical doubt fuels the pessimist's refusal of existence, just as pessimistic incredulity fuels the skeptic's mantra "I refrain." But if the pessimist tends towards disenchantment and despondency, the skeptic retains a certain cheerfulness, the cheerfulness of refraining, of opting-out, of not playing the game to begin with.

Locating Montaigne along this spectrum is difficult. Through he was prone to bouts of melancholy, he remained socially active and even lauds personal relationships in several of his essays. But for every essay on friendship there is another on solitude; for every essay on honor there is another on vanity; for every essay on conscience there is another on drunkenness. For other philosophers, skeptical doubt was a means to an end – for Descartes, doubt served as a by-way to the rational foundation of self-consciousness, whereas for Pascal, doubt was the jumping-off point for an affirmation of religious faith. However, Montaigne seems to indicate his adherence to another type of doubt, a doubt that is not a means to an end, but an end in itself. If there is a through line in the *Essays*, it is this idea of a pervasive, all-embracing doubt, a doubt without end. Even the titles of his essays espouse this type of doubt: "It is folly to measure the true and false by our own capacity", "Of the uncertainty of our judgment", "Of the vanity of words."

But it was in the lengthy "Apology for Raymond

Sebond" that we see Montaigne comment extensively on a particular type of skepticism, that of the Greek philosopher Pyrrho (c. 360 BC – c. 270 BC): "Pyrrho and the other Skeptics… say that they are still in search for the truth. These men judge that those who think they have found it are infinitely mistaken; and that there is also an overbold vanity in that second class that assures us that human powers are not capable of attaining it."

The response of the Pyrrhonian was a double refusal, a refusal of both sides, doubting every assertion, resulting in an absurdist chess match: "If they win, your proposition is lame; if you win, theirs is. If they lose, they confirm ignorance, if you lose, you confirm it." Montaigne summarizes the Pyrrhonian method: "Their expressions are: I establish nothing; it is no more thus than thus, or than neither way; I do not understand it; the appearances are equal on all sides; it is equally legitimate to speak for and against… Their sacramental word is ἐπέχω, that is to say, 'I hold back, I do not budge.'"

The philosophy of Pyrrho entered Montaigne's life through the writings of the second-century Greek physician and philosopher Sextus Empiricus, whose *Outlines of Pyrrhonism* details the elements of philosophical skepticism. Montaigne had read a Latin translation made by Henri Estienne in the 1560s, and it served as the source for the citations in his writing, both in his essays and on the numerous inscriptions he made on the ceiling beams of his library at home. The *Outlines of Pyrrhonism* defines skepticism as follows:

Skepticism is an ability, or mental attitude,

149

which opposes appearances to judgments in any way whatsoever, with the result that, owing to the equipollence of the objects and reasons thus opposed, we are brought firstly to a state of mental suspense and next to a state of unperturbedness or quietude.

Of "suspense" Sextus Empiricus says "a state of mental rest owing to which we neither deny nor affirm anything." And of "quietude" he says "an untroubled and tranquil condition of soul."

Doubt reveals nothing but an invariably modern faith in the reliability of doubt, in its usefulness in the service of philosophy. But in the fourth century, we find Pyrrho of Elis: doubt doesn't stop, or, doubt stops at tranquility. It is said that, finding himself unable to decide which of the philosophical schools of his day to support, Pyrrho discovered a state of stillness and quiet.

~ * ~

Doubtful. Where does doubt stop? Every philosopher must answer this question. Descartes: doubt stops at self-consciousness, the *cogito* (doubt stops so that it can become constructive). Hume: doubt stops at the habitual repetition of cause and effect (doubt stops because it is constructed). Wittgenstein: doubt stops at language, a game played out to its end (doubt stops so that the game can go on).

Attaining such tranquility is, of course, easier said than done. In the "Apology" Montaigne tells of how

Pyrrho, when talking with someone, displayed such equanimity that, if the discussant walked away, Pyrrho would simply continue talking, as if nothing had changed.

~ * ~

I've always had the suspicion that Nietzsche's works are an extended attempt to "shake" pessimism.

~ * ~

You can only force a smile for so long until it becomes a grimace.

~ * ~

The other night I picked up a book of aphorisms, I forgot by who – Lichtenberg, Leopardi... no, it was Chamfort – and opened at random. I read something to the effect that reading a book of aphorisms is like eating nuts or berries – you start by picking out the best ones. But gradually, reading becomes an act of laconic grazing.

~ * ~

Talking to K one day after lunch. Conversation turns to Surrealism, as I'm writing an article on the poet Robert Desnos, known for his ability to put himself into a sleep trance and then write fantastical stories. K reminds me of René Crevel, also adept at such "automatism," and who, when he committed suicide on June 18 of 1935, left only a short note: "Please cremate my body. Loathing."

~ * ~

"...nothing else can be stated as the aim of our existence except the knowledge that it would be better for us not to exist" (Schopenhauer). A realization that, of course, can only be arrived at by existing.

~ * ~

For all its claims to being the cultural and financial center of the world, New York City is remarkably disordered, dirty, and full of unpleasant people. As P and I walk down to the G train station, we are greeted by litter, rats, and the smell of urine. These are the twilight years of our culture. P says to me: "It's like we live in an *undeveloping* country."

~ * ~

Eliminativism (I). Some pessimist thinkers argue that consciousness is an aberration, that we are nothing more than neuro-cognitive automatons, and that our highest values are nothing more than ephemeral epiphenomena of an equally ephemeral notion of self, all undermined by the myriad impersonal atoms, quarks, strings, and bosons that dissolve the self into so many unnamable particles.

I find all this compelling. The problem is that even

this scientific pessimism still believes in the explanatory power of science. (Is this not the ultimate form of hubris?)

~ * ~

Eliminativism (II). The reduction of the mind to the brain, the reduction of the brain to the body, of the body to matter, of matter to silted dust, of dust to...

~ * ~

Eliminativism (III). In the philosophy of mind, "eliminativism" is the position that our common-sense, everyday notions of the mind are false, including mental states such as those of belief or doubt. But how could someone develop a philosophy of elimination, and then have such grand ambitions for it?

~ * ~

Eliminativism (IV). What always strikes me is how simple-minded neuropsychological explanations are.

~ * ~

Eliminativism (V). We are so easily rendered insignificant by time, so effortlessly reduced to matter. The only question that remains is which will go first, my body or my mind?

~ * ~

Against the Species. If we are indeed living in the era of the anthropocene, it seems sensible to invent forms of discrimination adequate to it. Let us cast off all forms of racism, sexism, nationalism, and the like, in favor of a new kind of discrimination – that of a *speciesism*. A disgust and revulsion towards the species that has, as a further qualification, the disgust towards ourselves. (Is this still too helpful, still carried out with too much good conscience?)

~ * ~

Dostoevsky. The trick to reading his novels is that the characters in them are less interesting than their misfortunes. It's taken me a while to appreciate this. So many plans, so many schemes, so many mishaps along the way...

~ * ~

Cavalcades of dying stars, dirtied ivory skulls caprioled, roaring diadem cataracts. From the gentle splashing, black wings brush against my face. What is our inertia compared to the stillness of suspended planets?

~ * ~

Read in a book on mysticism: "There is nothing in this world which does not speak." The world as idle chatter.

~ * ~

Pessimism is misanthropy as an end, not a means – misanthropy without origin.

~ * ~

Study of Failed Epiphanies. Walking home from work one day. I'm listening to music on headphones. I hear the sung lyric "Cathedral quiet and narcotic seas..." just as I was walking by the old church north of the park. The doors were open – a modest sign reads "Evening Silent Meditation." I'd always been meaning to go in, just to see what it looked like inside. So why didn't I go inside, sit down in an empty pew, and listen to the cathedral quiet? Maybe because I already did, because it was sadly meaningful before it even had the chance to happen. On the other hand, maybe I simply felt insecure, awkward, or just lazy.

Most of the epiphanies I have are, like this, failed ones.

~ * ~

One who has ceased being irritated by others, but who remains a misanthrope.

~ * ~

The downside of teaching the texts of Nietzsche, Leopardi, or Cioran is that they inspire students to produce their own texts of fragments and aphorisms. I caught myself the other day in a moment of condescension – clearly the student's writing "wasn't quite there," obviously they "didn't get it," and so on. And then the usual reflexive turn – am I any different? What makes me so sure my writing is worthwhile – simply because it's published? (And what more delusional reason for writing is there?) And the student, who am I to judge them? Wasn't Schopenhauer similarly dismissed? Wasn't Cioran once a student who had abandoned his thesis? Wasn't Nietzsche perennially dismissed *because of his writing*? Maybe the secret of the pessimist aphorism is actually quite simple, even formulaic: one is always pretending to be a writer.

~ * ~

While reading in a café, I came across this passage from Cioran: "I long to be free – desperately free. Free as the stillborn are free." Something strange happened – I sort of zoned out on this one passage for what seemed like an eternity. Everything around me became motionless and ambient. People still passed by outside, and I could still hear the faint clinking of cups, the distant din of the radio. My whole body felt relaxed and numb. I kept looking at the words on the page, aware that they were there, that they were words, words that said something, and yet I was not reading them – maybe I was hearing them, physically sensing the resonant flash of a long dead thought. Or maybe it was just that late afternoon slump.

~ * ~

Anyone can end their own life – for good reasons, for

bad reasons, or for no reason at all. Suicides can be intentional but also, sometimes, accidental – they can be personal or political, carefully planned or haphazard, tragic or comic, dramatic or absurd, spectacular or forgotten... Then there are the rest of us who die a little every day by living... There is a universality to suicide...

~ * ~

Schopenhauer's pessimism harbors within itself a secret optimism – the discovery of something unhuman at the core of the human: "...it would have been much better if the sun had been able to call up the phenomenon of life as little on the earth as on the moon; and if, here as there, the surface were still in a crystalline condition."

~ * ~

On the bustling street outside the café, a scene is taking place. An old homeless man is lethargically pushing a towering shopping cart, filled with black trash bags holding innumerable cans and plastic bottles. I watch him, slowly and silently pushing the cart as others walk by. At one point, his baggy and worn black pants fall down around his ankles. Unperturbed, he bends down, pulls up his pants, and then slowly turns and walks back, leaving the shopping cart. About half a block away are two more oversized trash bags, also full. He proceeds to drag the two extra bags along the sidewalk, towards the shopping cart. Once he reaches the shopping cart, he then proceeds to push the cart, leaving the two bags behind. He pushes the cart about half a block until his pants again fall down around his ankles. The entire pantomime starts all over again, all at the same, slow and even pace. He never asks for help and no one stops to help him.

~ * ~

Schopenhauer's paradox: that one lives, in spite of the fact that life is not worth living.

~ * ~

Nietzsche's paradox: the best one can hope for is the worst.

~ * ~

Cioran's paradox: existence has no meaning, and this is meaningful.

~ * ~

Pessoa's paradox: that everything amounts to nothing, and that this itself is something.

~ * ~

A Bad Mood (VII). There will always be someone who will see the futility of your actions. There will always be someone who is irritated by what you do, whatever you do. In this way we participate in a kind of shared, communal pessimism.

~ * ~

Pessimists are religious only by virtue of profound sarcasm, by the frustration that all religions are, in the end, solipsistic. Brahman into Atman, God incarnated as Christ, the Word made Flesh – that *any* people at all should be a chosen people is the most depressing thought. Must everything that indifferently transcends the human always be brought back to it?

~ * ~

We should be content with personal facts, false certitudes, forecasts and trivia, wagers and reveries, divinations and ciphers. Our consolation should be wisdom without philosophy.

~ * ~

If I ever wrote a self-help book I would begin with these words from Cioran: "The more you live, the less useful it seems to have lived."

~ * ~

We are a shapeless and hideous mass, a mass that might also be exhaled, which obscure theologians would call by obscure names, like a fine and rarified stellar dust.

~ * ~

How To Get Through The Day. Pessimism emerges out of a basic tension between the world as we think it should be and the world as it is. The tension cannot hold, and so we change the former, though it never quite matches the latter. Little did we expect that the world would also change.

~ * ~

After the lecture, D suggests to me another definition of pessimism – a "negative epiphany." I have been to places that I know I will never visit again. I have met people I know I will never see again. I have read books I know I will never read again. The negative epiphany is the moment one realizes, "I will never do this…", "I will never go here…", "I will never finish…" As if life were a prolonged expectation of such epiphanies.

~ * ~

In his book of aphorisms, *Cool Memories*, Jean Baudrillard writes: "the real joy of writing lies in the opportunity of being able to sacrifice a whole chapter for a single sentence, a complete sentence for a single word." Writing then becomes a process of relinquishing language, marred by the suspicion that each sacrifice is somehow insufficient, that there is still another thought, another phrase, still something to give – to give away…

~ * ~

There is no surer sign of pessimism than an overly-optimistic person.

~ * ~

The Misanthrope's Dilemma. When I laugh, it's usually among other people, unless I'm laughing at myself. When I cry, I'm usually alone, even if I'm around others.

~ * ~

The Slumber of Oblivion. Why does it feel so effortless, so natural, to lay down and sleep?

~ * ~

To be let down by life – one of pessimism's greatest affirmations.

~ * ~

Could it be that the world has inclinations that have nothing to do with being human? Could it be that being human has inclinations that have nothing to do with being human?

~ * ~

"Feeling of well-being after completed daily work" (Nietzsche). One has said too much, or too little.

~ * ~

We Philosophers. Eager to help, trained to be ineffectual.

~ * ~

The fragment is pessimism's *realism* showing through.

~ * ~

If Schopenhauer agrees *to* the indifference of the world, Nietzsche agrees *with* it. Schopenhauer lived to a ripe old age, grumbling the entire way; Nietzsche's life was cut short by madness and disease – was it worth it – for either of them?

~ * ~

Honest questions, dishonest replies.

~ * ~

Enthusiasm is the vulgarity of the few. Depression the luxury of the many.

~ * ~

God, the Plagiarist. "If there is anyone who owes everything to Bach, it is certainly God" (Cioran).

~ * ~

Just once, if you have been sad *for no reason*…

~ * ~

Enthusiasm as a form of depression.

~ * ~

The prolongation of suffering beyond death. Where pessimism stops and mysticism begins.

~ * ~

The human displays itself; the unhuman proves itself.

~ * ~

A paraphrase of Schopenhauer: Misanthropy and love of solitude are not the same. The pessimist's dilemma.

~ * ~

A year prior to his death Kafka writes in his journal: "February 20. Unnoticeable life. Noticeable failure."

~ * ~

Laying down on my back, acupuncture needles constellating both arms. An itch on my left temple.

~ * ~

The Age of Enlightenment. "He seemed to me like a man who was caged in the edifice of his own words and was pompously gesticulating in his prison."

~ * ~

Jotting down some notes, I misspelled "Confucianism" as "Confusionism" – which I like better.

~ * ~

Even the carnivorous plants of a thousand fingertipped moons are skeptical of all my efforts.

~ * ~

Another paraphrase of Schopenhauer: For the pessimist, the dead are envied. The old are only half-envied.

~ * ~

Pessimist of thought, optimist of books.

~ * ~

In a café I saw two signs: "Seat Yourself" and "Help Wanted."

~ * ~

Respectfully Decline. Is there a polite way to say no? Or is negation always impolite?

~ * ~

Pessimism: the poverty of philosophy.

~ * ~

"How are things going?" "Oh, I can't complain..." The greatest complaint of all.

~ * ~

A Happy Death. In spite of his pessimistic views on life, Schopenhauer famously argued against suicide, noting that, if the conditions of one's life changed for the better, we would likely call it off.

~ * ~

We misunderstand the café if we think only of the romanticized images of community at the Café de Flore, Les Deux Magots, the Gaslight, Café Reggio, Café Tingis. (We have, unfortunately, updated this image with the post-capitalist version of freelancers, laptops, and conference calls from "the office.") Arguably, "solitude" is an urban word. The café is the urban equivalent of the desert cave.

~ * ~

An Inventory of Affects (VII). In the "news" I read about a person on drugs, found crouched and naked in an alleyway, eating another person's face. Another item:

a person, perhaps also on drugs (and I am in awe of the possibility they weren't on drugs), is confronted by the police. In response he cuts open his abdomen, tears out his intestines, and hurls them violently at the police. One of my students tells me of a person who walks into a large hardware store, takes up a table saw, and proceeds to cut off both arms (I am amazed, even impressed, by the lack of foresight here...).

~ * ~

At the right scale, everything exists in relation to me, and everything makes sense. When things are scaled up or scaled down, the macrocosm and the microcosm gradually become indistinct from each other, rendering me as nothing more than the trace of stellar dust towards which I and everyone around me must ultimately return.

Sadly, the insignificance of all this remains profound.

~ * ~

During the last of our seminars, S and I attempt to summarize the main themes of the semester. S encapsulates our sentiments with the question, "What would philosophy have to become in order to take mysticism seriously?"

In commenting on our differences in teaching style, S notes my habit of neatly-arranged writing in my notebook, versus his "unwieldy" printed pages, his fondness for the "manic tradition" in philosophy and my "spiritual minimalism."

   At one point, in response to a question, I think S said, "we become mystics every time we sleep"...

~ * ~

There are two kinds of pessimism – one based on experience and one separate from experience. This latter kind of pessimism is unconditional – there is no experience that can adequately account for it. One can easily mistake it for inspiration.

~ * ~

Tranquility in a void. Equanimity in vastness.

~ * ~

We are the species that has sacrificed breath for speech.

~ * ~

In his journal Mário de Sà-Carneiro writes: "I imagine the utter devastation of my life as a series of zinc lozenges, bruised and twisted, spattered with various colors, in particular, by a shade of dirty red." And then this: "And many a night, in bed, reviewing the stagnant nausea of my existence, a ridiculous longing arises in me to make of my body a triangle and to have the vertices honed into sharp steel blades." A latticework of futility, a geometry of failure.

~ * ~

I am an embalmed version of my life.

~ * ~

The silence of refusal.

~ * ~

A character in Thomas Bernhard's *The Loser* rumi-
nates on his friend's recent suicide: "...the fact remains
that people are more unhappy than happy, he said, I
thought. He was an *aphorism writer*, there are countless aphorisms of his, I thought, one can assume he
destroyed them, *I write aphorisms*, he said over and
over, I thought, which is a minor art of the intellectual asthma from which certain people, above all in
France, have lived and still live, so-called half philosophers for nurses' night tables, I could also say calen-
dar philosophers for everybody and anybody, whose
sayings eventually find their way onto the walls of
every dentist's waiting room..." The monologue continues: "But I haven't been able to get rid of my habit
of writing aphorisms, in the end I'm afraid I will have
written millions of them, he said, I thought, and I'd
be well advised to start destroying them since I don't
plan to have the walls of every dentist's office and
church papered with them one day, as they are now
with Goethe, Lichtenberg, and comrades, he said, I
thought." To which is added: "Since I wasn't born to be
a philosopher I turned myself into an aphorist..." And

then: "If we look at things squarely the only thing left from the greatest philosophical enterprises is a pitiful aphoristic aftertaste…" And: "Our great philosophers, our greatest poets, shrivel down to a single successful sentence…" And finally: "Fundamentally we are capable of everything, equally fundamentally we fail at everything…" (But this is not "finally" because the entirety of Bernhard's book is a single, unending monologue.)

~ * ~

The human being – a living sacrifice.

~ * ~

Something to do, something to say, something I'd rather not to do, something I prefer not to say.

~ * ~

Stairways that one can neither ascend nor descend.

~ * ~

Nietzsche's Proof of God. "There would have to be creatures of more spirit than human beings, simply in order to savor the humor that lies in humans seeing themselves as the purpose of the whole existing world…"

~ * ~

The profanity of presence.

~ * ~

The planet rests in silent meditation. The terror of the species its proof.

~ * ~

Morbidity. I used to be afraid of exercising. That was before I was dealing with these health problems. Now I'm afraid of not exercising. The fear is the same.

~ * ~

If one fails one succeeds; if one succeeds one fails. What pessimism seeks is neither one nor the other. Ecstasy of the null state.

~ * ~

Baptism of time.

~ * ~

The stupidity of human beings is astounding. It requires an almost spiritual attitude to accept it – especially in ourselves.

~ * ~

As a philosopher, I'm much more interested in those

moments when a philosophy fails (and *all* philosophy fails... eventually).

~ * ~

Mea culpa. How can everything be so loud and yet so insignificant?

~ * ~

Few sights are more awkward (or embarrassing) than that of human beings in nature.

~ * ~

When asked a thought-provoking question, some look up at the ceiling, while others look down at the ground. Some close their eyes.

~ * ~

From Joubert's notebook of 1810: "All cries and all complaints exhale a vapor, and from this vapor a cloud is formed, and from these heaped-up clouds come thunder, storms, the inclemencies that destroy everything." Mountains made out of molehills.

~ * ~

The Philosophy of No. It's a cold but clear late-January day. I'm putting together the reading list for my pessimism seminar (called, "Pessimism"). It occurs to me that, after reading all these philosophers of futility, it will be nearly impossible for anyone in the class to turn in a final paper. After reading all these unfinished or fragmentary works – after Pascal and Pessoa, after the *Zibaldone* and the *Sudelbücher*, after the diaries of Kierkegaard, Kafka, Zürn, after the rantish indictments of Schopenhauer, Bernhard, Takuboku, after the one-liners of Chamfort or Cioran, after all this, why in the world would anyone write a finished paper? I should only pass those students incapable of finishing the course.

~ * ~

Everything – our very existence – is just for show.

~ * ~

"Generally, I lack the patience to live…" (Kierkegaard).

~ * ~

To die of old age – no matter how old you are.

~ * ~

Depression is the final stimulus of life.

~ * ~

The Spiritual Brain. "Logic is in essence optimism" (Nietzsche).

~ * ~

Our hunched-over backs mottled with indecipherable erosions, giving way beneath the slightest sigh. Sad things deprived even of decomposition.

~ * ~

For every day of philosophy there is a somnambulistic night of the aphorism.

~ * ~

What the title "PhD" indicates: much reading and little retention.

~ * ~

Epigraph/Epitaph. "Life is a disagreeable thing. I have set myself to spend it in thinking about it" (Schopenhauer, aged twenty-two, speaking to the seventy-eight-year-old poet Christoph Martin Wieland).

~ * ~

The solipsism of the species increases in inverse proportion to its relevance.

~ * ~

Half-full, Half-empty. What happens to me is not part of me.

~ * ~

"Not to be surprised at anything, they say, is a sign of great intelligence. In my opinion, it might as well be a sign of great stupidity" (Dostoevsky, *The Idiot*).

~ * ~

C tells me of a man he passed on his way to work this morning. He was standing on the corner, holding up a giant, handwritten sign: "I HATE MY LIFE." There wasn't even a hat or container for spare change.

~ * ~

I've never liked kids – even when I was a kid. But that doesn't absolve me from being an adult.

~ * ~

What Pascal said of those enamored of religion could also apply to those enamored of philosophy: "We lift our eyes on high, but lean upon the sand; and the earth will dissolve, and we shall fall whilst looking at the heavens."

~ * ~

Expressions of mute suffering.

~ * ~

In his journal the Viscount Lagano Tegui once noted that a book is the vegetal pulp of its author. He means it, I think, literally.

~ * ~

On the Vanity of Existence. People walking slower than me are idiots. People walking faster than me are assholes. And nothing is more annoying that a stranger walking at exactly my pace.

~ * ~

I am in the same café I've been going to for the past few weeks. "The usual?" "Yes," I say, holding back a smile. As I leave the barista says "See you tomorrow…" I already know that, for some reason, I'll go to a different café tomorrow.

~ * ~

Thursday, 4:05am. The most elevated type of suffering simply the marking of time by the body.

~ * ~

Wreaths of sleep-fed plankton calmly seep from every pore.

~ * ~

The exclamation point is the banalization of language.

(I long for someone to invent a punctuation mark for despondency...)

~ * ~

When someone casually asks me "How are you doing?", I sometimes find myself hesitating, as if caught in a micro-catatonia. The question is both petty and cosmic at the same time. Then I remember: just say "Fine."

~ * ~

Corpus mysticum. In spite of all our efforts, it seems difficult to truly get rid of corpses. In Western cultures, funerary practices play a game of hide and seek – we bury the body and then mark the hiding with a headstone (...why aren't there more hidden cemeteries?). We do all sorts of things to corpses – bury them, burn them, embalm them, we make death masks from them and donate them to science or to an exhibition. But cemeteries can be flooded, or the land might be purchased and the graves unearthed. And so the corpses keep coming back. Even in cremation one is still left with ashes and the urn, a sort of coffin-in-miniature. With cremation there are the winds that blow back in the wrong direction, or the weightlessness of ashes as the urn bobs up and down along the banks of a river out to sea. It is the persistence of the corpse that gives testimony to the notion that death is not the end. And the persistence of the corpse is perhaps the greatest tragicomedy.

~ * ~

"Only optimists commit suicide" (Cioran). And only pessimists think of it.

~ * ~

The miracle of birth is that one hasn't yet died. The miracle of death is that one didn't die sooner.

~ * ~

Sighs that eclipse living entirely.

~ * ~

Riding the subway. It rises above ground. Looking down, I see the streets, stores, people walking. The train passes by the massive expanse of a cemetery, almost endlessly populated by tombstones, carefully aligned yet overgrown and ruinous. It seems larger than all the streets and all the stores lining the streets. I imagine it imperceptibly expanding according to a logic unknown to even the most conniving realtors. Cemeteries like this – so vast – it reinforces Montaigne's observation: that our only occupation is to die.

~ * ~

Which is the least discouraging? To move from a contempt for others to a contempt for oneself, or the reverse?

~ * ~

De profundis. Schopenhauer frequently refers to blind, impersonal "Will" that drives everything that exists to exist, and that originates in a kind of primordial, anonymous abyss. Likewise, mystics such as Hadewijch, Mechthild of Madgeburg, and Marguerite of Porete frequently allude to divine love as a mutual abyss. In each instance, one *plummets* into the divine.

~ * ~

The universality of suffering. It is with either compassion or spite that I'm convinced life is idiotic, pedantic and, even in the best cases, barely worth the trouble. A confused irritation remorselessly extended in time, leaving not even an aching, writhing corpse – and then, mercifully, not even that.

~ * ~

Nietzsche pondering the uniqueness of human beings: we've suffered so much we were forced to invent laughter.

~ * ~

The only thing more terrifying than the person who has nothing is the person who has everything. Things can only get worse for them. The more you have, the more you have to lose. And in the end everything must be lost. Is it better to not want anything at all? Maybe, but what about the rest of us, who have some things, which we judiciously manage, like archivists?

~ * ~

Beasts of Indifference. The fable of "Schopenhauer's porcupine" provides one model for pessimist behavior: seeking warmth, the porcupines huddle together; but when they get too close their spines puff out, pushing each other away. But suppose the pessimist doesn't seek out others to begin with? What beast fable would be appropriate to such behavior? The hermit crab shuns not only others but the outside world, enclosing itself in a series of scavenged, discarded shells. Then there is the mole, constantly digging, refusing to acknowledge the world at all; or there is the moth, seeing everything and blinding itself in a luminous self-abnegation. Beyond this, there is the animal that does not hide or escape but that is impassive, supremely resigned, effortlessly authenticated in its mere quasi-existence – swarms of jellyfish, the imperceptible eukaryotes, weird lichen and fungi... Such beasts of indifference are the pessimist's spiritual guides, these insensate creatures of futility.

~ * ~

What is repulsive about children – all children – is not that they are not yet adults, but that they are already adults – whining, self-absorbed, demanding attention, unable to care for themselves, throwing tantrums when things don't go their way. Far from what we tell ourselves, children are the most concise expressions of humanity. At least children are unaware of this.

~ * ~

That not only I crumble but that the planet crumbles (…and the sun… and the stars… and the crumbling cosmos…) – is this what makes pessimism "philosophical"?

~ * ~

Reductionism is the guilty pleasure of philosophers. (Pessimism's shortcoming: it is too guilt-free to be philosophical.)

~ * ~

Aviaries of doubt.

~ * ~

Is it harder to watch other people age or oneself? Does my mortality seem more or less inevitable?

~ * ~

I don't believe in saying anything unless there's something to say. As time goes on, the less I speak. Boredom, depression, equanimity.

~ * ~

"The question of the purpose of human life has been raised countless times," Freud once wrote. "It has never yet received a satisfactory answer and perhaps does not admit of one." It is not only the irresolvable nature of the question that intrigues Freud, but its attendant urgency. "Some of those who have asked it have added that if it should turn out that life has *no* purpose, it would lose all value to them." The most urgent question, then, is also the one without a definitive answer.

"But this threat alters nothing," Freud replies. "It looks, on the contrary, as though one had a right to dismiss the question, for it seems to derive from the human presumptuousness, many other manifestations of which are already familiar to us." (He then observes: "Nobody talks about the purpose of the life of animals, unless, perhaps, it may be supposed to lie in being of service to mankind.")

~ * ~

The Copernican Paradox. The more we know about the world, the less we understand it.

~ * ~

"…what is called a reason for living is also an excellent reason for dying" (Camus).

~ * ~

A Manual of Meditation. Lying down on one's back, there's nothing to look at. Lying face-down produces the same effect (breathing is more difficult).

~ * ~

No one who has hoped for something has ever had their hopes perfectly realized. There are compromises, adjustments, contingencies. Eventually, hope becomes indistinguishable from resignation.

~ * ~

All our vespertine theologies are annulled by black-naped, ashen remorse.

~ * ~

I will pay extra to avoid bargaining.

~ * ~

At its best pessimism evokes the least noticeable smile.

~ * ~

Around 1913, Kafka, suffering from tuberculosis, stays with his sister's family on their farm, near the Swiss village of Zürau. There he writes aphorisms, perhaps as a form of convalescence. One of them reads: "A cage went in search of a bird."

~ * ~

Achy back, sore shoulders, tendonitis in my left elbow, and now I've discovered a strange pain in my thumb, no doubt from holding my pen too tight. There mouths all over my body, on my spine, my shoulders, elbow, knees, all moaning in a myriad of voices. It's as if my body refuses to write, a kind of corporeal Bartleby-ism.

~ * ~

There are times when I feel an antagonism that knows no limits – it is too sacred to simply call it "pessimism."

~ * ~

N sends me this line, from a book on mysticism: "Weep within continuously; outwardly remain normal and cheerful."

Horror of horrors – am I the reverse? Sullen on the outside, cheerful on the inside.

~ * ~

The human being: the animal that sighs.

~ * ~

There are times when the stupidity of our species is so suffocating that even extinction will not suffice. Then I understand, if only briefly, the other motive for suicide: the need – the desperate need – to be rid of other people.

~ * ~

The cosmos contemplates – we merely think.

~ * ~

The privilege of suffering.

~ * ~

"We have sufficient grounds for taking life mistrust-fully: it has defrauded us so often of our cherished expectations" (Shestov).

~ * ~

Thoughts as inexpressive as mist.

~ * ~

"Giving up is a revelation."

~ * ~

Everything I've written has been about one of two things – the unhuman outside the human, or the unhu-man inside the human.

~ * ~

J tells me about a nightmare he used to have as a child. Half-awake, in a kind of twilight sleep, he would feel everything around him "fill with emptiness." The room, his bed, even his own body – everything swelling with an infinite emptiness. It reminds me of meditating.

~ * ~

A Treatise on Humanism.
Human beings are capable of ruining anything.
Every thing is a "thing."

~ * ~

Religion Without God. Pascal: "Nothing is more intolerable than a state of complete repose, without desire, without work, without amusements, without occupation. In such a state one becomes aware of one's nothingness, one's abandonment, one's inadequacy, one's dependence, one's emptiness, one's futility. There at once wells up from the depths of the soul weariness, gloom, misery, exasperation, frustration, despair." In other words, divinity.

~ * ~

P and I are sleeping in the guestroom. The bed feels like an uneven lump of old cardboard and creaks like the hull of an old, derelict ship, making sleep an ache-ridden jumble of turbid dreams and sore muscles. Why is it that a bad attitude is effortless? – so effortless it is almost unconditional.

~ * ~

Kierkegaard once described faith as "floating over 70,000 fathoms." The weight of disappointment soon makes bottom-feeders of us all.

~ * ~

Aporia. One learns to laugh only after having learned to suffer. One learns to suffer only after having learned to laugh.

~ * ~

The pathos of the impersonal.

~ * ~

The obliteration of all necessity.

~ * ~

Some people attack life – they leap out onto the floor and dance with unbridled joy. Others recoil from life, sitting in the back corner, waiting for it all to pass. Both, however, regard living as something to deal with – like a wart, an abscess, a blemish.

~ * ~

To live in constant apprehension of life. Exhaustion before one has made the effort. To attempt to laugh at it all, until the laughter becomes slightly sad, until tedium covers everything with its tenebrous haze.

~ * ~

"There is nothing innocuous left" (Adorno).

~ * ~

From a book on nineteenth-century German philosophy: "In the Munich beer halls, when one student is heard laying down the law about something which he does not understand to a companion who cares not a rap on the subject, it is very generally taken for granted that the two are talking metaphysics." Which is the pessimist – the person talking or the person not listening?

~ * ~

Astral Projection. The more I talk to people, the less I see the point in conversation. I've often been in the midst of a conversation and have suddenly, unwillingly, been extracted mysteriously from it, as if I were observing the whole thing with a strange sense of detached melancholy, like an out-of-body experience. Why exactly are we talking? What exactly are we saying? And how long have we been talking? It's as if we talk in order to slow down time, thereby secretly extending our share of immortality just a little.

~ * ~

Lee Kiho's novel *At Least We Can Apologize* recounts the misadventures of a narrator and his companion Si-bong. Living in an unnamed institution, their daily activities seem to consist of labelling soap, packing socks, taking medication, and being periodically beaten by the caretakers. At one point the narrator and Si-bong realize that they will be beaten less the more they admit wrongdoing: "The caretakers said that committing the same wrong again was an ever greater wrong. So we had to come up with new wrongs every day. Some of them became 'wrongs,' while others became 'greater wrongs.' On days we committed wrongs, we were beaten less, on days we committed 'greater wrongs,' we were beaten a lot, and on days we admitted to nothing, we were beaten repeatedly all day long." The narrator adds: "After we confessed a wrong, we always made sure to commit it."

Later, after they leave the institution and are unable to find any work, the narrator and Si-bong come to the conclusion that they are only good at one thing. They make a sign and post it around the neighborhood: "We apologize for you! Parents, couples, siblings, acquaintances, friends, neighbors, coworkers, any relation! Whether you knew you were doing it or not, we offer apologies for any number of wrongs you've committed against someone. So don't hesitate, give us a call!"

~ * ~

In our contemporary mania for saving everything, we lose nothing. Gone are the days when a manuscript could be *burnt* – when writing could be reduced to ash and smoke...

~ * ~

An Inventory of Affects (VIII). Excessive sleeping or lack of sleep (hypersomnia or insomnia); lack of motivation; inadequate eating and/or significant weight change; decrease in enjoyment or pleasure in activity; irritable most of the day (or nearly every day); persistent feelings of sadness and/or emptiness; tearful appearance (observation made by others); feelings of excessive or inappropriate guilt; psychomotor agitation or retardation; thoughts of death or suicide (inclusive of suicidal ideation without a plan); fatigue and depletion of energy; persistent feelings of worthlessness; reduction in self-esteem and self-confidence; pervasive anxiety and/or despair; withdrawal from society and social interaction; diminished ability to think or concentrate; morbid preoccupation with feelings of hopelessness; debilitating indecisiveness every day (or nearly every day); quiet, negative, and oppositional behavior in social settings; constant fear that something awful might happen.

~ * ~

From a book review: "...the stammerings of an old man who does not seem to have achieved a full psychic victory over an awkward adolescence..."

~ * ~

Nietzsche dubbed his own brand of pessimism "Dionysian pessimism." It would retain the vitriol and misanthropy of Schopenhauer's philosophy, while jettisoning its world-weariness. This Dionysian pessimism would become – for Nietzsche – a source of joy, of the greatest and most difficult affirmation. All that we esteem would exist indifferently alongside all that we decry, the highest and the lowest, the most meaningful and the most meaningless... exclaiming a reverberant, even musical "yes" to all that is, as it is...

Few of us have the capacity for such a pessimism – truthfully, not even Nietzsche did. But what emerges from it is a strange, vaporous, vacuous sense of the unhuman. Even Nietzsche was aware of this. In one of the last notebooks, he writes: "This pessimism of strength ends in a *theodicy*."

~ * ~

I often succumb to that most secular of religious creeds: that religious people have ruined religion. I have an excuse, however. A farce is taking place just outside our building. A group from one of the neighborhood churches has set up a PA system. What ensues is a demonic cacophony of proselytizing and off-key singing, complete with microphone feedback. It's impossible for P and I to do anything – read, work, talk, sleep... I can't even hear myself think. I want nothing else than for them to please stop. I wish for a sudden thunderstorm, precisely targeted lightning, an air raid, a power failure, riot police, swarms of muggers, a bulldozer, anything... a miracle.

Amidst the chaos my one consolation is the strange and sovereign indifference of the day – buses stop and pick up passengers, people walk by with groceries, kids play at the playground, the air cools and the sun sets. The indifference of the everyday gets the better of us all.

~ * ~

At an outdoor café, fresh ground coffee and late afternoon drowsiness. For the rest of the world – the stone, the plant, this notebook, that chair, a cup of coffee, the sounds of crickets, the stray cat, the stray cigarette smoke – existing suffices. Only human beings have had the misfortune of inventing something called "life" on top of it all.

~ * ~

Afraid to be happy. Content to be sad.

~ * ~

To decide is to compromise.

~ * ~

To admire a misanthrope.

~ * ~

I'm never as optimistic or as pessimistic as I think I am.

~ * ~

Teeming forests in our anodyne skulls, a nocturnal

expanse that can be quietly heard, echoing gently down the long, vaulted, moss-ridden arches of our calcified anatomies.

~ * ~

A paraphrase of La Rochefoucauld, Leopardi, Lichtenberg: human communication is the sequential vomiting of information. We do not listen so much as gorge ourselves. We do not speak so much as burp, drool, and wail. Unfortunately we've also learned to read and write.

~ * ~

Cheerfulness to endure my own suffering. Fortitude to endure the cheerfulness of others.

~ * ~

Signs of the Times. It is more important to be seen than to exist.

~ * ~

A bit of philosophizing leads to a wonderment of life. A lot of philosophizing leads to a contempt of it.

~ * ~

Nietzsche was adamant about distinguishing his own brand of pessimism from the melancholic, "romantic pessimism" he associated with Schopenhauer. Being a philosopher, Nietzsche knew this required a method. Being a poet, he also knew that every method harbors within itself a certain frivolity. And so Nietzsche attempted to move beyond pessimism by moving through it – but the trick was to not simply come out the other end, as an optimist. Of the aphorisms he wrote in *Human, All Too Human* he says: "There speaks out of them a pessimist whose insights have often made him jump out of his skin but who has always known how to get back into it again, a pessimist, that is to say, well disposed *towards* pessimism…"

~ * ~

I thought I would be wiser. Instead I'm just older.

~ * ~

There is a special kind of Purgatory that involves waiting for something *not to happen*.

~ * ~

"Only the scrupulously rational are entitled to skepticism about reason… Anything less is complaint, not critique" (Brassier). Without realizing it, pessimism has passed, almost effortlessly, from the former to the latter.

~ * ~

In the face of good fortune there can be nothing but despair.

~ * ~

We know too much about ourselves as a species to be truly optimistic.

~ * ~

The present – not worth the time.

~ * ~

St. Paul: "When I am weak I am strong."

Nietzsche: "What doesn't kill me makes me stronger."

Cioran: "Only the idiot is equipped to breathe."

~ * ~

Morbism. That pessimism may have a medical basis is proved by the innumerable studies of clinical depression (not so long ago one used terms like "melancholia," or as the ancient Greeks would say, "black bile"). Some studies have even been devoted to examining artists, writers, philosophers. I would love to hear Schopenhauer's reply to his diagnosis – maybe he would even agree with the physicians…

The scientist Alfred Ziegler presents the case for a pessimist medicine. For Ziegler, the human being's natural state is not health but morbidity: "…humanity is chronically ill by nature." Our obsessions over exercise and healthy eating are simply an unconscious confirmation of an essentially afflicted constitution. Our corporeal predilection towards morbidity over-reaches any "Rousseauian optimism." Ziegler coins the term "morbism" to describe this view, the view that "the human species is by nature morbid and can escape its fate only in death."

So there is hope after all.

~ * ~

A crying baby is the purest expression of the inanity of being human.

~ * ~

Overheard on the subway: "…yeah, I've been there, you know? I'm tired of being tired of *being* tired…"

~ * ~

The certitude of doubt, the accretions of withering and spectral organisms.

~ * ~

No epiphanies here.

~ * ~

Confusion, frustration, depression, spite. Confusion about what I am supposed to do, frustration at my conditions, depression at feeling frustrated and confused, and a general spitefulness towards the world and all people. Every day. Only going for walks and writing in this pedantic notebook help, a little.

~ * ~

Our inability to change, matched only by our capacity for suffering.

~ * ~

The anthropocene: an accomplished ruin.

~ * ~

Philosophy as reducible to an alibi for one's existence – for all existents. Hubris. Fear.

~ * ~

"…most of us die because we know no way to keep from dying" (La Rochefoucauld).

~ * ~

Prospect Park, Sunday afternoon. To feel claustrophobia even in "nature."

~ * ~

On Reading Dostoevsky. Everyone is guilty. Especially the innocent.

~ * ~

To have mistaken enthusiasm for optimism…

~ * ~

"I'm not teaching you anything."
"Yes! – you're not teaching us anything!…"

~ * ~

Contra what all the scholars say, Schopenhauer was right about Buddhism – at its core, it is pessimistic, unconditionally pessimistic. But no one believes this…

~ * ~

There is no A_1, there is no A_2, there is no A_3…there is no A_x…

~ * ~

Human expression is so desperate–

~ * ~

Pessoa titled one of his texts "Chapter on Indifference or Something Like That." In the manuscript he placed the title in parentheses.

~ * ~

If there are several options for relieving pain, it usually means none of them work. The same for suffering.

~ * ~

The further we go in an argument, the details matter more, the differences matter less, and the colors of thought fade, until there is no luster left in them at all. And then everything is still.

~ * ~

I recently read a kōan – I think by Dōgen – that describes our thoughts as a breeze that blows across one's face. In meditation one simply lets them pass.

Later that day I go into the city. Cold November winds barrel through the corridor streets, making it difficult to walk. I find it irritating – I become annoyed at the wind.

~ * ~

Aphorisms, maxims, proverbs, adages, idioms, witticisms, platitudes, mottos, maxims, epigrams, epithets, and fragments… in writing, I feel a strange euphoria… there are so many ways to say nothing.

~ * ~

An argument for or against suicide? One lives, in *spite*

of life.

~ * ~

Sincerity is as disgusting as all forms of irony. One fools oneself too well.

~ * ~

The face – stigmata of life.

~ * ~

When someone complains that their life has come to nothing, we should reward them, not console them.

~ * ~

The allure of having beliefs outstrips having to live with them.

~ * ~

A philosopher – Shestov I think – once noted that, since philosophy deals with the most difficult and important issues concerning existence, philosophers think themselves the most important people. He then notes: "A bank clerk, who is always handing money out, might just as well consider himself a millionaire."

~ * ~

Anthropocentrism – as banal as an advertisement, as devastating as a flash-flood, as insignificant as time.

~ * ~

In February of 1942 Camus writes in one of his note-books: "What prevents a work from being completed becomes the work itself." It is one of the last entries.

~ * ~

It is often said that the more spiritual a person becomes, the more unassuming they are. Eventually, they vanish entirely.

~ * ~

To live: the pinnacle of "cruel optimism."

~ * ~

A Principle of Sufficient Reason. The fragility of time is nothing next to that of the body.

~ * ~

A saying from the Desert Fathers reads: "It is frighten-ing to die, it is even more perilous to live a long life." If only pessimism had the devotion of the ascetics.

~ * ~

What pessimism really is: a temper-tantrum restated in the soothing tones of enigma.

~ * ~

Faith, like reason, lies just beyond the range of human hearing.

~ * ~

Knowledge exists in inverse proportion to meaning.

~ * ~

There are those phrases so concise that they render superfluous everything you've written. Cioran: "The multiplication of our kind borders on the obscene; the duty to love them, on the preposterous."

~ * ~

Chamfort once noted that four-fifths of Parisians die of grief. Perhaps the other one-fifth – the rest of the world – dies by simply passing the time, no less blameworthy than their bilious neighbors.

~ * ~

Inexhaustible indifference.

~ * ~

Swaying tendrils of blackwood acacias. Burnt pods of raintree and camphor. Musical immobility. Doubt, sullenness. Sea hibiscus and satin leaves.

~ * ~

Descartes' demon, Kant's deathbed sigh, Nietzsche's mad laughter – if philosophy amounts to anything, it is a testament to the stark realization that thought is an aberration. We are mistaken if we think that thought serves us as human beings, our hopes and desires. Thought fails us – thought works too well for our own good. What hubris to think that thought is "inside" our cavernous, hollowed-out skulls…

~ * ~

"How are you?"
"Good–"
"Give it time…"

~ * ~

Thought – the shortest path between being and non-being.

~ * ~

One of the greatest things I learned as a student was how to teach myself. My punishment for this was to become a teacher.

~ * ~

Kierkegaard is fond of noting that one arrives at faith "by virtue of the absurd" – "the absurd" I take to mean that which cannot happen and yet does happen. "I, a rational being, must act in a case where my reason, my powers of reflection, tell me: you can just as well do one thing as the other."

But isn't the absurd that anything happens at all?

~ * ~

The aphorism: profoundly reductive.

~ * ~

Awkwardness at having nothing to say.

~ * ~

Existence is tiring.

~ * ~

Age, injury, illness, aches and pains and the passing of time. The breakdown of the body is terrifying because it's nothing personal.

~ * ~

Attentive insignificance.

~ * ~

The human body – the strangest geography on the planet.

~ * ~

"You are dead after life, but during life you are dying" (Montaigne).

~ * ~

The only thing worse than human culture is human nature.

~ * ~

Walking, running, hiking, cycling, climbing, canoeing, camping, sailing, flying – we seem enamored of finding ourselves everywhere, even in the most remote settings. (P and I travel to a remote forest, only to find crowded trails and chatty tourists.)

A proposal – all of nature should be a nature reserve, for a true nature reserve would disallow any human presence whatsoever – but then it would no longer be either nature or a reserve. It would simply be a place without people (and thus nothing natural...).

~ * ~

The act of speech itself is patronizing.

~ * ~

Early morning. Dark, cold, and clear outside. P and I laying there, half-asleep, tired. Creaky joints, slow breaths. All the little rituals we have for just maintaining. On her way to the bathroom P says to me, "How did we get duped into living?"

~ * ~

Reading Melville's "Bartleby the Scrivener," I was led to Vila-Matas' book *Bartleby & Co.*, which catalogs the "writers of the No." Thinking of Thomas Chatterton, Eric Stenbock, Jacques Rigaut, Juan Rulfo, Sakutaru Hagiwara, and of course Arthur Rimbaud, I begin to wonder if the reason writers quit writing is also the reason they begin writing: futility, boredom, laziness, disillusion, aches and pains...

~ * ~

Do I have high expectations and low standards, or low standards and high expectations?

~ * ~

Lagerkvist's *The Dwarf* is a masterpiece of misanthropy. The dwarf holds such a disdain for human beings that he places himself *beneath* them.

~ * ~

Swimming in the lake, floating on my back, motionless and still – falling into the sky.

~ * ~

Caves and cathedrals the same shape as the roof of our mouths. (If only our silences were so enigmatic.)

~ * ~

Horror temporis. Energy expended, wasted time.

~ * ~

Letting go. Giving up. Resignation.

~ * ~

Bliss of ignorance, ignorance of bliss.

~ * ~

To be so fatigued by daily living that one accepts anything. A *spiritual* failure.

~ * ~

"It is always easy to be logical. It is almost impossible to be logical to the bitter end" (Camus).

~ * ~

Blotted-Out Thought. Winter, Tuesday morning, 8:41am. While meditating – while trying to meditate – I allow all thoughts to empty themselves out of my head. Gradually, an indistinct point – an abyss – begins to form. I am looking at it but not looking at it. Slowly, imperceptibly, it blots out all other thoughts, everything in me and everything around me. I begin to notice, through half-closed eyes, waves upon waves of concentric circles, dark blurry obsidian expanding outwards. A dark, fuzzy, blotting out of all thought. (Really, I think I was just falling asleep.)

~ * ~

Outward movement, inner stillness.

~ * ~

There is something farcical about the autobiography – especially the multi-volume, thousand-page exercise in self-examination, from Proust to Knausgård. The more seriously the work takes itself, the greater the farce. I'm assuming the authors are aware of this – blissfully aware of it.

Where are our great aphoristic autobiographies? The Japanese philosopher Kitaro Nishida once wrote: "I spent the first half of my life facing the blackboard, the second half with my back to it."

~ * ~

Summer afternoon, Prospect Park. What strikes me is

how boisterous and belligerent we are, blissfully unaware of how we have intruded upon a "nature" that we
have created. We are above all an invasive species.

~ * ~

The vast and indifferent clouds, the twilight hours, the
languorous movement of jellyfish swarms. For every
personification of the world we should reply with an
equal depersonification of ourselves – until the tentative, half-witted, unfortunate shape calling itself
human is nothing but the aftereffects of climate or the
elements.

~ * ~

Sift and Sort. The original manuscript is some eight
hundred pages. The second draft is around two hundred and fifty pages. The third about eighty pages. A
fourth under ten pages. There is no fifth. Writing as a
process of elimination.

~ * ~

All accidents are happy accidents… Some accidents are
unfortunate… There are no happy accidents…

~ * ~

"This is the supreme wisdom – to despise the world and
draw daily nearer the kingdom of heaven" (Thomas à
Kempis). I excel in the former but fall short in the latter

– so much so that I also despise the kingdom of heaven.

~ * ~

Wednesday, 10:40am – This morning I brought in a bunch of books to sell to The Strand. They divide the books into a large pile, for which they can give me about $30 in store credit ($27 cash), and a small pile of four to five books which they can't take. The small pile they tell me I can either take back with me, or they can put them outside in the dollar bins. Among the books in the small pile is a copy of my first book, written years ago – an extra copy I have no use for. I pause for a moment, wondering to myself what lesson I should glean from this. If they can't buy back a book it either means that the book is in poor physical condition, or it means that there is no one that will want to pay more than a dollar for it. I attempt to console myself by noting that one of the other books they can't take is a copy of Schopenhauer's *Essays and Aphorisms* (another extra copy). But this book is heavily foxed and dog-eared, the cover is creased, and the spine cracked. My book, on the other hand, is brand new. I tell them they can go ahead and put the books in the dollar bin, and get my store credit.

~ * ~

Each night a seraphic theater that neutralizes muscle, nerve, and flesh in a black stellar pause. A thousand points of numbness gently quiver in anonymity.

~ * ~

A meeting with R at a café. We talk of philosophies whose first commitment is to non-being rather than being. He reminds me of the enigmatic philosopher Pyrrho, for whom negation knew no end – nothing can be known for certainty, and even this is uncertain, thus a vacuous non-being must lie at the root of all being. (The next day I recall the example of Gorgias, who – I have to look this up – asserts that (i) nothing exists, (ii) even if something does exist, nothing can be known about it, and (iii) even if something can be known about it, it can't be communicated.) But all this is still thought. For me, thought isn't all that special, which is why I often walk away from the game before it's finished. (This is my shortcoming, not R's.) It's early evening. He's drinking a beer, I'm drinking coffee.

~ * ~

With pessimism, there are no proselytes, only acolytes.

~ * ~

Tired. Same difference.

~ * ~

There are those adventurers who experiment with life. I count myself in another group – I have the constant suspicion that life is experimenting with me.

~ * ~

The awkwardness of anatomy.

~ * ~

In eternal night, we each burned a forest in order to better see. Clouds of ravens drift silently upward, blotting out the stars.

~ * ~

The pessimist grieves for everything in general and nothing in particular.

~ * ~

"Happiness" is the feeling you have just before something goes wrong.

~ * ~

To feign thoughts one does not have.

~ * ~

To have begun in system and to have ended in solipsism.

~ * ~

Pessimism – the luxury of doubting the obvious.

~ * ~

The obligation to not weep.

~ * ~

The wager without result.

~ * ~

"Learned helplessness." A *clinical* term.

~ * ~

A systematic philosophy constructed by accident.

~ * ~

Banalities secretly attributed to illustrious names.

~ * ~

Winter. Snow outside. P says to me, "imagine how quiet it would be if we spoke without judgment…"

~ * ~

The impact of what one seems to have said.

~ * ~

We live in a time when we are capable of producing more bad news than in any other era.

~ * ~

There is something overly-precious about the aphorism, as if it were some ineffably-wrought gem of
poignant and wizened contemplation. The aphorism is
not sacred, but profane. Aphorisms are written out of
the lowest of sentiments – impatience, laziness, frustration, spite, bewilderment, resignation. Go to a café, a
restaurant, a park, go for a walk, anywhere where there
are people (and there are always people). Writing aphorisms is almost not worth the trouble.

In an interview Cioran once remarked that one
throws out an aphorism – they are discarded…

~ * ~

Behind every philosophy is Philosophy (with a capital
P) – which is the more pretentious?

~ * ~

From *The Brothers Karamazov:*

"For the last time, definitely: is there a God or not?
It's the last time I'll ask."
"For the last time – no."
"Then who is laughing at mankind?"

~ * ~

An old man in one of Strindberg's chamber plays notes,
"I have made people unhappy and people have made

me unhappy – the one cancels out the other."

~ * ~

"…the dread of something after death…"

~ * ~

The human species is a failed species. What would a philosophy have to become to *begin* from this position, rather than to have arrived at it?

~ * ~

Spite as superficial as deep space, as patient as deep time.

~ * ~

Lichtenberg once noted that there are two ways of extending life, one in which birth and death are set as far apart as possible from each other, and another in which birth and death are left where they are, but the time between them is lived more slowly.

To this we can add a third – silence, stillness, and the absolute quietude of a non-time: the quiet of 3am, early Sunday autumn mornings, dusk in winter.

~ * ~

At our best, human beings are imperfect. At our worst, we ennoble this as a virtue.

~ * ~

Thought at the moment it discovers it is unfounded.

~ * ~

All philosophers are armchair philosophers.

~ * ~

A hatred of humanity so all-encompassing it forms an embrace.

~ * ~

"We" is just another way of saying "I" – solipsism ramified by the arithmetic of futility.

~ * ~

A rheumatism of concepts. A philosophy of aches and pains.

~ * ~

The greatest terror is that there are only human beings, that only human beings are meaningful. A religious terror.

~ * ~

Why is it that at some moments everything around

you seems filled with significance? I find it annoying; I become apprehensive. P and I are walking through the subway, on our way to a doctor's appointment. I see the words "faith" and "fate" next to each other on the wall, a woman walks by wearing a black t-shirt that says "Cats" on it, a patch on the side of a backpack in front of me says "Alone" with the "A" depicted as an anarchy symbol… and then more signs jump out from magazine covers, as graffiti, as storefront signs – "your story," "a new beginning," "useless" (or was it "use less"?)… Neither epiphanies nor trivialities, I feel fatigued by so much signification; it exceeds all interpretation.

~ * ~

To have lived a life that amounts to nothing and yet to be burdened with something – like ashes.

~ * ~

Knowledge that exists in inverse proportion to mastery.

~ * ~

Suicide: there is hope…

~ * ~

The criteria for failure. The promises of futility.

~ * ~

Only my incapacity is mine (even that is sheer hubris).

~ * ~

Scribbled on a stall in an airport bathroom:

> LIFE
> ~~do stuff~~
> ~~do stuff~~
> ~~do stuff~~
> ~~do stuff~~
> do stuff
> do stuff
> die

~ * ~

The Schopenhauer Guide to Life. The question isn't whether you will suffer, the question is whether your suffering will have meaning. So I tell myself.

~ * ~

A writer never finishes a book – they abandon it.

~ * ~

I support the cause – I just don't believe in it.

~ * ~

This morning, over coffee, P casually says, "I think I'm

a lazy self-starter…"

~ * ~

Hans Jonas' *The Gnostic Religion* gives us hints of a pessimist religion. The world is neither order and harmony (the Greek cosmos) nor is it preordained and destined (the Judaic *logos*). The world is alien and absurd, caught between an unknowable "Depth" and an unspeakable "Silence," that together produce the haphazard and arbitrary "Pleroma" of worldly existence. From ancient thinkers like Valentius one can even extract a dogmatic pessimism: all gods are suffering, the world is an error, and the human is unconditionally estranged. In such a situation, the one and only benefit of *gnosis* lies in its adamant refusal of everything… but this is already too modern…

~ * ~

The pessimist – the person who has dispensed with reason but not with philosophy.

~ * ~

Despondent limbs, sullen organs, a slow and steady skeletal sorrow.

~ * ~

The theophany of indifference. Trees, clouds, rocks.

~ * ~

My regrets as a writer change with each book I write.

~ * ~

It's just as erroneous for us to describe the world in terms of masses of cells or subatomic particles as it is to wax poetic about a forlorn autumn sky or the melancholy of a forest. Even in the most hardened of the sciences there is an occult form of personification, and the best that literature can do is to yearn for a poetics of the impersonal. The more I write, the more I feel an overwhelming urge to accept the obvious, which is that we are forever cut off from a world we neither have access to nor whose existence we can affirm or deny. The resignation provides a bit of motivation...

~ * ~

Walking down Waverly Avenue with P, we pass two old men sitting on a stoop. One of them says to the other: "...and then they told me I have a crass disposition – can you fucking believe that?"

~ * ~

Bartleby's paradox: acceptance through refusal.

~ * ~

La Rochefoucauld: "We have many reasons for being

disgusted with life, but we never have any for despising death." Except that death comes *after* life.

~ * ~

Young enough to keep trying, old enough to know better.

~ * ~

Always wanting more, always having less.

~ * ~

At the acupuncturist. My neck, shoulders, and back are a glacier of stress. Maps that point to no territory.

~ * ~

"It is impossible to see everything, impossible to know everything, impossible to rise too high above the earth, impossible to penetrate too deeply down. What has been is hidden away, what will be we cannot anticipate, and we know for certain that we shall never grow wings" (Shestov).

~ * ~

The sincerity of the impersonal.

~ * ~

It must be good to know that everything is bad…

~ ✳ ~

On Optimism. In the winter of 1915 Kafka writes in his diary: "After days of uninterrupted headaches, finally a little easier and more confident. If I were another person observing myself and the course of my life, I should be compelled to say that it must all end unavailingly, be consumed in incessant doubt, creative only in its self-torment. But, an interested party, I go on hoping."

~ * ~

How conscientious would we have to be to appreciate the impersonal all around us?

~ * ~

Bernhard's paradox: to correct a work to the point of effacing it.

~ * ~

Our deep and sedentary breaths undulate with all the patience of regret.

~ * ~

Language falters where contempt flourishes.

~ * ~

"My head is as empty and dead as a theatre when the play is over" (Kierkegaard).

~ * ~

Philosophers remembered only for their most significant errors.

~ * ~

"Unhappiness is much less difficult to experience" (Freud).

~ * ~

Individual people as irritating as people in general.

~ * ~

Life as a terminal illness.

~ * ~

Gogol, Beckett, Bernhard, Krasznahorkai … the fecundity of negation…

~ * ~

Everything dissipates. Diligence.

~ * ~

A character in Sartre's *Huis Clos* notes: "Death is only a word. Life is much, much worse."

~ * ~

Tuesday, 3:09am. Silence annuls time, producing a stillness that borders on vertigo.

~ * ~

In a fragment entitled "Resignation," Adorno encapsulates the futility at the center of pessimism: "…thought achieves happiness in the expression of unhappiness…"

It is unclear whether this is happiness in the service of unhappiness, or the reverse.

~ * ~

Doubts that outstrip all argument.

~ * ~

The tenuousness of rituals of celebration.

~ * ~

Black volcanic sands. In arenophile dreams, limpets of basalt and gypsum languorously drift upwards, in doubtful recitals of quiet inactivity.

~ * ~

No redemption worth its weight in suffering.

~ * ~

"Extinction" can only be comprehended from within the tomb.

~ * ~

When he was strongest, Nietzsche was the most frail – he tried to solve the problem of nihilism. Did he not comprehend the significance of his phrase "all too human"?

~ * ~

To interpret sincerity as sarcasm.

~ * ~

Pedagogy of the Worst. One summer afternoon, the Zen master Hakuju was conducting a class on Chinese philosophy at the Tendai Sect College. During his lecture, he noticed that several of the students were dozing off, their heads bobbing like river reeds. He stopped his lecture midsentence and said "I can't blame you for going to sleep – mind if I join you?" With this, he shut his book, leaned back into his chair, and promptly fell asleep. The class was dumbfounded, and those who were asleep woke up at the sudden silence. Everyone sat up in their seats, rapt with attention. (As a teacher, I dream of a class so attentive.)

~ * ~

Attached detachment.

~ * ~

A dark surface can give the illusion of depth.

~ * ~

Interpretation is misinterpretation.

~ * ~

Dostoevsky's Axioms. (1) Everyone suffers. Some are aware of it, others not. (2) What is irritating in individual people is equally so in humanity in general. (3) It is impossible to speak honestly and directly, especially when lying. (4) We are pushed and pulled by impersonal forces of which we are only dimly aware.

~ * ~

Deep Time. On New Year's Day, D sends me this, from the nineteenth-century Japanese poet Shiki:

> New Year's Day
> nothing good or bad –
> just human beings

~ * ~

To never have hope or to keep losing it. Which is more profound? The more futile?

~ * ~

Grumbling incessantly: a categorical imperative.

~ * ~

Humanism and Anti-Humanism. One's training leads to the negation of that training.

~ * ~

The other day someone asked me if I exercised. I said, "I run... but I'm not very good at it..." It struck me how absurd that was, like saying "I like breathing, but I'm not very good at it..." (...a situation we will all find ourselves in sooner or later...)

~ * ~

"A *Miserere* sung in common by a multitude flailed by destiny is worth a whole philosophy" (Unamuno).

~ * ~

Doubts that prompt disbelief.

~ * ~

Aphorism. *Aphorismi.* Concise incompleteness.

~ * ~

The stupidity of suffering. The more poignant, the more cruel.

~ * ~

Lichtenberg: "To obtain an idea of the non-existence following death, I imagine the state in which I was before being born." Schopenhauer notes something similar, that the nothingness before my birth is equal to the nothingness after my death, with only an "ephemeral life-dream" in between. Still, it is hard not to find a profound significance in nothingness, especially in the moment of our failure to think it. Lichtenberg again: "One is equally well off, I suppose, in either case."

~ * ~

Meandering slabs of diatomic shale weave their way across the moss-ridden trellises of our latticed anatomies.

~ * ~

Turning Around To The Next Set Of Lives. Late evening, Fall. P and I are sitting together after dinner. It's strangely quiet. On the stereo a slow passage from *The Art of Fugue* is playing. We both listen, tranquil and enchanted. The music reminds me of my father's studio, which I associate with the sound of string quartets, rows of records and books, drawings on the wall and hours of conversation in the dimly-lit evening. The sense of stillness makes me all the more aware of the ephemeral. I think of the rows of tall and slowly swaying Cascadian fir trees around the house where I grew up.

~ * ~

For some, the pessimist outlook is unconditional. For others, it is purely conditional, prey to all the subtleties and nuances of everyday life. The former shouldn't surprise us any more than the latter. Camus: "We get into the habit of living before acquiring the habit of thinking."

~ * ~

Falling asleep. Waking up.

~ * ~

An Ungrounded Earth. In a letter written near the end of his life, Kant comments: "Life is short, especially what is left after seventy years have passed, to bring it to an untroubled close, some corner of the earth can be found, I suppose."

Was he assuming too much?

~ * ~

There is a sense of relief – tragic relief – in what life refuses us.

~ * ~

Often I tried to lift myself, only to plunge the deeper.

~ * ~

"Let future generations reject us, let history stigmatize our names, as the names of traitors to the human cause – still we will compose hymns to deformity, destruction, madness, chaos, darkness. And after that – let the grass grow" (Shestov).

~ * ~

The aphorism – abyss without precipice.

~ * ~

Is it easier to hate humanity in general or individual people?

~ * ~

Dostoevsky – poet, engineer, prison inmate...

~ * ~

Matter more melancholy than the mind.

~ * ~

Life as a near-death experience. Living deprives us

even of this.

~ * ~

De corpore politico. Illness and injury, aches and pains, passions, gravity, and the passing of time. The logic of pessimism is a corporeal logic – a secret disputation in which we hear only the final proofs.

~ * ~

Let us sleep, let us sleep. How else to discover the wisdom of somnambulists?

~ * ~

Murmur of the Sullen. There is a voice that the pessimist secretly longs to hear, the faintest of echoes heard only in the cavernous heights of resignation. For some, the voice will say: "You have said 'no' enough and your struggle is finished; now it is time to cease saying 'no' and to let things be what they are, as they are." To others the voice will say: "You have said 'no' in a way that has fulfilled all the requirements of negation; now you may realize that your saying 'no' is really a saying 'yes,' and that this will be more than sufficient for you." And to still others the voice will say: "You have said 'no' perfectly, that is to say unconditionally, and in this you will be sufficient in your insufficiency."

In addition there is another voice, one that has never ceased speaking, though few really have ears for it. It simply murmurs, sighs, hums.

~ * ~

Camus once noted that Schopenhauer "praised suicide while seated at a well-set table." Nietzsche, on the other hand, dealt with stomach problems his whole life.

~ * ~

Happiness in other people makes me suspicious.

~ * ~

Happiness in myself makes me apprehensive.

~ * ~

The correlation between being and non-being with the positive and the negative is one of the most debilitating platitudes of philosophy. Kafka was acutely aware of this: "What is laid upon us is to accomplish the negative; the positive is already given."

~ * ~

Written in the Hall of Mosses. Thought wanders in eerie shapes, growing in unexpected, verdant directions. Slowly, imperceptibly, it covers the entire surface of the brain. It drapes itself like a viscous and dazzling early morning moss.

~ * ~

I'm reviewing De Quincey's *Confessions of an English Opium Eater* to prepare for class. In it De Quincey describes his hallucinations of vast black oceans as having a physical effect on him: "...these images haunted me so much, that I feared some dropsical state or tendency of the brain might thus be making itself (to use a metaphysical word) *objective*; and the sentient organ *project* itself on its own object."

The frequency with which suffering arrives in physical form – an anonymous, indifferent, and "objective" experience of horror. No reasons given, no one to blame, nothing to do. Infinite resignation.

~ * ~

Hope is suffering. Suffering is suffering.

~ * ~

P and I are en route to the Olympic Rainforest. In the early morning, the sight of low clouds among fir trees gives the impression of the entire sky having been subtracted from the world. It is the same with mist that rolls in with the low tide, or with high bridges that pass over ravines of dense fog, in which neither ground nor sky can be detected. There is an impersonal drama to all these sights, as if the planet has, for a moment, revealed some other non-respiratory dimension both breathlessly still and lyrically impassive.

~ * ~

A spite of humanity so profound it becomes spiritual.

~ * ~

To have arrived at estrangement...

~ * ~

A book with the title *How To Read Books* – or, better yet, a book called *How To Stop Reading Books*.

~ * ~

The pessimist despairs not of failing but of having had to make an effort in the first place. The tedium of effort – the secret link between pessimism and the aphorism, the fragment, the stray thought.

~ * ~

When you're born, you cry. When you die, others cry.

~ * ~

The cruelty of time. It will fix you in place, force you to watch as those around you lose their memory and their bodies wither. All the while you imagine you're fixed in place.

~ * ~

An Inventory of Affects (ix). At what point do you

233

become concerned? In roughly one trillion, trillion, trillion years, the expansion of the universe will obliterate all matter, including the galaxies, planets, and all forms of life... In approximately 4.5 trillion years the sun will die out, leaving behind a cold and uninhabitable earth... In one billion years the Earth's oceans will dry out due to rising temperatures... Given projected increases in global population and projected decreases in resources, the human species could become extinct by the year 3000... The average human life span is eighty-six years... Next week, you have plans...

~ * ~

Writing is proof of the pessimist's optimism.

~ * ~

Kafka's diary entry for March 15th, 1914: "Only this everlasting waiting, eternal helplessness."

~ * ~

I've been a misanthrope since before I was born.

~ * ~

To become overgrown – like a ruin.

~ * ~

Pessoa: "All I ask of life is that it ask nothing of me."

~ * ~

What is "religious" to me: manifestations of human insignificance.

~ * ~

One always *admits* to being a pessimist.

~ * ~

There are writers who are so depressing it's inspiring.

~ * ~

Dare one hope for a philosophy of futility?

~ * ~

There is no unpretentious emotion.

~ * ~

The gulf separating resignation from acceptance.

~ * ~

All philosophies live in Kafka's castle, built on slate and mist.

~ * ~

Attached detachment.

~ * ~

Human beings deep in thought look like corpses.

~ * ~

Saying "yes" in order to say "no."

~ * ~

A phrase often attributed to Camus: "Should I commit suicide or should I have a cup of coffee?" Depends on the coffee.

~ * ~

This sarcophagus of breathable air.

~ * ~

Kant (of all people) once defined laughter as "an affect resulting from the sudden transformation of a heightened expectation into nothing." Strange, I always thought that was the definition of sorrow.

~ * ~

The absurd: irritation irritated with itself.

~ * ~

Derision spilling over into humility.

~ * ~

"…the fanaticism of the worst…" (Cioran)

~ * ~

The brain – the persecution of thought.

~ * ~

Deep space – the only place worthy of depression.

~ * ~

I find expressions of futility inspiring – it almost makes life worth living.

~ * ~

The putrefaction of fresh ideas.

~ * ~

Phosphorescent, moss-ridden aphorisms inseparable from the ossification of our own bodies.

~ * ~

Which do I choose, the Principle of Sufficient Reason or the forest at dusk? Disappointment…

~ * ~

Breath that secretly desires asphyxiation.

~ * ~

The empiricism of *ennui*.

~ * ~

The silent glow of resignation.

~ * ~

Joyless calm.

~ * ~

"I have never been able to meet anyone without an accompaniment of painful smiles, the buffoonery of defeat" (Dazai).

~ * ~

Sullen jewels dubiously crawl around us in our moonlit mesmerism.

~ * ~

Utterances just indelicate enough so they are spoken with a weak smile.

~ * ~

Why do one thing as opposed to another? At what point does "doing nothing" eclipse "doing something"? At best we seem to be marionettes with slackened strings, strings that ascend into a dark and doubtful ether. Kierkegaard concisely expresses this in a parable:

> Something wonderful has happened to me. I was caught up into the seventh heaven. There sat all the gods in assembly. By special grace I was granted the privilege of making a wish. "Wilt thou," said Mercury, "Have youth or beauty or power or a long life or the most beautiful maiden or any of the other glories we have in the chest? Choose, but only one thing." For a moment I was at a loss. Then I addressed myself to the gods as follows: "Most honorable contemporaries. I choose this one thing, that I may always have the laugh on my side." Not one of the gods said a word; on the contrary, they all began to laugh. From that I concluded that my wish was granted, and found that the gods knew how to express themselves with taste; for it would hardly have been suitable for them to have answered gravely: "Thy wish is granted."

~ * ~

Days and nights when even the stars softly grumble to themselves.

~ * ~

No amount of suffering is worth the expression that validates it.

~ * ~

There are too many ways of refusing the world to be involved in it.

~ * ~

The notion of an American pessimism is an oxymoron, which is as good a reason as any to undertake it.

~ * ~

Pessimism is the last refuge of hope.

~ * ~

The pessimist is farthest from pessimism at the very moment it is expressed.

~ * ~

Disgust, contempt, disdain, complacency, indifference, whatever...

~ * ~

Cioran: "Without the idea of suicide, I'd have killed

myself right away."

~ * ~

A refusal so absolute that nothing will suffice. How vindicated pessimism would be if only the rock, the cloud, and the tree would also complain... The sorrowful sigh of every climate, a climate of refusal.

~ * ~

If you make yourself still enough, the clouds start to move.

~ * ~

Help me appreciate how helpless I am.

~ * ~

Misanthropy fueled by a hatred of suffering.

~ * ~

Under forests of futility there are no conclusions, no resolutions, no revelations, no epiphanies. There is not even a last page. One finishes writing a book by walking away from it.

~ * ~

"Are you a pessimist?"

"On my better days…"

~ * ~

At once the strongest and the weakest argument for pessimism: non-existence doesn't hurt.

~ * ~

Thoughts that wither.

~ * ~

In his enigmatically-titled book *The Pinnacle of the Abyss*, Lev Shestov writes: "When a person is young he writes because it seems to him he has discovered a new almighty truth which he must make haste to impart to forlorn humankind. Later, becoming more modest, he begins to doubt his truths: and then he tries to convince himself. A few more years go by, and he knows he was mistaken all round, so there is no need to convince himself. Nevertheless he continues to write, because he is not fit for any other work, and to be accounted a superfluous person is so horrible."

~ * ~

The weariness of faith.

~ * ~

The incredulity of facts.

~ * ~

Somber incandescence.

~ * ~

Every person has a point beyond which life is no longer worth living. In this way we are all covert pessimists.

~ * ~

A philosophy that consists entirely in what it refuses.

~ * ~

An Inventory of Affects (X). There are approximately 37 trillion cells in the human body. There are approximately 100 billion galaxies in the universe. We look down on what is smaller than us with the same feebleness that we look up at what is bigger than us.

~ * ~

At first I had planned to write a book about pessimism, a clearly written, judiciously researched history, with names and dates and titles of obscure books few have bothered to read. But it seemed so tedious, and not worth the effort. Not that this is better, of course. It's possible I've simply arrived at the same destination by another path.

~ * ~

To have such tranquility that one ceases to exist.

~ * ~

I am a pessimist about everything, except pessimism.

~ * ~

A whirlwind of crystal, kelp, and moss closes gently around my wrists.

~ * ~

Let all that I live be as a forgotten dream.

~ * ~

Resignation is the residue of failure.

~ * ~

There is no philosophy of pessimism, only the reverse.

~ * ~

THE PATRON SAINTS OF PESSIMISM

The patron saints of pessimism watch over our suffering. Laconic and sullen, they never seem to do a good job at protecting, interceding, or advocating for those who suffer. Perhaps they need us more than we need them.

There are patron saints of philosophy, but their stories are not happy ones. For instance, there is the fourth-century Saint Catherine of Alexandria, or Catherine of the Wheel, named after the torture device used on her. A precocious fourteen-year-old scholar, Catherine was subject to continual persecution. After all forms of torture failed – including the "breaking wheel" – the emperor finally settled for her decapitation, a violent yet appropriate allegory for the protector of philosophers.

Does pessimism not deserve its own patron saints, even if they are unworthy of martyrdom? In our search, however, even the most ardent nay-sayers lapse into brief moments of enthusiasm – Pascal's love of solitude, Leopardi's love of poetry, Schopenhauer's love of music, Nietzsche's love of Schopenhauer, and so on. Should one then focus on individual works? We could include Kierkegaard's trilogy of existential horror: *Sickness Unto Death*, *The Concept of Dread*, and *Fear and Trembling* – but these are complicated by their fabricated and unreliable authors. And how can one separate the pessimist from the optimist in works like Unamuno's *The Tragic Sense of Life*, Camus' *The Myth of Sisyphus*, or even Adorno's *Minima Moralia*? And what of the many forgotten philosophical histories of pessimism, of which Edgar Saltus' *The Philosophy of Disenchantment* is emblematic? Even in cases where the entire corpus of an author is pessimistic, the project always seems incomplete, as if there was still one more thing to say, one last indictment...

And this is to say nothing of literary pessimism, from Goethe's sorrowful Werther, to Dostoevsky's burrowing creature, to Pessoa's disquiet scribbler; Baudelaire's spleen and *ennui*; the mystical pessimism of Huysmans and Strindberg; the stark and unhuman lyricism of Meng Jiao, Georg Trakl, Xavier Villarrutia; the frenetic obfuscations of Sakutaro Hagiwara, Ladislav Klíma, Fyodor Sologub; the haunted and scintillating prose of Mário de Sá-Carneiro, Izumi Kyōka, Clarice Lispector; the misanthropic rigor of Lautréamont's *Maldoror* or of Bonaventura's *Nightwatches*; the crumbling of reason in Artaud's *The Umbilicus of Limbo* or Unica Zürn's *The House of Illnesses*. Grumpy old Beckett. The list quickly expands, soon encompassing the entirety of literature itself, and beyond (...even the great pessimist stand-up comedians). In the end it's overwhelming; all of literature becomes a candidate. All that remains are singular, anomalous statements, a litany of quotes and citations crammed into arborous fortune cookies read by no one.

So I confine myself, somewhat arbitrarily, to pessimist "philosophers," dubious though this distinction is. But a cursory look at the history of philosophy reveals something quite different. Philosophers that stumble and trip over their own feet. Philosophers that curse themselves. Philosophers that laugh at themselves. Philosophers that abandon philosophy, but still remain "philosophers." They deserve better than biographies, those exhaustive and tedious narratives of heroic intellectual progress. Only hagiographies will do. But the tradition of hagiography, or lives of the saints, is a peculiar kind of writing. Unlike the modern biography, hagiographies are not comprehensive or chronological. Unlike modern historiography, hagiographies often contain second-hand accounts of miraculous events, and are unconcerned with verification or "proof." Popular medieval hagiographies such as the *Legenda sanctorum* are exemplary of the genre; they highlight particular moments in the life of a saint, but they do so in an anecdotal, almost haphazard way. In a way, they are more faithful to life. Cioran: "One only troubles oneself with saints because one has been disappointed by the paradoxes of earthly life... without realizing that this journey is merely a brief side trip and that everything in the world is a disappointment, even saintliness."

My list is, clearly, neither inclusive nor exhaustive. And, it has not escaped my attention that these are philosophers with a capital P, often enmeshed in the very sites of privilege that they either refuse or fail to live up to. (Shouldn't there be, for example, a pessimism of race or gender, a political or economic or historical pessimism? Absolutely. In fact, I dream of an indo-pessimism, a sino-pessimism, an afro-pessimism, a gyno-pessimism, a queer pessimism, a techno-pessimism, an eco-pessimism... I suddenly feel quite generous, as if pessimism belongs to everyone, simply by virtue of undergoing the burden of being...) At the same time, what I find equally appealing in my failed saints are those instances in which "Philosophy" is whittled down to "philosophy," and even that status becoming dubious.

In the hagiography tradition, patron saints are traditionally named after a locale, either a place of birth or the site of a mystical experience. Perhaps the better approach is to focus on those sites where pessimists were forced to live out their pessimism – Schopenhauer facing an empty Berlin lecture hall, Nietzsche mute and convalescent at the home of his sister, Wittgenstein the relinquished professor and solitary gardener, Cioran grappling with Alzheimer's in his tiny writing alcove in the Latin Quarter.

Nicolas Chamfort

10 September 1793

~ * ~

"In studying the ills of nature, one acquires a contempt for death. In studying the ills of society, one acquires a contempt for life."

~ * ~

"Society, which is called the world, is nothing but the contention of a thousand petty interests, an eternal conflict of all the vanities that cross each other, strike against each other, are wounded and humiliated by each other in turn, and expiate on the morrow, in the bitterness of defeat, the triumph of the day before."

~ * ~

"We must know how to perform the foolishness that our characters require."

~ * ~

"False modesty is the most decent of all lies."

~ * ~

"A philosopher looks upon 'his place in the world' as Tartars look upon cities: as a prison. It is a circle in which the ideas shrink, draw together, meanwhile robbing the soul and the mind of breadth and development. A man whose place in the world is large has a larger and more ornate prison."

~ * ~

"Philosophy, like medicine, can offer a great many drugs, a very few good remedies, and almost no specifics."

~ * ~

"Living is an ailment which is relieved every sixteen hours by sleep. A palliative. Death is the cure"

~ * ~

Historians of eighteenth-century French literature often speak of the *moralistes*, writers working both within and against the Enlightenment, using reason to shine a light on the many curious behaviors, absurdities, and hypocrisies of "modern" culture. As writers, the French moralists excelled in the short form – witty observations crystallized into aphorisms, maxims, epigrams, and anecdotes. Neither a movement nor a school of thought, the French moralist tradition spans decades, bringing together authors as wide-ranging as Voltaire, La Rochefoucauld, and Joseph Joubert.

Of the French moralists, none captured the sardonic,

gallows humor of pessimism better than Sébastien Roch Nicolas Chamfort. La Bruyère is known for his literary observations of the human character; La Rochefoucauld known for his taut and witty maxims on culture and society; Vauvenargues formulates concise statements about the limits of human knowledge; and thinkers such as Voltaire are known for their sprite, ironic stance towards all of humanity. But it is Chamfort who truly distills the dark underbelly of the Enlightenment into the short form of the aphorism. It is Chamfort that we later find cited in the pages of authors such as Camus, Céline, Cioran, Nietzsche, and Schopenhauer.

Chamfort was very much a product of his time, and like many of the French moralists, the writings for which he is now known were not published during his lifetime. The son of a noblewoman and a priest, young Chamfort was abandoned as an infant and taken in by a local grocer, who raised him with his wife. A precocious student, he was drawn to the study of classical languages, and seemed determined to rise above his circumstances through his studies and his writing. As a young adult Chamfort quickly learned how to navigate the labyrinthine twists and turns of Parisian court life, and became notorious both for his verbal acrobatics in conversation and his amorous acrobatics in the boudoir. As he would later write, "one must admit the impossibility of living in the world without acting a part from time to time." Patronages followed for the upstart playwright, as did recognition from France's top institutions, including the Académie Française. But things took a dark turn in his late twenties – he contracted several venereal diseases, which took their toll on his health and his appearance. His increasing intolerance for courtly life led to a growing sense of alienation and paranoia, and his plays – when they were staged – were critical and financial flops. He eventually ceased writing altogether, and was reduced to taking petty jobs for the aristocracy – for a time he was even secretary for the king's sister – and then as a librarian for the Bibliothèque Nationale.

It is around this time that Chamfort writes the maxims for which is now known. One of them provides a sort of method: "The best of philosophies, with regard to the world, must combine the sarcasm of good humor with the indulgence of contempt."

~ * ~

Chamfort seemed to be perpetually stuck in the wrong place at the wrong time. Years of political controversy had left Chamfort exasperated, as he, like many, witnessed the transition from the Revolution to the Terror. An early supporter of the Revolution, and a stubborn adherent to its idealistic principles, Chamfort became vilified by both sides, variously accused of being a revolutionary subversive and an aristocrat of the Ancien Régime. Though Chamfort did have ties to the aristocracy, he was among the first to write against the Ancien Régime and in favor of a republican government – he became a street orator, stormed the Bastille, and was arrested several times for refusing to recant his statements. He is one of those unique figures of the period to have been accused of being both a revolutionary and a counter-revolutionary. A plethora of editorials, letters, missives, and pamphlets testify to the dizzying political debates of the period. So when the tides turned, he found himself again on the losing side.

~ * ~

The most startling thing about Chamfort's life was his death – that is, his failed death. Never a favorite with the ruling order, Chamfort's criticisms of the new regime did not go unnoticed. He had already been imprisoned under charges of sedition, and the prison he stayed in – dank, filthy, disease-ridden, overflowing with prisoners in the corridors and stairwells – was so bad that he vowed he would never go back. One winter evening, Chamfort was hosting several guests at dinner. A gendarme arrived, with orders that Chamfort be taken back to prison "for questioning." According to second-hand accounts, Chamfort calmly finished his after-dinner coffee before retiring to his dressing room, ordering his housekeeper to pack his bag. He locked the door of the room, took out a pistol from its hiding place, loaded it, and fired at his forehead. But he missed. The recoil of the shot jarred his arm, the bullet smashing the upper part of his nose and bursting his right eye. Surprised to find himself alive, he then took an ivory-handled razor and slit his throat – several times, each time pressing harder. Blood covered his clothing, but still nothing. Grabbing another razor, he then stabbed himself in the chest, thighs, and calves, before attempting to cut both wrists. Still he was alive. Blood began to soak the floor and seep under the door. In a fit of either pain or frustration, Chamfort finally let out a desperate moan before collapsing into a nearby chair, exhausted, but alive.

Alarmed at all the blood, the housekeeper attempted to open the door. When it wouldn't give, she went to fetch her husband, who tried to break it down. When this failed, Chamfort himself got up and unlocked the door – according to a friend, he emerged "like a ghost" before staggering back into the blood-soaked room. Chamfort was taken to his bed, where the housekeeper attempted to bandage his wounds. In the meantime, someone had gone out to get a doctor and, ironically, the police. A local policeman refused to come, referring the matter to the district commissioner. The commissioner eventually arrived with a clerk. They first took the gendarme's statement, before going to Chamfort's bedside. They then began asking Chamfort – whose larynx was protruding through his throat – a series of routine questions. One question was "By whom were you wounded?", to which Chamfort calmly replied "By myself..." The questioning continued, and when it was finished the commissioner asked Chamfort to re-read it over and give his approval. When the doctors arrived, they surveyed the damage and shook their heads. In addition to the twenty-odd wounds he had sustained, the doctors were unable to locate the bullet still lodged in Chamfort's head. The doctors ordered that Chamfort not be returned to prison. And so Chamfort was left in his bed to die.

~ * ~

"Civilization, in many respects, is like cooking. When one sees on the table light dishes, wholesome and well prepared, one is happy indeed that cooking has become a science. But when one sees gravies, rich bouillons, truffled patés, one curses the cooks and their morbid art…"

~ * ~

Soon after the attempted suicide, Pierre-Louis Ginguené, a close friend of Chamfort and his first biographer, arrived at the house. While Chamfort was dictating his last wishes, he sat up and said: "What can you expect? That's what it is to be clumsy with one's hands. One never manages to do anything successfully, even killing oneself."

~ * ~

E.M. Cioran

14 February 1993

~ * ~

We like to imagine that poets die poetic deaths. One thinks of Shelley, who, after having reportedly seen his doppelgänger, drowned off the coast of Tuscany while sailing out to sea in his boat, the *Don Juan*. Or Nietzsche, the "mad" philosopher and iconoclast who suddenly collapses in Turin while witnessing the flogging of a horse, his tear-leaden arms thrown around the animal's neck. In mid-February of 1993, an emaciated, elderly man with sharp eyes and wavy hair is found sitting on the side of the street somewhere in Paris's Latin Quarter. He is lost. He cannot recall his address, and his own neighborhood is unfamiliar to him. Eventually he is taken home. A few days pass, and he stops eating. After an accidental fall, he is brought to a hospital. He drifts in and out of lucidity, rarely recognizing those closest to him. He stops speaking entirely. After slipping into a coma, Emil Cioran dies on June 20, 1995.

For Cioran, the twilight philosopher who once noted "the stillborn are the most free," the end came not with melodramatic flair, but gradually, even routinely. For several years, the Romanian-born writer had been grappling with Alzheimer's. Writing became more and more difficult. Traveling, lectures, and interviews were impractical. Even a walk down the street took on an almost absurd risk. But Cioran's final silence was, in a way, a long time coming. By the early 1980s, he was finding it difficult to write, though the themes of his writing – pessimism, despair, melancholy, and an almost ecstatic antagonism towards the world – continued to find their way into his increasingly sparse works. Now well into his seventies, he and his companion Simone Boué continued to live in their Rue de l'Odéon apartment, where he divided his time between long walks in the Jardin du Luxembourg, and writing aphorisms in the cheap, multi-colored Joseph Gibert notebooks he had been using for years, and that piled up on his desk in the hazy light of his top-floor writing alcove.

~ * ~

Cioran is among those writers whose books form an extended autobiography of the mind. Though he lived a modest life, the real austerities of Cioran are to be found in his writings. In 1986, the solitary stroller who once wrote – "Solitude: so fulfilling that the merest rendezvous is a crucifixion" – published a book about friends and colleagues entitled *Exercises d'admiration*. It collected short articles written between the 1950s and the 1980s, many of them about other writers (Samuel Beckett, Jorge Luis Borges, Mircea Eliade, Henri Michaux).

Of Beckett, for instance, Cioran had this to say: "He lives not in time but parallel to it, which is why it has never occurred to me to ask him what he thinks of events." Of Borges, he wrote: "The misfortune of being *recognized* has befallen him. He deserved better. He deserved to remain in obscurity, in the Imperceptible, to remain as ineffable and unpopular as nuance itself."

~ * ~

Struggling with the gradual loss of his memory, in 1987 Cioran published *Aveux et anathèmes* (which could be translated as "Confessions and Curses"). Composed of short, staccato fragments, the writing has all the urgency of a last word, and yet the almost tranquil distance of a documentarian: "How age simplifies everything! At the library I ask for four books. Two are set in type that is too small; I discard them without even considering their contents. The third, too... serious, seems unreadable to me. I carry off the fourth without conviction." Following the publication of *Aveux et anathèmes*, Cioran decides to stop writing altogether. But it is a gesture already in his mind early on. In a 1980 letter to a friend he notes: "The very idea of writing makes me queasy, and with it comes a sour feeling of disgust, failure, and a total lack of satisfaction."

~ * ~

One day, while an aging Cioran was on his routine walk, a stranger stopped him and asked "Are you by any chance Cioran?" His reply: "I used to be."

~ * ~

In an interview given near the end of his life, Cioran is asked why most of his books are written in fragments and aphorisms. His reply:

> Because I'm lazy. To write a book, one must be an active person. But I was *born* in the fragment. I've written fuller, more completed texts, but they're not worth mentioning. These days I write only aphorisms: I'm a victim of my own ideas. Since all I've done as a writer is to attack literature, to attack life, to attack God, what's the point of writing a book about it? To prove what exactly? There was an inexorable logic that brought me to this point, but it's also just something that fits my temperament…

Cioran even adds to this a note on his method for writing aphorisms: you go to a restaurant, someone says something particularly stupid, then you go home and write it down. Eventually you have a book. "At any rate," he concludes, "the advantage of the aphorism is that there is no point in proving anything. One throws out an aphorism – like an insult."

~ * ~

There is a scene Cioran recounts in a number of interviews, a scene almost fit for a film. It is Paris, the winter of 1944, and in order to stay warm, many of the writers, artists, and students in the neighborhood huddle in the cafés that line Boulevard Saint-Germain. At the Café de Flore, existentialism is brewing out of the malcontent

of war, ignited by new ideas both political and philosophical. Near the radiating warmth of the café stove,
Jean-Paul Sartre and Simone de Beauvoir sit with others
around the small marble tables, talking, writing, smoking. Next to Sartre is a young man, neat and modestly
dressed, a pack of Gauloises nearby. He is there every
morning, afternoon, and evening – in his own words,
"like a clerk." Whenever de Beauvoir takes out a cigarette, he politely stands, leans over, and lights it for
her, receiving a nod of thanks in return. All the while
he barely says a word, even though at night he is filling
notebooks. He barely says a word; instead, he listens.

The scene at Café de Flore, however romantic it
may seem, speaks volumes about Cioran as a thinker.
If Cioran had a period of tutelage perhaps this was
it – but it was a tutelage of antagonism, allowing the
upstart author to write against both existentialism and
its critics. It suggests someone who, while he enjoyed
being near the center, always preferred to keep his
distance, even if it meant his own voice might not be
heard. It also suggests a certain outer calmness, a tranquility, and a determination not to get too caught up
in the moment, which will, like all things, soon pass.
But this outer calmness also covets an inner passion for
"thinking against oneself," a sort of ecstatic nay-say-
ing leveled at both reason and unreason: "Let us speak
plainly: everything which keeps us from self-dissolu-
tion, every lie which protects us against our unbreatha-
ble certitudes is religious."

~ * ~

During the early years he spent in Paris, Cioran had to piece together small grants and ad-hoc translation jobs to make ends meet; he and Boué were constantly moving around the Latin Quarter, from one tiny lodging to the next. In interviews, Cioran is fond of relating how he was able to use his student ID card from the Sorbonne to get cheap meals in the student dining hall, a practice he continued for years.

~ * ~

Cioran's book *The Temptation to Exist* was published by Gallimard in 1956 – the same year as the student uprisings in Bucharest and a year before the death of Cioran's father, a prominent orthodox priest. Its title flirted with the vogue for existentialism at the time, but Cioran was careful to label such a trend a "temptation," as if the pessimist author were insinuating that one would do better to resist existentialism – and even existence itself. In style it differs from the fragments of *A Short History of Decay* and the aphorisms of *All Gall Is Divided*, for in *The Temptation to Exist* Cioran comes nearer to the classical essay as pioneered by Montaigne. Insofar as the book has a theme, it is that "to exist" is to be tempted to exist – to exist in time, to exist with plans, to exist in a human-centric world of our own making, propelled towards an unforeseen future and pining for a lost past. If Cioran is a "pessimist," it is because he refuses to place his faith in human beings, let alone God or science. This alone distinguishes him from his existentialist colleagues – always at a distance, but always within hearing range.

~ * ~

An informal meeting of friends outside a café – winter, Paris, 1977. They are old schoolmates, each a Romanian exile in France. Eugène Ionesco is a playwright and leading figure of the theater of the absurd; Mircea Eliade, a historian of religion and author of *The Sacred and the Profane*; and with them Cioran, wayward philosopher and aphorist. Though their books are found on different shelves in Parisian bookshops, they all speak to the key issues of postwar European culture – an existential crisis brought on by a loss of faith in humanist ideals; alienation from one's self and others, in part triggered by the chaotic pace of modern life; weariness over the dominance of scientific and technical rationality; and an emerging awareness of a new and unrecognizable world, a world at once post-industrial and postmodern.

Cioran, now in his sixties, seemed especially aware of the changing tides; the reclusive prowler of the Latin Quarter began giving more and more interviews, some of them for radio and television. In 1979 Cioran published a book with the stark title *Écartèlement* (translated as *Drawn and Quartered*). The pessimistic statements are there, true, but there is a sharpness to them, a contentiousness absent in the earlier, more lyrical books:

Left to its own devices, depression would demolish even the fingernails.

There is no other world, nor even this one.

Enough to be in a crowd, in order to feel that you side with all the dead planets.

Existing is plagiarism.

Cioran's fragments are themselves so fragmented, so shattered (and shattering), that they sometimes seem less than a fragment: more a particle, a speck of dust, the debris of thought.

~ * ~

In June of 1969, the French newspaper *Le Monde* published a two-page spread entitled "Cioran, or the Contemplative Nihilist." The title was ambiguous; it was difficult to tell if it was meant as an accolade or an accusation.

~ * ~

In early October of 1965, Mircea Eliade wrote this in his journal:

I found in Junod's *Moeurs et coutumes des Bantous* these details which would delight Cioran. In the region of Thonga, the chief of a village "overcome with sadness and devoid of everything" shows the gods his misery by making them an offering of his own spittle. It is called "the offering of bitterness." The man hopes to arouse the pity of the gods by this derisory gift.

~ * ~

Cioran published *De l'inconvénient d'être né* (translated as *The Trouble with Being Born*) in 1973. It was a time of loss and refusals. A few years before, Cioran's mother and sister had died. Cioran's close friend, the playwright Arthur Adamov, committed suicide. The year also saw the death of another close friend, the existentialist philosopher Gabriel Marcel. A year later, the poet Paul Celan, who had translated Cioran's work into German, also committed suicide. It was a period of refusals. Cioran proudly spurned several gestures of monetary support, as well as numerous literary prizes, many of them financially significant (there is an anecdote of Beckett lending Cioran money while chiding him for refusing such prizes). All the while Cioran continued to live modestly in his rented apartment, working at his compact and cluttered desk, writing in his multi-colored notebooks, taking his frequent walks.

In *The Trouble with Being Born* Cioran grapples with an age-old philosophical dilemma – the problem with being here, in this moment, thrown into an existence that one has neither asked for nor desired, in a world that we have difficulty whole-heartedly accepting or rejecting. Today, in the early years of the new millennium, academics discuss the problems of global climate change, sustainability, and over-population, taking sides in philosophical debates on natalism and anti-natalism. Such debates are not new. In the 1970s, journalists and public thinkers frequently discussed the "population bomb" and the "end of history." But in *The Trouble with Being Born* Cioran remains skeptical of such a myopic emphasis on the present – his writing asks whether such issues are not simply a symptom of a fraught relationship to our own mortality – the latest stage in Western culture's "fall into time." *The Trouble with Being Born* is an extended meditation on the problem of time and temporality that begins with Cioran's own devastating realization late one night, in the slow seconds of his life-long struggle with insomnia: "Three in the morning. I realize this second, then this one, then the next: I draw up a balance sheet for each minute. And why all this? *Because I was born.* It is a special type of sleeplessness that produces the indictment of birth."

~ * ~

There are writers that one seeks out, and there are writers that one stumbles upon. Cioran is arguably of the latter kind. Such was my own introduction to his work, as a student meandering one rainy afternoon in a used bookstore in Seattle. In the philosophy section, squeezed between "Cicero" and "Confucius," was a book that jumped out simply by its title: *A Short History of Decay*. Spine-creased and dog-eared, it was by an author I knew nothing about. But the title was evocative. Decay, decline, decadence – these are never popular topics, especially in an era such as ours, equally enamored with the explanatory power of science as we are with an almost religious preoccupation with self-help. But how can one write a "short" history of decay? And is there not something contradictory in assembling a "history" of decay? Even the original French title – *Précis de décomposition* – is curious. In French, one often gives the title *Précis* to textbook summaries – for exam-ple, a *Précis de littérature française* or a *Précis de mathéma-tiques*. But a "précis" of decay? It seemed absurd to write such a book. And so I bought it.

That used bookstore no longer exists, though I still have my copy of Cioran's book. Originally published in 1949, *A Short History of Decay* was the first book Cioran wrote in French. Born in the small Romanian village of Rășinari in 1911, Cioran attended university in Bucharest, where he discovered the works of Pascal and Nietzsche. While there, he befriended Mircea Eliade and Eugène Ionesco, who would remain life-long friends. In the early 1930s Cioran was awarded a fellowship to study in Berlin. There, the misanthropy already evident in his writing found further expression in the extreme right-wing politics of the period. On his return to Bucharest, he expressed support for the Iron Guard, a far-right political organization, and published *The Transfiguration of Romania*, a book that employs impassioned prose in its evocation of a "messianic fury." As the decade wore on, however, Cioran repudi-ated his political views – and indeed politics altogether – and would continue to express bitterness and remorse over his activity during this period to the end of his life. (Elliptical as ever, in a 1935 letter to Eliade he once wrote, "My formula for politics is: to fight *sincerely* for that in which I do not believe.")

By the late 1930s, with the support of Bucharest's French Institute, Cioran was in Paris, ostensibly to write his philosophy thesis. Instead, he spent many of his days bicycling around the outskirts of the city. It was a time of intense poverty; not only was it difficult to make ends meet, but he experienced both a cultural and linguistic self-exile, writing in a language not his own, in a style composed entirely of fragments, during long nights of insomnia. In the 1940s, against the backdrop of war, Cioran began a project originally entitled *Exercices négatifs* (*Negative Exercises*), then changed the title to *Penseur d'occasion* (*Second-Hand Thinker*), before finally settling on *Précis de décomposition*. The project resulted in some eight hundred manuscript pages and four different manuscript versions of the book.

When *A Short History of Decay* was published in French, it tended to polarize readers. Many dismissed it as overly morose and pessimistic, completely out of tune with the obligatory optimism of postwar European culture. Others praised it for precisely these reasons (in his review of the book, the editor Maurice Nadeau proclaimed Cioran "the harbinger of bad news par excellence..."). The original impact of Cioran's book can still be felt today. Like Nietzsche, Cioran is intent on exposing the hypocrisies of the human condition; but unlike Nietzsche, Cioran never once offers a way out, or even words of inspiration. And yet, there is a kind of enthusiasm in Cioran's prose that peeks through, in spite of his predilection for pessimism and despair: "It is because it rests on nothing, because it lacks even the shadow of an argument that we persevere in life"; "How invent a remedy for existence, how conclude this endless cure? And how recover from your own birth?" There is an ecstasy of the worst in Cioran's writing that manifests itself in his many voices – sometimes philosophical, sometimes poetic, always polemical. *A Short History of Decay* is at once a work of philosophy and yet a sort of song, a conflicted and agonistic testament of the "magnificent futility" that is humanity – and the ambivalence the book expresses is, arguably, more and more relevant today in our own era of end-of-the-world scenarios.

Though his books are well-regarded today, and though he received many literary prizes for them – nearly all of which he refused – Cioran always held the worlds of literature and philosophy at arm's length. His willful experiment with style has largely prevented his work from being easily recognized: neither philosophy nor poetry, neither essay nor novel, neither manifesto nor confession. Perhaps he preferred it this way. Of course, in our digital age is quite easy to find Cioran's books. The real question is why one would read them. In this sense, perhaps the *only* way to encounter Cioran is to stumble across him, as if by accident, or by fate.

~ * ~

Joseph Joubert

31 October 1818

~ * ~

An entry from one of Joubert's notebooks reads: "I am an Aeolian harp. No wind has passed through me."

~ * ~

Søren Kierkegaard

25 September 1855

~ * ~

There are two noteworthy facts about Kierkegaard's life: first, that nothing much happened, and second, that this has been exhaustively detailed and documented – especially by Kierkegaard himself. By contrast with other writers of his generation, with Kierkegaard we get no travels to far-away places, no accounts of erotic adventures, no bouts of substance abuse and addiction, no incarceration by the State, no tragic tales of madness or suicide, not even anecdotes of being expelled from school or rebelling against one's parents. With Kierkegaard, what one finds is a solitary figure intensely captivated by the basic spiritual relationship of a single, fragile individual before an opaque and indifferent God. All the drama is within.

Certainly Kierkegaard experienced the sort of ups and downs that one experiences, but these simply constitute "a life," nothing more, nothing less. We know about his birth into a prosperous Copenhagen family, the strict father, the gentle mother, his education, his inability to decide on a career, his inheritance and the independence it afforded, his engagement and his breaking off of the engagement, his participation in the intellectual debates of his day – especially concerning religion and the institutions of religion – his illness and death at the relatively young age of forty-two, and of course the writings, often penned under various pseudonyms.

While Kierkegaard himself never denied these more mundane aspects of his life, he also went to great lengths to highlight what he regarded as key events in his development as an individual: the emotional turmoil of his relationship with and engagement to Regine Olsen from 1840 to 1841; the brief scandal with the Danish newspaper *The Corsair* in 1845 and 1846; and, in 1854, the polemics against the Danish Church. But these were more at Kierkegaard's instigation than anything else. It was a twenty-seven-year-old Kierkegaard – Kierkegaard the lover – who made the proposal of marriage and who, a year later, rescinded the proposal, for reasons that were unclear even to him (Kierkegaard blamed his "melancholy"). And, a few years later, it was Kierkegaard the writer who intentionally courted scandal by daring *The Corsair* to publicly satirize him. The same would happen near the end of his life as he indicted the Danish Church authorities for smothering the "true Christianity" of the individual.

Kierkegaard not only "authored" the drama in his life, but he willingly – perhaps enthusiastically – suffered it as well. However, such drama is not, relatively speaking, all that dramatic. Kierkegaard simply suffered a break-up and some bad press. "Join the club," one is tempted to say. And yet, his published writings and the journals display such attentiveness to the nuances of spiritual craving and the absurdities of modern life, that one cannot help but to be moved.

There is a sense that Kierkegaard was, if anything, the master of making a mountain out of a molehill.

~ * ~

Is Kierkegaard's life a life of great drama and little consequence, or is it a life of little drama and great consequence? If the latter, is this an argument for a more authentic, more spiritual life? Everyday life as a passion-play? His voluminous journals would seem to offer answers to such questions. In one early entry, he writes: "The whole of existence frightens me, from the smallest fly to the mystery of the Incarnation; everything is unintelligible to me, most of all myself; the whole of existence is poisoned in my sight, particularly myself."

If Kierkegaard's life was unexceptional, the extent to which biographers have meticulously detailed the life of Kierkegaard is striking: Walter Lowrie's much-referenced, two-volume biography is over one thousand pages, and Joakim Garff's more recent biography clocks in at just under nine hundred pages (by contrast Alastair Hannay's classic biography is brief, at five hundred pages).

As for Kierkegaard, the entries in his journals titled "About Myself" are numerous, though they often boil down to a single formula: ...without my melancholy I would have not become a philosopher, much less a Christian...

~ * ~

Kierkegaard kept journals throughout most of his adult life. Though he wrote books, pamphlets, essays, and newspaper articles, his journals remain at once the alpha and omega of the works for which he is now known. The edition of the *Søren Kierkegaards Papirer*, which began in 1909 and continued, under different editors, until 1970, comprises thirteen volumes in twenty-five bindings. However the project was begun as early as the late 1850s, just after Kierkegaard's death, when his brother, the Bishop of Aalborg, began to collate various unpublished papers and manuscripts. Another editor took up the project in the mid-1860s, but, bizarrely, threw away the originals after they had been transcribed. If one adds to this the fact that many of Kierkegaard's journal entries lack dates, then it becomes clear that if Kierkegaard had not intentionally created a labyrinth for the reader, he certainly had done so by accident.

Despite its magnitude, the journals are themselves not a "work," and the problem of how one should read them has kept Kierkegaard scholars busy for generations. Should the journals be read alongside the published works or can they be read on their own terms? For that matter, the question of the status of the journals remains unclear. Kierkegaard left no explicit instructions concerning the publication of his journals, and, though we might be inclined to think of his journals as "private," there are numerous instances in which Kierkegaard clearly seems to be writing for an imagined audience. Given Kierkegaard's self-reflexivity – his publishing under clever pseudonyms like "Johannes de Silentio" (John of Silence) or "Victor Eremetia" (Victor the Hermit) – it is entirely possible that he knew, and hoped, that the journals would be his final, posthumous "work."

The journals vary in their content, from everyday observations, to condensed philosophical essays, to drafts of letters to friends and colleagues. A number of journal entries display the sort of melancholy for which Kierkegaard is now well-known:

> Deep down in every person there dwells a dread that he become alone in the world, forgotten by God, overlooked among this huge household's millions upon millions. One keeps this dread at bay by seeing many people around one who are bound to one as kin and friends. But the dread is there all the same. One dare hardly think what it would feel like if all this were taken away.

But these weighty and angst-ridden comments are often counter-balanced by pedantic complaints about constipation or the latest society gossip. And then there are comments that seem to come from an altogether different place: "Now and then I get a strange desire to make an entrechat with my legs, to snap my fingers, and then die."

~ * ~

Kierkegaard rarely travelled outside of his dear Copenhagen, though he owned a floor-standing globe and numerous reference books, including the *Compendious General Atlas of the Entire World*. The one exception he made was a visit to Berlin, where the young Kierkegaard stayed for some five months between 1841 and 1842. The motive for the trip was philosophical. The influence of German Idealism had been felt not only within Germany but beyond it as well, and as a student Kierkegaard fell briefly under its spell. His reading of Hegel, in particular, piqued his interest so much that he resolved to study in Berlin. Once there, he attended lectures by several then-prominent, but now-forgotten philosophers in the Hegelian tradition. Kierkegaard also attended the lectures of Friedrich Schelling, whose turn to religion had also piqued the interest of the melancholy Dane. Hope quickly turned to disappointment, however, as Kierkegaard found himself increasingly impatient, critical, and simply bored.

There was another problem as well. While Kierkegaard loved exploring the neighborhoods of Berlin, the lack of public restrooms made it all but impossible for him to take extensive walks around the city. He would inevitably walk a number of blocks and then be forced to turn back home to urinate. (No doubt this was due, in part, to the steady stream of coffee Kierkegaard enjoyed during the day.) One wonders if the brevity of his walks curbed the intellectual labor of the peripatetic philosopher. Were there profound thoughts or key insights that were suddenly cut short by the urgency of a full bladder? A further, no less philosophical, disappointment.

~ * ~

For every leap there is a fall. Too often, perhaps, we have been told to find great wisdom in Kierkegaard's now-cliché leap of faith. But what about the art of fall-ing? In *Fear and Trembling* Kierkegaard offers the fol-lowing parable:

> The knights of infinity are ballet dancers and have elevation. They make the upward movement and come down again, and this, too, is not an unhappy diversion and is not unlovely to see. But every time they come down, they are unable to assume the posture immediately, they waver for a moment, and this wavering shows that they are aliens in the world. It is more or less conspicuous according to their skill, but even the most skillful of these knights cannot hide this wavering. One does not need to see them in the air; one needs only to see them the instant they touch and have touched the earth – and then one recognizes them. But to be able to come down in such a way that instantaneously one seems to stand and to walk, to change the leap into life into walking, abso-lutely to express the sublime in the pedestrian – only that knight can do it, and this is the one and only marvel.

~ * ~

The writer and scholar Israel Levin, who served as Kier-kegaard's research assistant in the late 1840s, related his mentor's fondness for coffee. After their evening meal, Kierkegaard would open a cupboard filled with a dizzying array of cups and saucers. After selecting a set himself, Kierkegaard would ask Levin which he preferred – and why. Then Kierkegaard would set down his empty cup, pouring sugar into it until it formed a neat, conical shape that just peeked out of the top of the cup. Strong, hot, black coffee would then be poured over this sugary cone, where it was then swiftly downed in a few swallows. The night's work could then begin.

~ * ~

Kierkegaard's own brand of melancholy was not unrelated to his day-to-day experiences, especially the experience of his body. All throughout his life Kierkegaard experienced minor ailments, but near the end of the 1840s his letters and journals dwell more and more on constant annoyance caused by arthritis, back pain, constipation, eye strain, headaches, hemorrhoids, indigestion, insomnia, stomach cramps, and spells of vertigo. Things would get more serious later on, but even at this early point what Kierkegaard notes is the cumulative effect of the body's finitude, the often irritating reminder of the body's mortality, marked daily by the passing of time and the routine of daily movements, gestures, and acts:

> Like the invalid who longs to get rid of his bandages, so my healthy spirit longs to throw off my body's languor… Like the one who in danger at sea, when another drowning man tries to seize hold of his leg, pushes him away with all his might, so too my body like a heavy weight which drags me down clings to my spirit, and it will end in death.

In the margins of the journal Kierkegaard adds: "…the clammy, sweat-soaked poultice that is the body and its languor…"

~ * ~

A year prior to his death, Kierkegaard began reading Schopenhauer. His health getting worse, the discovery of Schopenhauer seemed to provide a brief boon to the ailing Dane, sparking new turns in his religious thinking. While he had certainly heard of Schopenhauer before, it remains noteworthy that around 1854 Kierkegaard began to purchase all available books by and about Schopenhauer – and this at a time when the former bibliophile had largely abandoned the purchase of books.

In a journal entry from this period Kierkegaard is careful to note both similarities as well as differences, referring to Schopenhauer by his initials "A.S." and to himself by the initials "S.A." (Søren Aabye): "A.S. (Note: Oddly enough, I am called S.A. No doubt we ourselves are also inversely related)…" Kierkegaard was an eclectic reader of Schopenhauer; weary of the latter's turn to mysticism and ascetic refusal, Kierkegaard criticizes Schopenhauer – not for being a pessimist, but for not being pessimist enough:

> …one arrives at asceticism by way of an original intellectuality because one sees into the misery of everything or, more properly, the misery which is existence, or is brought through suffering to the point where it seems a relief to let the

whole thing come to a breaking point, breaking
with everything, with existence itself – that is,
with the desire for existence (asceticism, mortification)…

Schopenhauer had not gone far enough. He had questioned religion and philosophy, but had not questioned
his own "religion" and his own philosophy – "a class
of men in philosophy, just like the priests in religion."

This is, of course, the extreme point that fascinates
Kierkegaard, especially the later Kierkegaard who
writes both *Training in Christianity* and *Attack Upon
Christendom*. At what point does philosophical argument cease and religious faith begin? His indictment of
Schopenhauer is curt and tinged with irony: "But how
then does S. live? He lives in retreat and once in a while
sends out a thunder of rudeness – which is ignored;
well, yes, there you have it." "If I could talk with him,"
Kierkegaard teases, "I am sure he would either shud-
der or laugh if I measured him with this yardstick."

~ * ~

Near the end of 1847, as Kierkegaard finished *Works of
Love*, he was reminded of how his work had taken him
away from his frequent walks around Copenhagen. As
a sort of compensation, Kierkegaard treated himself to
specially-reserved, country carriage rides outside the
city. Some of the destinations were farther than others
(Fredensborg, Frederiksborg, Northern Zealand),
while other destinations were closer to home (Bellevue,
Deer Park, Fortunen, Lyngby, Nyholte, Rudersdal, or

the aptly-named Hermitage). He referred to such out-ings as "air baths."

~ * ~

Though his work would become more and more aus-tere in its spiritual vision, Kierkegaard was fond of his effects. This was especially the case with his collection of walking sticks and umbrellas, as evidenced by a short, parodic text written in the 1840s, "My Umbrella, My Friendship":

> It was a terrible storm; I stood alone and aban-doned by all on the Kongens-Nytorv; then my umbrella also turned on me. I was at my wits' end, not knowing whether I should let go of it for its act of perfidy and become a misanthrope or not. It has become so dear to me that I always carry it whether it is rainy weather or sunny; and so as to show it that I do not love it merely from utilitar-ian motives I sometimes walk up and down in my room and behave as though I were out, lean upon it, open it up, lean my chin against the crook, put it up to my lips, and so on and so forth.

Colleagues of Kierkegaard, while they enjoyed walk-ing and talking with him, were often taken aback by the highly energetic gesticulations Kierkegaard would make with his walking stick, giving the effect of a kind of fencing philosopher, a sword-wielding Socrates. (His companions on his walks always noted the vari-ety of walking sticks made available, from polished bamboo to black silk umbrellas.) And yet, in spite of his melancholic musings and religious despair, the street philosopher of Copenhagen reveled in his daily excursion. In his early work *The Concept of Irony* Kierkegaard described Socrates as "a master of the casual encounter."

~ * ~

If Kierkegaard took an interest in Schopenhauer late in his life, it not only had to do with the latter's pessimism – it also had to do with their shared animosity towards German academic philosophy, symbolized by the figure of Hegel. Schopenhauer wrote entire diatribes against German Idealism, at one point even calling Hegel a "windbag" (*Schwätzer*), a poetry of insult Kierkegaard took note of:

> It's a remarkable word: I can envy the Germans it. It's particularly excellent also because it can be used as an adjective and a verb. A. Schopenhauer makes first-class use of it – yes, I must say Schopenhauer would be in a fix if he didn't have that word, having to discuss Hegelian philosophy and all the professor-philosophy.

A small consolation perhaps. But Kierkegaard continues:

> We Danes do not have this word, but neither is what the word designates typical of us Danes. Being a windbag isn't part of the Danish national

character. However, we Danes do have another fault, a *corresponding* fault, and the Danish language also has a word for it, a word which the German language perhaps does not have: windsucker (*Vindsluger*). It is used mainly of horses but can be adopted generally. This is just about the way it is – a German to make wind and a Dane to swallow it.

Hence, in spite of their differences, the shared, philosophical misanthropy of both thinkers: "…if Schopenhauer had windbags to deal with, I have to cope with windsuckers."

~ * ~

Upon returning from the hospital for the treatment of partial paralysis, Kierkegaard remarked to a friend: "The doctors do not understand my illness. It is psychical, and now they want to treat it in the usual medical fashion."

~ * ~

Kierkegaard was more apt to describe himself as a melancholic than as a pessimist. Melancholy was at once his ground and his downfall. But behind this melancholy is a secret suspicion that things will not work out, and therefore that it is better to not bother trying at all – marriage, family life, academic life, professional life, the religious vocation… one does everything with a great sense of tenuousness, as if at any moment it might all fall apart. If we were to come up with Kierkegaard-ian-like terms, we might say that Kierkegaard's pessimism is a "conditional unconditionality": that is, there will always be some reason that things will not work out, if not now, then later. This leaves one with one of two options: either, in a fit of superstition, one pre-empts things not working out by causing their downfall oneself, or, in a fit of apathy, one does nothing.

Throughout his life, Kierkegaard was bent to spells of severe depression, in which even doing nothing was too much of a burden. In a journal entry from the autumn of 1837 he writes:

> I don't feel like lying down, because then I would either remain lying down for a long time, and I don't feel like doing that, or I would get up again, and I don't feel like doing that either. I don't feel like going riding, it involves motion that is too strenuous for my apathy. I just want to go for a drive in a carriage and let a great many objects glide by while I experience a steady, comfortable, rocking motion, pausing at each beautiful spot merely in order to feel my own lassitude. My ideas and impulses are as fruitless as the lust of a eunuch...

Kierkegaard caps off the entry with: "...I don't even feel like writing what I have just written, nor do I feel like erasing it..."

~ * ~

In the 1830s, while still a student, Kierkegaard became obsessed with books. He made frequent visits to Reitzel's Bookshop, where he purchased books in philosophy, theology, literature, and other subjects. On his shelves were to be found literary classics such as Dante's *Divine Comedy*, Hoffmann's tales, Shakespeare's plays, and the poetry of Byron, Heine, and Petrarch. Among the numerous books of theology and spirituality were Pascal's *Pensées* and the works of Jean Paul. Of German philosophy one finds Hegel, Schlegel, and Novalis. In addition to a collection of modern Danish and Swedish literature, Kierkegaard also seemed to be fond of fairy tales, from *A Thousand and One Nights* to the Brothers Grimm. And then there are those hard to classify, "miscellaneous" books, often anonymously authored: books such as *Strange Questions* or the enigmatically-titled *Fun to Listen to and Read*.

By the end of the decade Kierkegaard's personal library was estimated at approximately two thousand books. The books were often bound in leather, often with glazed paper and decoration to the spine. This attention to detail was echoed in how Kierkegaard read his books. There are dog-eared pages (sometimes at the top, sometimes at the bottom), and the texts of the books include notation in various colors of ink (black, blue, red) as well as marginalia in pencil.

About six months after his death, Kierkegaard's personal library went out to auction. On April 8th, the three-day auction of 2,748 books began, held in the empty rooms of Kierkegaard's last home. A large crowd was in attendance, including everyone from local book dealers to representatives from the Royal Library. One bookseller noted how everything in Kierkegaard's library went for "enormously high prices" – even Kierkegaard's own writings were sold for three times their bookstore price.

~ * ~

All through the autumn of 1855 Kierkegaard had been suffering from chronic digestive ailments. On one occasion, while on one of his many walks about town, he suddenly felt a numbness in his legs, then a shooting pain down into his toes. On another occasion, as he shifted in his chair at home, his entire lower body went numb, as he helplessly slid from his chair to the floor. At times simple acts such as putting on his trousers or shoes became unbearably painful. His earlier bouts with constipation returned, his stomach in knots. Urination became difficult – or he would urinate and defecate involuntarily. Doctors either provided opaque diagnoses or else simply threw up their hands. By October, as his condition became more and more unpredictable, Kierkegaard was taken to a room at Royal Frederick's Hospital, where he would spend the final month of his life. Again the diagnoses were inconclusive. In between visits from family and friends, the doctors regularly administered laxative injections to treat the constipation. An argument ensued between Søren and his brother Peter over the former receiving last communion. They would never be reconciled. Now almost totally paralyzed from the waist down, the doctors made a final attempt to electrocute Kierkegaard's lower body, but to no avail. Eventually, by the first week of November, his heart rate slowed, and the paralysis reached up his body to his face, freezing it in place. Kierkegaard entered into a coma shortly after, and died on the 11th of November.

In February Henrik Lund sent a letter to Peter Kierkegaard, noting that, among his brother's effects were several locks of Søren's hair. Lund asked Peter if he wanted one of these "hair relics." A month later Peter answered in the affirmative.

~ * ~

In September of 1855, in failing health but good spirits, Kierkegaard wrote in his journal: "Our destiny in this life is to be brought to the highest pitch of world-weariness." But that is not all, Kierkegaard asserts; weariness is the means, not the end. "He who when brought to that point can insist that it is God who has brought him there, out of love, has passed life's examination and is ripe for eternity."

But whether Kierkegaard included himself in this select group is unclear. In the very next line, he writes, "It was through a crime that I came into the world, I came against God's will... The punishment fits the crime: to be bereft of all lust for life, to be led to the extremity of world-weariness..."

Then others come under Kierkegaard's depressive spell: "Most people these days are so spiritless, so deserted by grace, that the punishment simply isn't used on them. Lost in life they cling to this life, out of nothing they become nothing, their life is a waste." In the concluding paragraph Kierkegaard simply writes

"What then does God want?" Kierkegaard's answer: "...God sits in heaven listening. And every time he hears someone praise him, someone he brings to the extremity of world-weariness, God says to himself: Here is the voice..."

This was to be Kierkegaard's last journal entry. After this, there is only the silence of illness, paralysis, and unconsciousness.

~ * ~

Kierkegaard evokes little sympathy but a great deal of empathy. Even his apathy is strangely inspiring.

~ * ~

It appears that, early on, Kierkegaard had formulated many of the themes that would occupy him as a philosopher and writer. More than that, he had found a variety of ingenious ways of presenting his ideas, through his many pseudonyms and their crypto-bibliographic references. In one of his journal entries, the thirty-year-old Kierkegaard writes what could very well serve as his epitaph:

> After my death, no one will find in my papers (this is my consolation) the least information about what has really filled my life, find the inscription of my innermost being which explains everything, and what, more often than not, makes what the world would call trifles into, for me, events of immense importance, and which I too consider

of no significance once I take away the secret note
which explains it.

~ * ~

Giacomo Leopardi

1 December 1828

~ * ~

Often hailed as the greatest Italian poet since Dante, Giacomo Taldegardo Francesco di Sales Saverio Pietro Leopardi had no real reason to be a pessimist. He was born into a noble family and received a first-class education – though his father had a severe gambling habit that was countermanded by the equal severity and coldness of his mother. The family's prominent home was in Recanati, on the eastern coast of Italy – but for years Leopardi wished for nothing else than to leave. In his letters and poems he expresses nothing but dread for the stifling, provincial, conservative atmosphere of his home life. As a teenager Leopardi made several attempts to run away from home, but was always caught and placed under a sort of house arrest. In a diary entry Leopardi refers to his home as "a hermitage, or better, a prison." In another entry he considers suicide, but finds himself without the courage to carry it out, preferring instead the "live burial" of Recanati.

This nagging sense of *ennui* was only assuaged by the family's library, which a young Leopardi omnivorously devoured, eventually enabling him to read and write Greek and Latin with ease (in addition to Spanish, French, German, and Hebrew). Tutelage under a local priest, and then with a classics scholar, helped to foster Leopardi's interest in language and philology. It is from this period that he produces his first poems, and in the following years Leopardi would live the life of an itinerate poet – Bologna, Florence, Milan, Naples, Pisa, Rome. The poems for which he is known have since become a mainstay of Italian literature textbooks: *L'appressamento della morte* ("On the Approach of Death"), *L'infinito* ("The Infinite"), *Sopra il Monumento di Dante* ("Above the Monument of Dante"), *Risorgimento* ("The Resurgence"), *Le Recordanze* ("Memories"), and *Aspasia*. Publication of his poems gave Leopardi the freedom to live away from Recanati, but recurring illness and a weak constitution prevented him from doing much else – there were his sporadic episodes of blindness and recurring bouts of depression, in addition to asthma, persistent coughing, kidney and intestinal problems, dropsy, and defective bone growths on his spine, no doubt made "this troubled and travailed sleep we call life" more difficult. Leopardi's death came during a cholera outbreak in 1837, just a few years after the publication of his *Canti*, the work for which he is today most known.

~ * ~

One of Leopardi's poems contains the lines: "Fate has bequeathed unto our race / no gift except to die." The poem is titled "To Himself."

~ * ~

Even if one grants Leopardi the misfortune of a dys-
functional home life and frequent illness, it is still hard
to pinpoint the source of his pessimistic outlook – an
attitude already apparent in his first poems, written
between the ages of fifteen and eighteen. The sense of
being trapped produced wild mood swings, between
frenetic study and inertial apathy. Of his ailments it
was depression that most concerned Leopardi, what he
once described as "the obstinate, black, horrible, barba-
rous melancholy which consumes, grinds, and devours
me, and which is aggravated by study, and which, if
I abstain from study, increases." For several months
the teenage Leopardi was convinced he was dying. "At
night, in the midst of grief," he wrote a poem reflecting
his own sense of mortality: "So I must die, and yet I
have not seen / Full twenty times the snow upon the
roof / Nor twenty times the swallows build their nests."

One could, of course, simply attribute Leopardi's
pessimism to teen angst – but if so, it would be a tone
he would strike in nearly all his subsequent writings,
whether lyrical poetry or philosophical essay. What
does change over the years is the tone of Leopardi's
pessimism. In the early poems, Leopardi's pessimism
is drenched in dread and despair, as in *La vita solitaria*
("The Solitary Life") or *Lo spavento notturno* ("Night-
time Terror"). These, however, are contradicted by
later poems like *Il pensiero dominante* ("The Dominating Thought"), which persistently affirms life, even in
the face of tragedy and death. But not all of Leopardi's
writings have this sort of uplifting ending. A passage
from one of the dialogues, collected in the *Operette
morali*, reads: "Life is a thing of so little moment that

a man, thinking of himself, should not be greatly concerned either to retain it or to leave it." Scholars have even gone so far as to create a typology of pessimism in Leopardi's writings. This so-called *pessimismo leopardiano* goes through different stages – an individual pessimism, characterized by the early poems and their struggle between individual desires and the constraints of the world; a historical pessimism, which bemoans the ills of contemporary society; a metaphysical pessimism, which meditates on the frailty and ephemeral character of life itself; and even a final stage, a heroic pessimism, in which Leopardi affirms life, in spite of its pervasive suffering.

But how then to account for Leopardi's comments, at once stark and absurd, on death? "There are two truths which most men will never believe: one, that they know nothing, and the other, that they are nothing. And there is a third, which proceeds from the second – that there is nothing to hope for after death."

~ * ~

Leopardi's pessimism is indicative of the era in which he lived. Like many pessimist thinkers, he is at once a product of and a bulwark against the Enlightenment ideals of reason and scientific progress. Nowhere is this more evident than in the massive tome of miscellany Leopardi wrote, known as the *Zibaldone*.

Leopardi began the *Zibaldone* in the summer of 1817 and continued making entries in it until 1832, just a few years prior to his death. The term "zibaldone" itself indicated a sort of casual miscellany or hodgepodge; it also referred to the type of commonplace books often found in the later Middle Ages, books that might contain everything from poetry and prayers to accounts and grocery lists. The idea for the *Zibaldone* appears to have come to Leopardi from a local priest, Don Giuseppe Antonio Vogel, who once noted that "every literary man should have a *written chaos* such as this, a notebook containing pleasantries, arguments, extracts, counter-propositions, commentaries…" Initially Leopardi proposed for his notebooks the title *Thoughts on Various Forms of Philosophy and Fine Literature*, but later settled for the more condensed, and, perhaps, more honest *Zibaldone*.

The *Zibaldone* is one of the most profoundly incomplete works in the history of literature. True to its title, it is indeed a massive, heterogeneous treasure-trove of aphorisms, diary entries, essays in miniature, observations and meditations, literary criticism, anecdotes, parables, quotations from other poets, and stray fragments of popular songs. As a whole, the manuscript of the *Zibaldone* comprises over four thousand pages. Nearly every topic is discussed – poetry, philosophy, philology, politics, religion, science, art, love, culture, and even the *Zibaldone* itself. In it, Leopardi reveals much not only about his trajectory as a thinker and poet, but as a person: we read about his fondness for solitary walks and eating alone (this latter, as he notes, would have condemned by the ancient Romans as *inhumanum*); how he was often anxious, even superstitious, whenever any good fortune came his way; how he preferred to gaze at the night sky outdoors in complete darkness, rather than from a balcony or a window; how, in middle age, he feels embarrassment and revulsion at seeing younger poets or scholars presenting their ideas. But whatever the topic of discussion, the unmistakable tone of the *pessimismo leopardiano* blankets each of the texts. An early entry encapsulates much of this observational pessimism:

> Imagining that we are the most important of nature's beings and that the world was created for us is a natural consequence of the self-love that is necessarily intrinsic to us and necessarily unlimited. So it is natural that every species of animal should imagine, if not explicitly then certainly confusedly and fundamentally, the same thing. This happens in one species or genus with regard to every other species or genus. But, correspondingly, the same thing is visible in individuals...

Another, later entry is exemplary of the way Leopardi drew inspiration from his daily walks:

> In my solitary walks around cities, the view into rooms which I see from the street below, through their open windows, arouses within me very pleasurable sensations and beautiful images. Such rooms would arouse nothing in me if I saw them from inside. Is this not an image of human life, of its conditions, its goods and its delights?

Though it remained unpublished during his lifetime, the *Zibaldone* is in every way a document of the complexities and contradictions of pessimist thinking. But

it is not a completed work, and there is every indication that Leopardi did not intend it as such. There is
repetition and contradiction, failed attempts at philosophical argument, half-formed thoughts and half-fin-
ished poems, and, above all, a persistent tone of sorrow
and crisis. Yet the *Zibaldone* is not simply a confession;
in fact, what makes it such an interesting work is the
uncanny mixture of pervasive melancholy and an energetic, almost ecstatic inventiveness.

~ * ~

It is worth noting that, in spite of the amount of scholarship on Leopardi and his pessimism, Leopardi himself rarely used the term. Instead, he was more apt to
use the term optimism, and to stridently attack it, especially as incarnated in philosophers such as Leibniz. In
one of his notebook entries Leopardi breaks in with the
assertion:

> Everything is evil. That is to say everything that
> is, is evil; that each thing exists is an evil; each
> thing exists only for an evil end... There is no
> other good except nonbeing; there is nothing good
> except what is not... All existence; the complex of
> so many worlds that exist; the universe; is only a
> spot, a speck in metaphysics... Existence, by its
> nature and essence and generally, is an imperfec-
> tion, an irregularity, a monstrosity... This system,
> although it clashes with those ideas of ours that
> the end can be no other than good, is probably
> more sustainable than that of Leibniz, Pope, etc.,

that *everything is good…*

Leopardi attacked optimism – even though he didn't really believe in pessimism. This is, of course, what all pessimists do – they do not so much affirm pessimism as they negate optimism. And in the end, they secretly know that both positions are compromised.

~ * ~

On the 17th of April in 1827, Leopardi writes in his note-book (noting that it is Easter Tuesday):

I, for example, am idle for much of the time, and inclined to indolence, either by nature or by habit; yet in the midst of this deep inactivity, on a day when I have occasion to set to work, and have much to do, not only do I manage to finish everything, but I have time to spare, and in that spare time I find (and it has happened to me several times) a true need, a restlessness, to do something, a horror of doing nothing, which seems unbearable, as if I were unaccustomed to passing hours and, so to speak, months in my room with my arms crossed.

~ * ~

Georg Christoph Lichtenberg

24 March 1786

~ * ~

Lichtenberg was a hunchback, a hypochondriac, and a depressive, and the book of aphorisms for which he is now known – *The Waste Books* – was posthumously published. Lichtenberg was also known for his cheerful, witty disposition towards others, and during his life he enjoyed great notoriety as a scientist and mathematician. How someone who was, during his life, a paragon of scientific progress could also pen the caustic indictments of *The Waste Books* is one of the central enigmas in the history of pessimism. One of Lichtenberg's aphorisms reads: "Human beings live in three places – in the past, in the present and in the future – and are capable of being unhappy if one of these three is worthless. Religion has even added a fourth – eternity."

~ * ~

Lichtenberg's aphorisms have been cited by Kierkegaard, Schopenhauer, Freud, Wittgenstein, and many others. Nietzsche once claimed that *The Waste Books* was one of only four German books worth reading a second time.

~ * ~

As a child, a deformation of the spine led to Lichtenberg's hunchbacked stature, and would eventually be the cause of severe respiratory problems. As a student, he was prone to bouts of severe depression (in school Lichtenberg notes how he would write elaborate Latin treatises on the defense of suicide). This was counterbalanced by periods of feverish activity, mostly in physics. But the flurry of ideas for experiments would be accompanied by almost pathological procrastination. Nevertheless, he wrote volumes of scientific articles, and, in addition to "serious" scientific articles, he also wrote pieces with titles like "Geological Fantasies," "A Most Gracious Epistle from the Earth to the Moon," "Attempts at a Natural History of Bad Poets, Particularly the Germans," and the inescapably self-reflexive "A Fragment on Tails."

~ * ~

Lichtenberg was a life-long hypochondriac, at one point believing he had fever, asthma, dropsy, jaundice, partial paralysis, heart disease, a tumor on his liver, excess water in his brain, and early senility – all at once. In his journal he wrote, "I see the entire world as a machine which has the purpose of making me feel my sickness and my suffering in every possible way. A pathological egotist. Pusillanimity is the right word for my illness, but can one get rid of it?" In another entry he is even more concise in his diagnosis: "He had names for his two slippers."

~ * ~

Lichtenberg, the scientist we no longer remember, first gained his reputation as a lecturer at the university in Göttingen. He edited what was, at the time, the standard textbook on physics, and his lectures were attended by the likes of Alessandro Volta, Karl Friedrich Gauss, Alexander von Humboldt, and Goethe. But he was no friend of intellectuals ("Everyone is a genius at least once a year," he once wrote, "so-called geniuses simply have their bright ideas closer together"). Elections to various Royal Societies of Science followed, as did a visit to London and meetings with the King and Queen, where his wit, charm, and social graces did not go unnoticed. But such company seemed only to inspire disdain: "How happily many people would live if they concerned themselves as little about others' affairs as about their own"

~ * ~

As a teacher Lichtenberg was among the first to introduce scientific apparatus and demonstration into his lectures, and he himself was an avid collector of scientific equipment. Neighbors knew the professor was at home from the various explosions that would periodically emanate from his laboratory (accompanied, no doubt, by outbursts of frustration), and in the 1780s he caused some concern by installing Göttingen's first lightning rod in the middle of the town square – as if it were an invocation.

~ * ~

The work for which Lichtenberg is known – the so-called *Waste Books* or *Sudelbücher* – is the kind of book that could only have been written haphazardly, almost carelessly, with little intention of publication, and even less concern for literary merit. That is the impression, at least. In reality they are carefully constructed, painstakingly whittled down to their sardonic quintessence. That Lichtenberg was conscious of his aphorisms as an autonomous "work" is exemplified early on in one of the entries. There he borrows the English term "waste book" from merchants who, at the end of the day, tally everything bought and sold. This is gradually put into a more systematic form – into a "journal," and finally an official "ledger." All accounts are settled; the day's activities accounted for. As Lichtenberg notes, "this deserves to be imitated by the scholar." He goes on to offer a more detailed description:

> First, a book in which I inscribe everything just as I see it or as my thoughts prompt me, then this can be transformed to another where the materials are more ordered and segregated, and the ledger can then contain a connected construction and the elucidation of the subject that flows from it expressed in an orderly fashion.

Lichtenberg's comment is at once a joke – contrasting the value of goods bought and sold with the supposed valuelessness of philosophical speculation – and at the same time a serious method for the kind of aphorisms one also finds in La Rochefoucauld, Chamfort, Leopardi, Kraus, and Cioran. But there is also a sense in which the method – as orderly and neat as it sounds – is also undermined by the stark, gallows-humor pessimism that drives it. Between 1764, when Lichtenberg, as a student, began his *Waste Books*, to 1799, the year of his death, he produced some twelve notebooks, designating them by letters. His comments about the term "waste book" come from Notebook E (1775-1776), about midway through. But in subsequent notebooks Lichtenberg never says anything else about his "waste book" method. If we are to take Lichtenberg seriously (and this is a problematic assertion, at best), then it appears that either he never had the time to transform his "waste books" into a polished "ledger," or it was all a practical joke – the "waste book" *was* the "ledger."

~ * ~

Lichtenberg, as we noted, was a hunchback. Much later, a group of astronomers would name a large crater on the moon's surface after him. According to one report, the Lichtenberg crater is known for its "Transient Lunar Phenomena."

~ * ~

Lichtenberg once described his face as a "worry-meter."

~ * ~

Philipp Mainländer

1 April 1876

~ * ~

On the evening of the first of April, 1876, thirty-four-year-old Philipp Batz gathered together copies of his book *Die Philosophie der Erlösung* (*The Philosophy of Redemption*), which had just arrived from the publisher. He had worked in the finance and banking sectors for nearly a decade, before quitting his job in disgust. He had been discharged from his military service due to exhaustion and fatigue. He had written several poems and literary works which remained unpublished. And, from the time he was a teenager, he had enthusiastically read Schopenhauer, in addition to Leopardi, Dante, and Heraclitus.

In his Offenbach apartment, Batz gathered together the copies of his nine-hundred-page book, but with how much premeditation it is impossible to know. The book, published under the pen name of Philipp Mainländer, talks of a pervasive "Will-to-Die" that indifferently drives everything that exists, to exist – to exist in order to be extinguished. Batz arranged the copies of his book on the floor into a single pile. He stepped up on top of his books, and hung himself from the ceiling beam of the room.

~ * ~

Though Schopenhauer's thought influenced a great deal of German philosophy in the nineteenth century, most of them attempted some kind of balance between, say, Schopenhauer and Hegel. There were two exceptions to this. One of them was Nietzsche, who sought to push Schopenhauer's negations into an affirmation. The other exception was Mainländer, who went in the other direction, pushing Schopenhauer's negation into a further negation.

At the core of Mainländer's philosophy is the idea that everything that exists, exists in order to not exist – not for some imagined and fantastical afterlife, and not in order to re-enter the cycle of birth, suffering, and death, but for pure annihilation – a "mortification of energy." Everything that exists, driven by a blind "Will-to-Death," exists only to achieve its own nullification. Mainländer calls this "redemption."

Presaging an idea that would become central to Nietzsche's thought, Mainländer asserts that everything that exists is the result not of a beneficent Creator, but of the death of God: "God is dead and his death was the life of the world."

More than this, God doesn't die accidentally, but kills himself. In this "self-cadaverization of God," Mainländer suggests that the world, life, our very selves, are all the rotting residue of God's suicide.

~ * ~

Though he was steeped in the philosophies of Spinoza

and Kant, it was the discovery of Schopenhauer that had the most significant impact on Mainländer. Mainländer himself recounts the happenstance encounter with Schopenhauer's philosophy in a bookstore. He describes how, paging through *The World as Will and Representation*, he read of the "denial of the Will" and was instantly entranced. "I stormed like a crazed person from the bookstore and went home, where I read it from beginning to end. It was dawn when I finished. I had read the whole night through. When I stood up, I felt reborn."

~ * ~

Though his philosophy aimed to be both visionary and rigorous, there is a sense in which Mainländer is constantly warding off the allure of religion. In one passage he writes: "The world-weary person who asks himself – to be or not to be? – and creates reasons for and against this question entirely from within the world." And, because one is always speaking and thinking from within the world, any gesture "outside" is at best hubris, since, "beyond the world is neither a place of peace, nor a place of agony, but only nothing." The allure of the null-state becomes at once the alpha and the omega of Mainländer's philosophy, an enigmatic non-being where there is "neither peace, nor movement, but stateless as in sleep, only with the enormous difference that what is in a stateless sleep also no longer exists: the Will is completely annihilated."

~ * ~

Though he made great claims for his *magnum opus*, Mainländer's book is neither systematic nor rigorous. Or rather, it is systematicity become delirious, rigor become rapture. Sections analyzing the philosophy of Kant or detailing ideas from the sciences suddenly break off into "Oh, this glimpse into absolute emptiness!"

Nevertheless, what Mainländer's book lacks in organization it makes up for in its motive: "I would like to destroy every dubious motive that could deter human beings from searching for the silent night of death."

~ * ~

For Mainländer, the pessimist was also a humorist – not a humorist of gaiety and lightness, but a gallows humorist. At times the pessimist may glimpse the "ether of transparent clarity," and yet "an irresistible force draws him back into the sludge of the world." If one perseveres, it is because the pessimist "approves of only one struggle, the struggle towards the peace of the grave." The pessimist, Mainländer notes, "belongs to both worlds because the power fails him to renounce either." The result is a strange kind of pessimism that even Schopenhauer did not consider. In one of his most concise formulations, Mainländer writes: "The pessimist is actually a well-taught optimist."

~ * ~

Around the grave of Philipp Batz one finds flowers,

mementos, poems, notebooks, photographs, drawings, even effigies. A group of "Sinkers" (*Senker*) has
emerged around Mainländer's philosophy – a Sinker
School, defined in one manifesto as "philosophers who
carry around coffins within themselves."

~ * ~

In the years following his suicide, Mainländer's sister
Minna served as literary executor and editor of her
brother's works, publishing the second volume of
The Philosophy of Redemption in 1886. Shortly after, she
killed herself.

~ * ~

Michel de Montaigne

28 February 1571

~ * ~

Aristocrat, statesman, businessman, diplomat, humanist, socialite, melancholic, tourist, bibliophile, translator, and essayist – Michel de Montaigne was by all standards a worldly person. Born near the Bordeaux region to a wealthy merchant family, he had been reared according to the highest standards of humanist education. As a young man he served in the Bordeaux Parliament, and then at the court of Charles IX. As an adult Montaigne would also become a wine-grower, editor and translator, and would serve as Mayor of Bordeaux. As a statesman he was often pulled into the national negotiations surrounding the religious and political conflicts of his time. He travelled extensively across the continent, sometimes making spiritual pilgrimages, sometimes seeking convalescence for health problems, sometimes out of curiosity.

It is perhaps strange, then, that, at the age of thirty-eight, Montaigne would decide to refuse the world. He shut himself in his library in order to write. So decisive is this refusal that Montaigne christens it with an inscription made on the wall of his library:

In the year of Christ 1571, at the age of thir-

ty-eight, on the last day of February, anniversary
of his birth, Michel de Montaigne, long weary of
the servitude of the court and of public employ-
ments, while still entire, retired to the bosom of
the learned Virgins, where in calm and freedom
from all cares he will spend what little remains of
his life now more than half run out. If the fates
permit he will complete this abode, this sweet
ancestral retreat; and he has consecrated it to his
freedom, tranquility, and leisure.

What does he write? As any reader of his *Essays*
can attest, Montaigne seems to have written about
everything – over a hundred essays in three books, cov-
ering everything from the art of conversation to canni-
balism, much of it written in the first eight years spent
in his retreat from the world. However, what is noteworthy among the pages and pages of observations
is Montaigne's often unfavorable view towards life
– human life in particular. The statesman so involved
in the politics of his time writes: "It is time to untie
ourselves from society, since we can contribute nothing to it." The diplomat so enamored of conversation
now writes: "We are nothing but ceremony; ceremony
carries us away, and we leave the substance of things;
we hang on to the branches and abandon the trunk and
body." The avid traveler who once embraced life's ups
and downs now states: "Life is an uneven, irregular,
and multiform movement. We are not friends to ourselves, and still less masters, we are slaves, if we follow
ourselves incessantly and are so caught in our inclinations that we cannot depart from them or twist them

about." And the humanist, once so dedicated to knowledge and the pursuit of truth, now concludes that "to
philosophize is to learn how to die."

~ * ~

It would seem that owning an estate and castle would
be more than a sufficient means of shutting out the
world. But the Château de Montaigne was still too
"worldly" for Montaigne. What is needed, as he notes,
is an *arrière-boutique*, a kind of room-within-a-room,
where one can recede from the governance of daily life:
"We must reserve a back shop all our own, entirely free,
in which to establish our real liberty and our principal
retreat and solitude."

Montaigne himself decides to spend most of his time
in "the Tower," a small circular abode located at the
southern tip of the castle. It is comprised of a central
tower and an adjoining smaller tower that serves as a
staircase. Montaigne himself provides a description:

> It is on the third floor of a tower; the first is my
> chapel, the second a bedroom and dressing room,
> where I often sleep in order to be alone. Above it is
> a great wardrobe. In the past it was the most use-
> less place in my house. In my library I spend most
> of the days of my life, and most of the hours of the
> day. I am never there at night… The shape of my
> library is round, the only flat side being the part
> needed for my table and chair; and curving round
> me it presents at a glance all my books, arranged
> in five rows of shelves on all sides. It offers rich

and free views in three directions, and sixteen paces of free space in diameter.

He caps off the passage with the following: "There is my throne. I try to make my authority over it absolute, and to withdraw this one corner from all society, conjugal, filial, and civil."

~ * ~

The building that served as Montaigne's hermitage still stands today, having been restored and transformed into a historic site with museum, tours, gift shop, and a wine-tasting from the Château de Montaigne vineyards.

~ * ~

It appears that Montaigne's bibliophilia extended to the physical space of his library as well. On forty-six of the forty-eight ceiling beams of the library Montaigne had inscribed almost seventy quotations in Latin or Greek, mostly from classical authors or the Bible. Among them one finds stark statements such as this, from Pliny the Elder: "Only one thing is certain – that nothing is certain. And nothing is more wretched or arrogant than man." Another, from Lucretius: "One prolongs life only to discover it offers no new pleasures." There are also quotations from Greek tragedians, such as this, from Euripides: "How can you think yourself a great man, when the first accident that comes along can wipe you out completely?" And this, from Sophocles: "The sweetest life is to not think about anything, for the absence of thought is truly a painless evil." And then there are an abundance of lines from Greek Skeptics, foremost among them Sextus Empiricus: "I decide nothing." "I understand nothing." "It is possible, it is not possible." Many of these find their way into Montaigne's essays, where one regularly finds quotations from the likes of Cicero, Seneca, Lucretius, Horace, and Plutarch.

But this peculiar form of graffiti also had a more practical purpose. Montaigne notes how he often paces around his library, occasionally glancing up at the beams for inspiration. His refuge is less a place of work, and more a space of wandering, in which the space of the library becomes the hollowed-out listlessness of the skull: "When at home, I turn aside a little more often to my library... There I leaf through now one book, now another, without order and without plan, by disconnected fragments. One moment I muse, another moment I set down or dictate, walking back and forth, these fancies of mine that you see here."

~ * ~

In 1570 Montaigne, out riding with friends, fell from a horse. He lay half-dead on the ground, and had to be carried back home. It was, in his own words, "the only swoon that I have experienced to this day." Fading in and out of consciousness, he distinctly recalls the thought that he was dying:

...my condition was, in truth, very pleasant and

peaceful; I felt no affliction either for others or for myself; it was a languor and an extreme weakness, without any pain. I saw my house without recognizing it. When they had put me to bed, I felt infinite sweetness in this repose, for I had been villainously yanked about by those poor fellows, who had taken the pains to carry me in their arms over a long and very bad road, and had tired themselves out two or three times in relays. They offered me many remedies, of which I accepted none, holding it for certain that I was mortally wounded in the head. It would, in truth, have been a very happy death; for the weakness of my understanding kept me from having any judgment of it, and that of my body from having any feeling of it.

"...a very happy death..." Perhaps no other phrase encapsulates Montaigne's reflections on mortality. Yet, the period around his horse-riding accident is also filled with death: the death of his close friend, the poet La Boétie in 1563, the death of Montaigne's father in 1568, the death of his brother a year later, and the birth of a stillborn child in 1570, just before he begins writing the *Essays*.

Taking his cue from classical authors like Cicero and Seneca, one often finds Montaigne musing on the arbitrariness of life in contrast to the certitude of death: "Amid feasting and gaiety let us ever keep in mind this refrain, the memory of our condition; and let us never allow ourselves to be so carried away by pleasure that we do not sometimes remember in how many ways this happiness of ours is a prey to death..." Religion gives him little consolation, except to affirm the ambivalence surrounding life and its attendant sufferings: "Our religion has no surer foundation than contempt for life. Not only do the arguments of reason invite us to it; for why should we fear to lose a thing which once lost cannot be regretted?"

Such thoughts lead Montaigne towards a kind of ethos of death. It is Cicero's maxim, "to philosophize is to learn how to die," that serves as Montaigne's starting point in his essay of same title. Death is not the opposite of life; rather, it is omnipresent in life – death "is" by virtue of being alive. As such, death is not to be feared (or rather, it cannot be feared). It leads Montaigne to his famous formulation: "It is uncertain where death awaits us; let us await it everywhere."

While he waits, Montaigne writes, and, as if grasping a fine-grained sand, he attempts different variations on this theme:

All the time you live you steal from life...

Living is at life's expense...

The constant work of our life is to build death...

You are in death while you are in life...

Whether or not such maxims were therapeutic for Montaigne is up for debate. In another, later essay, he reveals a slightly different attitude, one that can only be called superstitious:

I sometimes derive from nonchalance and laxity a way of strengthening myself against these considerations... It often happens that I imagine and await mortal dangers with some pleasure: I plunge head down, stupidly, into death, without looking at it and recognizing it, as into a silent and dark abyss which swallows me up at one leap and overwhelms me in an instant with a heavy sleep free from feeling and pain. And in these quick and violent deaths, the consequence that I foresee gives me more comfort than the occurrence gives me fear.

~ * ~

Which comes first, Montaigne the depressive, or Montaigne the skeptic?

~ * ~

Montaigne's *Essays* is a haphazard book. It is prompted by disillusionment, fatigue, world-weariness, idleness, listlessness, boredom. Against the all-too-modern idea of writing-as-therapy, the *Essays* offer something different: writing-as-distraction. A reader of the *Essays* will be disappointed if they go looking in it for the secret to healthy living.

And yet, for better or worse, the *Essays* have become part of the Western literary canon. Written intermittently over a twenty-year period, the first volume was published in 1580, with the second following in 1588, and the third published posthumously in 1595. By his own account, Montaigne seems to have conceived of the whole as a unified project, though the very term he uses to describe his writings – *essai* – denotes something more tentative, an experiment, an attempt, a "try," a whole less than the sum of its parts.

In addition, he again and again expresses ambivalence towards his writing, calling it a "chimera and monster," a "wild and monstrous plan," "these absurdities" and "this stupid enterprise."

So unimpressed does he seem with himself, that it fascinates him: "I am so good at forgetting that I forget even my own writings and compositions no less than the rest. People are all the time quoting me to myself without my knowing it."

~ * ~

Montaigne rises after seven, sometimes going back to sleep after breakfast. He reads on the toilet, often for long periods of time. He dresses in black and white. He cannot read or write with anyone else in the room. His walks are short and brisk. At the dinner table he is easily distracted if there are too many dishes. He eats impatiently, sometimes accidentally biting his tongue. Napkins are in abundance. Steak rare, even gamy. Oysters. Sauces. Melons. Radishes digest well one day, not so well another. Red wine one night, white wine another. Intermittent digestive problems, failing eyesight, nagging and painful kidney stones. He dislikes smoke and rarely drinks. He sleeps "hard and alone," buried under an avalanche of blankets.

Though he wrote against the enslavement of habit,

Montaigne also noted his predilection to daily routine. The slightest interruption could trigger a string of deleterious effects: "If my health smiles upon me and the brightness of a beautiful day, I am a fine fellow; if I have a corn bothering my toe, I are surly, unpleasant, and unapproachable."

~ * ~

Around 1576, as he is writing his essays, Montaigne has several *aide-mémoire* medallions made. Each contains the family coat of arms, the family name, and, in Greek, the Pyrrhonian motto "I refrain." Perhaps when traveling he took them along with him, like so many coins in a purse.

~ * ~

Friedrich Nietzsche

3 January 1889

~ * ~

Around 1885 Nietzsche writes in his notebook: "The opposition is dawning between the world we revere and the world which we live – which we are. It remains for us to abolish either our reverence or ourselves."

~ * ~

Nietzsche excels at his studies, but is always set apart – or always sets himself apart. In an account given by his sister, young Nietzsche would often walk about freely citing psalms and verses from the Bible, giving impromptu, mock-sermons to captivated fellow-students. Because of this his schoolmates christen him "the little pastor."

~ * ~

Nietzsche's father, Karl Ludwig Nietzsche, was a pastor at the church in the small village of Röcken, where young "Fritz" grew up. Nietzsche describes him as "the perfect picture of a country parson," who "led a quiet and simple but happy life." Nietzsche's father would die in 1849, when Friedrich was just five years old. The diagnosis was a "softening of the brain." Later, during one of his many bouts with illness, a thirty-two-year-old Nietzsche would confide to a friend: "My father died of an inflammation of the brain at age thirty-six. It is possible that it will happen to me even faster."

~ * ~

From a young age, Nietzsche experienced ongoing bouts of illness, producing, in his words, "the laughable diversity of my ailments." These reach their pitch on the third of January, 1889, when Nietzsche collapses in the streets of Turin after witnessing the flogging of a horse. According to some accounts, Nietzsche, in tears and sobbing, rushed to the horse and threw his arms around its neck, and then collapsed. He is taken back to his apartment, where, over the next few days, he writes several short letters. His friends Franz Overbeck and Jacob Burckhardt are disturbed by what they read. Eventually Nietzsche is taken to a sanatorium in Basel, where several treatments are attempted, including one by an art therapist (which fails). Nietzsche eventually falls mute, neither speaking nor writing. He is then sent to the care of his aged mother, before being sent to the care of his sister Elisabeth. In Turin, just prior to his collapse, Nietzsche writes of feeling in good spirits: "Wonder upon wonders!... On this perfect day a ray of sunlight has fallen on to my life."

However, this now-mythical event was preceded by a lifetime of illness. Nietzsche contracts scarlet fever at the age of nine. At boarding school he is plagued by frequent headaches, often forced to spend time in the infirmary (from 1859 to 1864 the school sickness register shows over twenty entries for the young student). The litany of ailments would only grow in the ensuing years: migraines, rheumatism, head congestion, catarrh, respiratory ailments, and a weak immune system. The migraines would sometimes last for days on end, inducing nausea and vomiting. His university days were likewise beset with illness, no doubt exacerbated by beer, tobacco, and brothels. He attempts rest cures, exercise, various tonics and medicines – at one point even prescribing chloral hydrate for himself, signing the prescription "Dr. Nietzsche." During his military service Nietzsche is injured in a riding accident. The pain from the injury leads him to take morphium, which induces foreboding visions: "What I fear is not the dreadful figure behind my chair, but its voice: not so much the words as the terrifyingly inarticulate and inhuman tone of that figure. Yes, if it only spoke the way people speak!"

~ * ~

In 1870, Nietzsche is a medical orderly in the Franco-Prussian war, carrying corpses or the bodies of the wounded. He contracts both diphtheria and dysentery, the latter of which would lead to the numerous digestive problems Nietzsche dealt with throughout his life. Bouts of insomnia follow. The illnesses, combined with the stress of the experience of war and the demands of his professorship, eventually take a toll on Nietzsche. In 1871 he writes, "What does it mean to be a scholar in the face of such earthquakes of culture!" A few years later, working on his never-completed book *Philosophy in the Tragic Age of the Greeks*, he is beset by an eye disease and forced to dictate much of his work to a friend. After his early retirement from the University of Basel, Nietzsche enters a period of wandering, seeking healthier climates – Genoa, Nice, Rapallo, Sils Maria, Tautenberg, Tunis, Turin. In an 1885 letter to a friend, he notes: "I do as sick animals do and *hide myself away* in my cave…"

~ * ~

Biblical texts were Nietzsche's first great influence as a child. In a way, his fondness for memorizing verses and psalms never left him, as is evident from the numerous parables, poetry, and songs from *Thus Spoke Zarathustra* to his "Dionysius Dithyrambs," among his last works. At the Pforta boarding school (a former Cistercian monastery), Nietzsche discovers the works of Jean Paul, whose combination of religious sentiment and incisive wit was to have a lasting impact. Nietzsche also discovers the poetry of Hölderlin, at the time relatively unknown (as one of his teachers noted, too "romantic"). For a time Nietzsche even befriended the poet, alcoholic, and vagrant Ernst Ortlepp, who one day would be found dead in a ditch during Nietzsche's schooldays at Pforta. While at university Nietzsche kindled his interest in Greek drama and music. This would eventually lead to his appointment, in 1869 (still in his twenties), to the University of Basel as a professor of classical philology – before Nietzsche had even finished his dissertation.

But the biggest revelation during Nietzsche's student days was his discovery of Schopenhauer. In one of his letters Nietzsche describes his morose state of mind during this period: "I lived then in a state of helpless indecision, alone with certain painful experiences and disappointments, without fundamental principles, without hope and without a single pleasant memory."

The fateful event took place in 1865, in a used bookstore in Leipzig. There Nietzsche innocently picks up a copy of Schopenhauer's *The World as Will and Representation*. "I do not know what demon whispered to me 'Take this book home with you...'" Nietzsche soberly notes that this was "contrary to my usual practice of hesitating over the purchase of books." But the purchase was to have a decisive impact. "Once at home, I threw myself onto the sofa with the newly-won treasure and began to let that energetic and gloomy genius operate upon me..." So great was the impact of Schopenhauer that Nietzsche initially felt he had discovered – or re-discovered – himself: "Here I saw a mirror in which I beheld the world, life, and my own nature in a terrifying grandeur..."

~ * ~

In one of his books, Nietzsche gives the reader a rare insight into his philosophical tutelage. He tells us that as a student he had made, like Odysseus, a journey to the underworld (to a library, perhaps) in order to hold council with the dead. "There were four pairs who did not deny themselves to me, the sacrificer: Epicurus and

Montaigne, Goethe and Spinoza, Plato and Rousseau, Pascal and Schopenhauer."

Judging by Nietzsche's later writings, what they had to say must not have been optimistic. And yet their dead voices were more alive for Nietzsche than the chatter of his contemporaries, those Professorial undertakers of dead philosophers. It is as if every phrase Nietzsche wrote aims to ward off philosophy, especially philosophy's corpse.

~ * ~

Nietzsche's influences, formative or not, have been well-documented. A year after his quasi-mystical "Schopenhauer experience" Nietzsche was reading Emerson, and a just-published book by the German Kantian philosopher Friedrich Albert Lange, entitled *History of Materialism and Critique of its Present Significance* (published in 1865). The former introduced ideas about nature and the eremitic life to Nietzsche, while the latter introduced him to the rigors of the philosophy of science. Readings of Rousseau, Darwin, Montaigne, and Pascal would follow. The reading of Russian philosopher Afrikan Spir's *Thought and Reality: An Attempt to Renew the Critical Philosophy* (published in 1873) extended Nietzsche's fascination with the rigor and austerity of Kantian philosophy. Later, the encounter of the works of Dostoevsky, Kierkegaard, and Strindberg. These and other references are found littered among Nietzsche's own writings and in statements by friends and colleagues. But after Schopenhauer, the other major influence on Nietzsche was his meeting

Richard Wagner in the fall of 1868. Their relationship has been exhaustively documented, both in Nietzsche's own works (*The Case of Wagner* and *Nietzsche Contra Wagner*), as well as in biographies and scholarly studies. As dominating as Wagner – and the Wagner cult – was, the influence of the composer was indicative of the centrality of music to Nietzsche's life, from his student days as an aspiring pianist to his last lyrical verses. His appreciation for Beethoven, Schubert, Schumann, the choral works of Bach, and the lieder of Brahms has been noted – though whether this was the appreciation of a musician or a philosopher is difficult to tell.

But with Wagner – as with Schopenhauer – the important point is that Nietzsche eventually went his own way – as if to indicate the fulfillment of an influence, rather than an abandonment. With Wagner in particular the break was decisive and bitter. Personal feelings were involved, anxieties and insecurities abounded, eclipsed only by the *gravitas* of egos. With Schopenhauer the "break" is more complicated. There is a sense that Nietzsche never stopped thinking against Schopenhauer, if not alongside him.

~ * ~

In the spring of 1888 Nietzsche – the prolific yet unknown philosopher – received some unexpected good news. At the University of Copenhagen, a scholar named Georg Brandes – with whom Nietzsche had been in correspondence – had given a series of lectures on Nietzsche's philosophy. The lectures attracted hundreds and constituted the first substantial exposure of

Nietzsche's philosophy to a broader audience. Brandes also introduced Nietzsche's philosophy to August Strindberg, the playwright widely recognized at the time for his stark and pessimistic rendition of modern alienation. Strindberg was so taken by the reading of Nietzsche's books that a brief correspondence ensued between the two. At first, their exchanges are enthusiastic and mutually respectful. But by December of 1888 – less than a month prior to Nietzsche's collapse in Turin – the letters become stranger. In a letter dated December 7th Nietzsche writes:

> When your letter reached me yesterday – the first time in my life a letter has reached me – I'd just finished the last revision of *Ecce Homo*. Since there is no longer any element of change in my life, it follows that this is no coincidence either. How do you come to write letters that arrive at such moments?

Strindberg, who recounts his own near-mental breakdown in his prose works *Inferno* (1898) and the posthumously-published *From an Occult Diary* (1896-1908), accepted the exchanges for what they were. Nietzsche sends a short letter: "Dear Sir: You will soon have an answer about your novella – it sounds like a rifle shot. I have ordered a convocation of princes in Rome – I mean to have the young emperor shot." The letter is signed "Nietzsche Caesar." Strindberg replies "Carissime doctor!" followed by a line from the lyric poet Anacreon, written in Greek: "I want to be mad!" This is followed by another quotation, in Latin, from Horace:

"Better wilt thou live, Licinus, by neither always pressing out to sea nor too closely hugging the dangerous
shore in cautious fear of storms." Strindberg then adds
his own line: *Interdum juvat insanire!*, which might be
rendered as "Sometimes it helps to be mad!" Nietzsche
replies with a short note signed "The Crucified."

~ * ~

Through biographers, we know of Nietzsche's family,
friends, and acquaintances. We know that Nietzsche's
reverence for his father was matched by his animosity
towards his mother and sister. And, it is fair to say that
Nietzsche's sister Elisabeth, in particular, did more to
botch Nietzsche's works than any subsequent editor.
Her conservatism found expression in her marriage
to the German Nationalist and anti-Semite Bernard
Förster (in the late 1880s the couple attempted – and
failed – to establish a German colony in Paraguay). Elisabeth not only took possession of Nietzsche's notebooks
and manuscripts after his mental collapse, but she also
served as the gatekeeper for the Nietzsche Archive. The
image of the convalescent, mute Nietzsche in the care of
his sister, dressing Nietzsche up in priestly white robes
so that followers could make pilgrimage to the "mad
philosopher" – is both absurd and sinister.

Nietzsche's relations with his friends fared somewhat better, though personal relationships seemed to
always be an on-and-off affair. For instance, there was
Karl von Gersdorff and Erwin Rohde, friends during
his student days in Bonn, with whom Nietzsche was
fond of playing music. At school Nietzsche attempted

to join a fraternity of sorts, though he quickly became alienated from what he called their "beer material-ism." They in turn would call Nietzsche "mad" because he spent all his free time inside, reading and playing music. He later joins the Philological Club, presumably more in line with both his interests and temperament.

During his stay in Basel, and later in Leipzig, Nietzsche not only befriends Wagner and his wife Cosima, but makes several other important con-tacts: the Protestant theologian Franz Overbeck (who would play an important role during Nietzsche's con-valescence), the philosopher Paul Rée, the historian Jacob Burckhardt, and the musician Heinrich Koselitz (who went by the name Peter Gast, a name suggested by Nietzsche, based on a music joke meaning "stone guest"), and who would often assist Nietzsche when we was too ill to physically write. Then there is Lou-An-dreas Salomé, a Russian-born psychoanalyst – fiery, intelligent, and independent, undoubtedly the most significant love interest of Nietzsche's life, though a love that was not to be returned – at least on Nietzsche's terms. For the biographer, these and other figures con-stellate themselves around Nietzsche like so many planets – near, but at a distance. In one of his letters to Salomé, Nietzsche writes, almost confessionally, "I don't want to be lonely anymore; I want to learn to be human again. Alas, in this field I have almost everything still to learn." In a later letter, feeling the pangs of rejec-tion, Nietzsche refers to Salomé as "a dried-up, dirty, ill-smelling monkey with false breasts."

~ * ~

In 1878, just prior to the publication of *Human, All Too Human*, Nietzsche contemplated using a pseudonym, in order to avoid the ire of the Wagner circle to which he was still attached. He even wrote up a fake biography of his pseudonym, Bernhard Cron:

> Herr Bernhard Cron is, so far as is known, a German from the Russian Baltic provinces, who of late years has been a continual traveler. In Italy, where among other things he devoted himself to philological and antiquarian studies, he made the acquaintance of Dr. Paul Rée. Through the latter's agency he came into contact with Herr Schmeitzner. As his address for the next few years is subject to constant changes, letters should be forwarded to Herr Cron's publisher. Herr Schmeitzner has never seen him personally.

Had Nietzsche forgotten how *confessional* pseudonyms are?

~ * ~

As with many pessimist thinkers, the key to biography is bibliography. While much has been made of Nietzsche's melodramatic life, the bulk of his adulthood was spent as an itinerant philosopher and writer – indeed, being a writer seemed as important to Nietzsche as being a philosopher. One of his earliest "philosophical" essays was written when he was just twelve years old. It was titled "On the Origin of Evil."

While a young professor in Basel, the title of

Nietzsche's lectures reflect his interests at the time: "Greek Music and Drama," "Homer's Contest," and "On Homer's Personality" (his inaugural lecture from 1869). Further lectures follow, on Aeschylus's *Choephorae*, Sophocles' *Oedipus the King* and the Greek lyric poets. And already, by 1870, Nietzsche is experimenting with a strange hybrid of the classical and the modern, writing his experimental essays "The Dionysian Worldview" and the "Manfred Meditations," in addition to poetry and even several autobiographical sketches.

Nietzsche's books are notorious for being anti-systematic, refusing to be pigeon-holed into a single argument or philosophical position. And yet, one can detect patterns. There are, for instance, the more "academic" writings, which favor the form of the essay, including *The Birth of Tragedy* (1872), *Untimely Meditations* (1876), and texts such as "On Truth and Lies in an Extramoral Sense" (ca. 1873). Here Nietzsche will take up a single theme – be it that of Greek tragedy or the work of Schopenhauer – and then proceed to elaborate, extend, contort, and disassemble it until it appears as something scarcely recognizable (a technique Nietzsche learned from Montaigne, no doubt). But calling these works "academic" is misleading, since books such as *The Birth of Tragedy* were staunchly dismissed by Nietzsche's professorial colleagues. Nietzsche's well-known essay from *Untimely Meditations* "Schopenhauer as Educator" is not only an attempt at a philosophical farewell but mixes the personal and philosophical in a way that is still unacceptable in philosophical circles today.

Things drastically change in Nietzsche's middle-period works (which some scholars have described as his "critical" phase). With *The Gay Science* (1882), *Beyond Good and Evil* (1886), and *The Genealogy of Morals* (1887), two changes are readily apparent. The first is that Nietzsche largely abandons the form of the essay for that of the aphorism, which not only allows for a great condensation of ideas, but also gives the impression of a book being multi-faceted, fragmented, and kaleidoscopic. Nietzsche scholars estimate that between 1876 and 1888 Nietzsche wrote approximately five thousand aphorisms.

But what is also apparent in these middle-period books is the way that Nietzsche becomes a philosophical marksman, zeroing in on the themes of morality and religion. There is a certain continuity to these works – they are much more musical in form, returning to themes again and again like a leitmotif, each time from a different vantage point, each time with themes and variations. The book that sets Nietzsche out on this course is *Human, All Too Human*, first published in 1878. It is a book that is written at an important juncture in Nietzsche's life. He is in the process of leaving academia for good; but he is also entering a prolonged period of illness and convalescence, wandering from one town to the next, from one room to another. Nietzsche is reading La Rochefoucauld on the train as he leaves Basel for the south of Italy, where he begins writing *Human, All Too Human*. And, while the influence of the French moralists is evident, the stylistic shift suggests something further. The essay and the maxim have something literary about them; the axiom and theorem have something scientific or mathematical about them. The aphorism stands in a grey zone, not quite lyrical enough to be literature, not quite systematic enough to be science. Beginning with *Human, All Too Human*, Nietzsche suggests that, precisely for this reason, the aphorism is the *only* properly philosophical style – at least for the kind of philosophy Nietzsche begins to formulate at this time.

But here again, we must double-back, because to simply characterize Nietzsche's middle-period works as "critical" ignores the shimmering exceptions – *Thus Spoke Zarathustra* (1883-1885) being the most obvious case. Perhaps Nietzsche's most widely-read book, *Zarathustra* dares to take up a critique of religion, in the form of religion. Nietzsche employs a range of stylistic devices, borrowing as he does from the prophecy, the sermon, and even a touch of mystical poetry (though often rendered as drinking songs...). God is dead, yes, but *Zarathustra* remains a profoundly religious book – or better, a profoundly *irreligious* book. It is as if Nietzsche's *Zarathustra* dares to put forth not only a religion without God, but a religion without religion. There is an overwhelming, even disconcerting enthusiasm to *Zarathustra*...

~ * ~

We do Nietzsche a dis-service if we credit him for the death of God. He just happened to be at the scene of the crime, and found the corpse. Actually, it wasn't even murder – it was a suicide. But how does God commit suicide?

~ * ~

Nietzsche discovered Dostoevsky's writing in February of 1887 while in France. In a bookshop he had come across a French translation of *Notes From Underground*. Nietzsche recounts the discovery in a letter to his friend Peter Gast: "Dostoevsky happened to me just as Stendhal did earlier, by sheer accident: a book casually flipped open in a shop, a name I'd never even heard before – and the sudden awareness that one has met with a brother."

Nietzsche becomes fascinated with Dostoevsky's life, his imprisonment, his poverty, his aptitude for psychological description, and in particular his unflinching depiction of human suffering. He describes *Notes From Underground* as a "frightening and ferocious mockery of the Delphic 'know thyself,' but tossed off with such an effortless audacity and joy in his superior powers that I was drunk with delight." A year later, Nietzsche is still reeling from the discovery, writing to a friend, "I count any Russian book, above all one by Dostoevsky (translated into French, for God's sake, not into German!!) among my greatest consolations."

But like many of Nietzsche's chance meetings with kindred spirits – including Pascal, Kierkegaard, Strindberg, and of course Schopenhauer – enthusiasm soon gives way to ambivalence. In November of 1888, Nietzsche is in Turin, a month prior to his mental collapse. Having just finished *Ecce Homo*, Nietzsche writes a response to his colleague Georg Brandes, a Danish scholar. Brandes has chided Nietzsche for his adoration of Dostoevsky, noting that "he is a great poet, but an abominable person, utterly Christian…" Nietzsche replies, "I believe every word you say about Dostoevsky; and yet he has given me my most precious psychological material…"

~ * ~

Digression from philosophy – in fact, digression in general – appears to inhabit all of Nietzsche's works of 1888, his final productive year. These are works marked by an unmooring of philosophy, both in content and form. *Ecce Homo: How One Becomes What One Is* extends Nietzsche's lifelong fascination with the genre of autobiography; the tone is so formless, nuanced, and obsessively textured, that it is impossible to locate Nietzsche the author or Nietzsche the character. When one reads through *Twilight of the Idols, or, How to Philosophize With a Hammer*, there is the impression of Nietzsche assembling a manual of style, operating at all registers, from well-chiseled essays to incisive aphorisms and ecstatic poetry – a poly-stylistic tour de force that encapsulates Nietzsche's interest in philosophy as style. And then there is the polemical voice of *Nietzsche Contra Wagner* and *The Case of Wagner*, chillingly distant yet amused prose definitively separating himself from Wagner, romanticism, idealism, nationalism, and nearly everything…

It is inevitable that, with a finale so mythical as that of Nietzsche's, a whole body of scholarship would grow around the unpublished works, as if to suggest that *corpus* and corpse might finally be fused in the pages upon pages of notebooks that Nietzsche kept throughout his life. The usual questions have long since been asked – should the *Nachlass* be considered a viable part of Nietzsche's works, and if so, how should one understand them? As unfinished masterpieces or simply as rough drafts and stray thoughts? Then there are the works that were either unpublished or incomplete – his early book on Greek tragedy, his lectures on the Presocratics, his many references to a book variously titled *The Will to Power* or *The Revaluation of All Values*, a book that would most likely have been Nietzsche's *magnum opus* (…and a book therefore destined to remain incomplete). And what of the book that Nietzsche's devious sister Elisabeth edited and published, *The Will to Power* – a book assembled and edited after Nietzsche's mental collapse, a book constructed with Elisabeth's own, proto-nationalist interests in mind? Finally, for those readers who cannot help but to find meaning in all aspects of Nietzsche, there are even the *Wahnbriefe* to consider, Nietzsche's final "madness letters," surreal and ecstatic missives shot out to friends, colleagues, complete strangers…A letter to Georg Brandes, postmarked a day after Nietzsche's collapse, reads: "To my friend Georg! Once you discovered me, it was no great feat to find me: the difficulty now is to lose me…"

~ * ~

Commenting on the influence of Nietzsche on him, Georges Bataille once wrote, "like him, I'm having fun laughing at the people on the shore from the perspective of a derelict ship…"

337

~ * ~

Though he is commonly regarded as a philosopher, Nietzsche himself was not so sure. With its mania for constructing elaborate systems, philosophy was perhaps too well-formed for Nietzsche. Perhaps what he sought was a philosophy with less integrity. An oft-repeated aphorism reads: "I mistrust all systematizers and I avoid them. The will to a system is a lack of integrity."

And yet, Nietzsche continued to write, up until he could no longer – or would no longer – write. A fragment from *Human, All Too Human* lauds the "incomplete thought":

> Just as it is not only adulthood but youth and childhood too that possess value *in themselves* and not merely as bridges and thoroughfares, so incomplete thoughts also have their value. That is why one must not torment a poet with subtle exegesis but content oneself with the uncertainty of his horizon, as though the way to many thoughts still lay open. Let one stand on the threshold; let one wait as at the excavation of a treasure: it is as though a lucky find of profound import were about to be made. The poet anticipates something of the joy of the thinker at the discovery of a vital idea and makes us desire it, so that we snatch at it; he, however, flutters by past our heads, displaying the loveliest butterfly-wings – and yet he eludes us.

~ * ~

Paul Deussen, a friend during Nietzsche's boarding school days at Pforta, and who would later, as a scholar, translate the *Upanishads* into German, once described Nietzsche's dwelling in Sils-Maria in 1887 as a "cramped and dingy cave," littered with "coffee cups, egg shells, manuscripts and toilet articles thrown together in confusion," set off against a perpetually unmade bed.

~ * ~

Blaise Pascal

23 November 1654

~ * ~

Of the life of Pascal much is known, thanks, in part, to the attentiveness of those around him who tried to make sense of a thinker who seemed to have one foot rooted in reason and the other in faith. As a result there are different images of Pascal – Pascal the scientist and Pascal the philosopher; Pascal the mathematician and Pascal the mystic; Pascal the activist and Pascal the hermit. There is the precocious student of science, who at the age of twelve, re-discovers the theorems of Pythagoras on his own. There is the engineer-inventor who, at barely nineteen years of age, designs and constructs a mechanical calculator (the "Pascaline"). There is the mathematician who does innovative work in geometry, arithmetic, calculus, and probability theory. As a young adult he begins a never-to-be-finished treatise of physics entitled *Traité du vide* (*Treatise on the Void*). Along the way Pascal comes into contact with the leading figures of philosophy and science (including a much-impressed Mersenne, and an unimpressed Descartes). All this in addition to miscellaneous work in civil engineering, linguistics, rhetoric, and meteorology.

But the central enigma of Pascal's life is religion.

Biographers often note of two "conversions" of Pascal, which took place roughly ten years apart from each other. The first occurred in 1646 when Pascal's father suffered a hip injury from a fall. The doctors who cared for his father and nursed him back to health were, as Pascal would discover, associates of the Jansenist religious community at Port-Royal-des-Champs. While Pascal, then a fervent student of mathematics and science, would remain skeptical of their religious ideas, one of his sisters, Jacqueline, would later join them. This first "conversion" is not, by any modern standards, a conversion. But the experience plants in Pascal the seed of a thought that would occupy him later in life – the relation between knowledge and healing, between reason and faith.

Pascal's real conversion would come some time later – on the evening of the 23rd of November, 1654, as Pascal himself notes. It is a vision in the tradition of the Medieval Christian mystics, and Pascal recounts it in a short text known as the *Memorial*. Pascal is quite precise in recording his own experience, noting, with almost scientific exactitude, a vision that lasts "from about half past ten in the evening until half past midnight." In addition to repeated references to Christological imagery, the *Memorial* is filled with brief, effusive flashes of ecstatic images: "Fire. God of Abraham, God of Isaac, God of Jacob, not of the philosophers and the scholars"; "Certainty, certainty, heartfelt, joy, peace"; "The world forgotten, and everything except God"; "'My God, wilt thou forsake me?'"; "Joy, joy, joy, tears of joy"; "Sweet and total renunciation."

~ * ~

In the aftermath of his mystical experience, Pascal ceases his work in mathematics and science almost entirely. He also takes several retreats at Port-Royal. When, in 1656 and 1657, the Port-Royal community comes under attack, Pascal defends them in a series of anonymously-written texts known as the *Provincial Letters*. Pascal, pretending to write to a friend of current events, uses wit and satire to ridicule the petty religious politics of his day, and in particular the ongoing infighting between Jansenists and Jesuits. The *Letters* were widely disseminated and read, making Pascal something of a local celebrity. The *Letters* also allowed Pascal to meditate on the complexities of religious experience, and over the next few years these thoughts would evolve into a plan for a major work on religion, which Pascal originally titled *Apologie de la réligion Chrêtienne* (*Apology for the Christian Religion*). Around 1658, now a central member of the Port-Royal community, Pascal presents an overview of the *Apology* to his colleagues.

But Pascal would never finish his *magnum opus*. What was left after his death perplexed both his family and his colleagues. Wishing to raise Pascal to the status of a saint or martyr, those at Port-Royal suggested that the *Apology* be published in its incomplete form. But even this proved to be difficult. To begin with, the papers Pascal left behind were in no particular order. Pascal's method of writing made things even more cumbersome. He wrote on large sheets of paper. After writing a fragment, he would draw a horizontal line. When a sheet was full, he would cut it into strips. The strips were stacked, and each stack was bound at the corner with thread. Pascal scholars refer to these as *liasses*, or simply "bundles."

The bundles are sometimes grouped around particular themes, and occasionally these themes correspond with one of the projected Tables of Contents Pascal provided. But often they don't, and many bundles don't appear to have any common theme at all. Arguments ensued about what to do with the bundles. One camp argued for publishing the material as it is, like an artifact – or a relic. Another camp argued for "finishing" the *Apology* for Pascal, using his 1658 presentation as a guide. In the end a compromise was achieved. The editors – from Port-Royal – selected the fragments they felt were the most complete, publishing them as is. Most of their intervention was in this selection process, and in the arrangement of the fragments under thematic headings (many which were not stipulated by Pascal himself). Finally, there were many other fragments that were not included, because, the editors note, they were "too obscure or too incomplete."

~ * ~

When, around 1669 or 1670, Pascal's colleagues at Port-Royal did finally publish the *Pensées de M. Pascal sur la réligion, et sur quelque autre sujets* (or the *Pensées* as it is now known), they expressed their own confusion and uncertainty in the book's Preface:

> As we knew of M. Pascal's intention to write about religion, we took very great care, after his death,

to collect everything that he had written on the subject. We found the papers all pinned together in different bundles, but without any order or arrangement because, as I have already said, they were only the first drafts of his thoughts which he wrote down on the little scraps of paper as they came to mind. And it was all so unfinished and so ill-written that we had the greatest difficulty imaginable in deciphering it at all.

There is a sense of disappointment in the Preface's tone, as if what many had hoped would be an epitome of mystical experience for the Enlightenment ended up crumbling into so many disparate fragments and hesitant confessions. (Their comments are given a further sense of irony in that, in French classrooms today, the *Pensées* is frequently studied as an exemplar of philosophical prose.) The Preface continues, noting that "when we saw them in that state, and were able to read and examine them with greater ease than in the originals, they appeared at first to be so shapeless, so lacking in order, and for the most part so little explained, that for a long time we never even gave a thought to the idea of having them printed..."

~ * ~

The fragments of the *Pensées* are filled with what appear to the modern reader as pessimistic statements on the human condition: "The only thing that consoles our miserable state is being distracted"; "We desire truth and find in ourselves nothing but uncertainty"; "Being unable to cure death, wretchedness and ignorance, we have decided, in order to be happy, not to think about such things"; "What amazes me most is to see that everyone is not amazed at their own weakness"; "We never actually live, but hope to live, and since we are always planning how to be happy, it is inevitable that we should never be so."

But these and other meditations on despair are a ruse for Pascal. Not that his despair was fake, quite the contrary. But every admission by Pascal of a life lived without God is always accompanied by the strange "reason" of faith and the life lived with and through God. Pascal utilizes a technique that Nietzsche would also leverage – he takes the reader into the absolute depths of despair, sorrow, and uncertainty, in order to come out the other side. This, of course, assumes that one does come out the other side, that the light at the end of the tunnel does not simply become the tunnel at the end of the light. What philosophers refer to as "Pascal's wager" is precisely this ruse – can you confront the "wretchedness and misery of life" and also accept the possibility that even then, in the depths of sorrow, you will be no closer to God than when you began? A fragment from the *Pensées* encapsulates this enigma:

When I consider the brief span on my life absorbed into the eternity which comes before and after – *as the remembrance of a guest that tarrieth but a day* – the small space I occupy and which I see swallowed up in the infinite immensity of spaces of which I know nothing and which know nothing of me, I take fright and am amazed to see myself here rather than there, now rather than then. Who put me here? By whose command and act were this time and place allotted to me?

If Pascal is a pessimist thinker, it is a pessimism that is always echoed by his devoutness.

~ * ~

For Pascal, there are two kinds of people in the world – those who "lament their doubt" and those who "live without a thought." Which live the more meaningful life? Which are happier, more content?

For a thinker like Pascal, both faith and reason dovetail into the question of the unhuman. There, all is obscurity. There is no beatific, shimmering, divine presence, only the *Deus absconditus*, only a hidden God.

For Pascal, it's all a ploy. Despair, doubt, and lament are a means to an end – Pascal wants to show us the depths of life without God, so that we will, in the depths of our sorrow, move towards a life with God. The *Deus absconditus* – a divine claustrophobia.

~ * ~

The deeply religious writer who meditated at length on the mysteries of mortality endured chronic illness throughout his whole life. In the final years of his relatively short life, complications that may have been the result of tuberculosis or cancer took their toll on Pascal. Unable to concentrate for any period of time, he became bed-ridden and eventually moved in with his sister Gilberte, where he spent his last days. Periodically wracked with spasms, his sister, who later would write a brief "Life of Monsieur Pascal," describes Pascal's traumatic physical condition: "...about midnight he was seized with such a violent convulsion that when it had passed, we thought he was dead." Père Beurrier, a priest from a nearby parish, attended Pascal, as did his colleagues and friends. But this comfort was offset by a string of opaque diagnoses and strange treatments by doctors, in perpetual conflict with Pascal's colleagues from the Port-Royal-des-Champs abbey, and who, in spite of Pascal's desperate pleas, stubbornly withheld the final sacraments from Pascal until it was almost too late. Added to this is the almost cultish curiosity over Pascal's corpse in the autopsy that followed his death. Pascal's religious colleagues were, no doubt, looking for signs of relics, while the doctors were more interested in the prodding gaze of medical science. It seems that the dual paths of religion and science followed Pascal's body up to and even after his death.

~ * ~

After his conversion, Pascal not only wrote down his experience in the *Memorial*, but took the parchment and had it sewn into the inside of his jacket so that it would always be near his heart (and "the heart," as Pascal famously wrote, "has its reasons, of which reason knows nothing"). But a problem arose. Sooner or later Pascal would have to change his jacket. His solution was simple. Pascal would re-sew the *Memorial* into the new jacket, repeating this as many times as necessary (unfortunately we do not know how many jackets Pascal owned, and how many times he changed them in a given day or week). That Pascal took this ritual seriously and executed it without exception is shown by the fact that, according to one account, the *Memorial* parchment was discovered in the jacket he was wearing when he died. It was a kind of mortification of the flesh, which Pascal practiced up to his death.

(I don't know why, but part of me is secretly disappointed that Pascal didn't actually sew the *Memorial* directly into his flesh, perhaps threading it just below his left nipple. There it might fester and flower forth from his chest in lyrical, tendril-like growths of unreflective black opal, gradually submerging his entire body – and later his corpse – into so many distillate specks of ashen thought.)

~ * ~

Arthur Schopenhauer

13 March 1820

~ * ~

Arthur Schopenhauer was the archetypal grumpy old man – even when he was young. In one of his books he writes: "…the world is by no means a necessary entity and something that ought to be… On the contrary, it presents itself even as something contingent, in other words as something that could just as well not exist; indeed it may well be regarded as something that really ought not to exist."

Those that knew him well, and those that only knew him by reputation, confirm the image of Schopenhauer as grumbling under his breath, scribbling on and on about a philosophy that was too pessimistic to be popular and too "mystical" or "Indian-sounding" (as his critics claimed) to be taken seriously in academia. This reputation was no doubt reaffirmed by the many elaborate insults Schopenhauer concocted for the philosophical trends of his day – indeed, Schopenhauer's many missives against philosophers deserve to be considered for their stylistic uniqueness. Negation runs through nearly all of Schopenhauer's works, whether it be in the form of criticisms of culture or a more ambitious desire to reveal the senselessness and "nothingness" of all existence. In 1846 the poet Hermann Rollet provided this description of the sixty-year-old misanthrope, who would often have lunch at the Englischer Hof restaurant in Frankfurt:

> He was a well-built and – albeit according to a somewhat outdated cut – invariably well-dressed man of medium height with short silvery hair, with whiskers trimmed in an almost military style, otherwise always smooth-shaven, of a rosy complexion and with bright, usually amused and exceedingly intelligent blue-flecked eyes... this comically disgruntled, but in fact harmless and good-naturedly gruff, table companion became the butt of the jokes of insignificant men about town, who would regularly – though admittedly not ill-meaningly – make fun of him.

~ * ~

Though as a philosopher he was steeped in the metaphysics of his day, Schopenhauer payed equal attention to the more prescient, yet less metaphysical aspects of physical existence. "There is only one inborn error, and that is the notion that we exist in order to be happy. It is inborn in us, because it coincides with our existence itself, and our whole being is only its paraphrase, indeed our body is its monogram."

~ * ~

On the 13th of March 1820, at one o'clock in the afternoon, a thirty-two-year-old Schopenhauer presented a lecture, on the philosophy of causality, before the faculty of the University of Berlin. It was a job interview. In attendance was none other than G.W.F. Hegel, then at the epicenter of a philosophical and cultural movement whose scope and ambition was matched only by an equally grandiose ego. Schopenhauer would get the job, but things didn't go smoothly. A heated argument followed, before he was finally granted permission to teach at the university.

For the students in Berlin – and indeed in European intellectual circles generally – Hegel was a celebrity, the philosopher who was already being written into the annals of the history of philosophy, the latest in a prestigious lineage that stretched back through Descartes, Aquinas, Plato and Aristotle. Schopenhauer had previously encountered Hegel and the other representatives of German Idealism, Fichte and Schelling. As a student at the University of Berlin some years earlier, a young Schopenhauer had attended lectures by Fichte and Schleiermacher, in addition to his own reading of Plato and Kant. But even as a student, he expressed nothing but contempt for philosophical fads, and especially German Idealism, a philosophy that Schopenhauer likened to "a cuttle-fish creating a cloud of obscurity around itself so that no one sees what it is." On Fichte's lectures, Schopenhauer would write "he said things that made me wish to place a pistol to his chest"; Schopenhauer's marginalia to one of Fichte's books is filled with hastily written reactions, such as "raving nonsense," "lunatic babbling," and so on.

The fact that the philosophy of Hegel and his colleagues was so in vogue at the time simply added fuel to the fire of Schopenhauer's discontent. He frequently refers to Fichte as a "windbag" and to Hegel – for whom Schopenhauer reserved his most virulent attacks – as a "crude, mindless charlatan" who had "made philosophy a tool of the State's purposes," preaching nothing but "obscurantism and protestant Jesuitry." To the large numbers of philosophers and students who followed these trends, Schopenhauer dismisses as "paid professors of Hegelry," mere "scribblers of non-sense" who were "sworn to the glorification of the bad." But the blame was always on Hegel, and the jargon-laden, "State philosophy" that his work represented for Schopenhauer. In one of his books Schopenhauer provides one of his more amusing rants, dismissing Hegelian philosophy as a "colossal mystification that will provide even posterity with the inexhaustible theme of ridiculing our age, a pseudo-philosophy that cripples all mental powers…" The result of such unbridled Hegelry was, for Schopenhauer, "to bring about the greatest stupefaction of people's heads" through "the hollowest word-mongering and the most senseless gibberish that has ever been heard, at least outside the madhouse."

The philosophy of Kant was difficult, yes, and Kant was no paragon of literary style – but at least the difficulty was offset by the architecture of Kant's system. With Hegel, Schopenhauer claims, we simply get intellectual posturing:

…the greatest disadvantage of Kant's occasionally obscure exposition is that…what was senseless and without meaning at once took refuge in obscure exposition and language. Fichte was the first to grasp and make vigorous use of this privilege; Schelling at least equaled him in this, and a host of hungry scribblers without intellect or honesty soon surpassed them both. But the greatest effrontery in serving up sheer nonsense, in scribbling together senseless and maddening webs of words, such as had previously been heard only in madhouses, finally appeared in Hegel. It became the instrument of the most ponderous and general mystification that had ever existed, with a result that will seem incredible to posterity, and be a lasting monument of German stupidity.

And yet, the controversy was mostly unidirectional; Hegel, by all accounts, appeared not to have even noticed the taunts of the younger Schopenhauer. The latter was, no doubt, just another nay-sayer gleaning satisfaction from chipping away at the heroic philosophical monument Hegel had constructed. Schopenhauer's invectives suddenly become a farce, a debate of one, an indictment with no accused. Still, Schopenhauer proposed as the title of his seminar something so general and ambitious it is hard not to believe it was a taunt to a mostly indifferent Hegel: "universal philosophy, i.e. the teaching of the essence of the world and of the human spirit."

~ * ~

At the core of Schopenhauer's philosophy is the basic intuition that we do not so much live, as we are lived.

From his earliest work in logic to his last aphoristic writings, his philosophy returns again and again to a basic gulf at the heart of human existence: we are in the world and of it at the same time. On the one hand, we are enmeshed in the world of which we are a part, and we observe it, measure it, interact with it, and even modify it towards our own ends. On the other hand, we are also aware that it is always we as human beings that do this, from our particular vantage point and with our particular interests at stake. Thus we have a minimal awareness that the world "out there," of which we are a part and towards which we act and interact, is also occluded from our particular frame of reference, a world "bigger" than us, scaled above and below our own perspective. On the one hand, a world towards which we direct ourselves, a world translated into our frame of reference, a world made in our own image – a world for us. On the other hand, a world that encompasses us, that is impassive and indifferent to us, a world that exists in the blind spot of humanity – a world in itself.

One of Schopenhauer's insights is that these two worlds are actually one, or two aspects of the same thing, the world for us he called "Representation" (*Vorstellung*) and the world in itself he called, simply, "Will" (*Wille*). For Schopenhauer, all the interminable, philosophical debates about idealism, realism, empiricism, and materialism missed this basic point, this black hole at the heart of existence – that we are forever occluded from the world at the very same time we construct knowledge about it.

This was not merely an academic interest for

Schopenhauer. For him, this irrevocable abyss at the core of existence was intimately related to the human experience of suffering. One of his late essays encapsulates this view:

> ...life by no means presents itself as a gift to be enjoyed, but as a task, a drudgery, to be worked through. According to this we see, on a large scale as well as on a small, universal need, restless exertion, constant pressure, endless strife, forced activity, with extreme exertion of all bodily and mental powers. Many millions, united into nations, strive for the common good, each individual for his own sake; but many thousands fall a sacrifice to it... All push and drive, some plotting and planning, others acting; the tumult is indescribable. But what is the ultimate aim of it all? To sustain ephemeral and harassed individuals through a short span of time, in the most fortunate case with endurable want and comparative painlessness, yet boredom is at once on the lookout for this... Seized by this, every living thing works with the utmost exertion of its strength for something that has no value...

Suffering is the alpha and omega of Schopenhauer's philosophy. His philosophy stands or falls on it (actually, it falls mostly, crumbles even, but its crumbling is what is most compelling about his philosophy). Not only did Schopenhauer agree with the classical Indian and Buddhist texts he had read that suffering was part and parcel of the human condition, but the very existence of suffering was enough for him to question the validity and meaningfulness of human existence altogether. His main target here is philosophical optimism: "...optimism is not only a false but also a pernicious doctrine, for it presents life as a desirable state and happiness as its aim and object...whereas it is far more correct to regard work, privation, misery, and suffering, crowned by death, as the aim and object of our life..." In other writings he is even more blunt: "In fact, nothing else can be stated as the aim of our existence except the knowledge that it would be better for us not to exist."

This is what Schopenhauer once called "the riddle of existence." What is it that compels us to live on, knowing full well the end result? We as human beings, endowed or burdened with consciousness, seem forever dangling between the poles of either striving or boredom:

> The striving after existence is what occupies all living things, and keeps them in motion. When existence is assured to them, they do not know what to do with it. Therefore the second thing that sets them in motion is the effort to get rid of the burden of existence, to make it no longer felt, to 'kill time,' in other words, to escape from boredom.

~ * ~

Reading Schopenhauer's philosophy, one has the sense that it's as if we are nothing more than lifeforms compelled to live, beings impelled to be, by some other, stranger, more diffuse and more impersonal force, even though we are well aware that, eventually, all will be for naught, and the self we have so carefully constructed will be eventually reduced to soil or ashes.

It is for this reason Schopenhauer calls this impersonal compulsion to exist the *Will* (which, in living organisms – and human beings in particular – becomes a "Will-to-Life"). "We are nothing more than the will-to-live" he notes. Elsewhere he states that "my body and the Will are one," and that the body is simply "objectified Will." But in using this term Schopenhauer intends no psychology. The Will is simply his name for this notion that we do not live, but are lived. The Will is not, therefore, desire, action, or volition (that is, it is not individual will). We may will certain things, and undertake actions based on this willing, but all this is for Schopenhauer secondary, derivative traces of the Will in itself.

Not only is the Will not human will, it is also impersonal, indifferent, and detached from the cares of any particular living being, human or not – as Schopenhauer puts it, the Will is "blind." The Will wills, and nothing more. It matters little whether it be through this species or that, through this existent or that. The Will wills, and for no reason. Its willing is not, strictly speaking, meaningful.

All this leads Schopenhauer to produce an ominous philosophy that gives one a sense of the incredible burden of existence, let alone life. "Being" – which so many philosophers have considered the pinnacle of philosophical inquiry – becomes, in Schopenhauer's hands, nothing more than a blind and indifferent urge, driven onward through different channels, manifesting itself in a myriad of ways in the deafening world into which we find ourselves thrown. What Schopenhauer calls "the inner antagonism" of human existence in particular is the awareness of this rift – between the world as Representation (our wants, hopes, and desires) and the world as Will (indifferent to those same wants, hopes, desires). The human being becomes little more than a striving, suffering epiphenomenon, behind which an oppressively raging Will urges itself forth.

~ * ~

Given the dire view of existence presented in his philosophy, it is no surprise that Schopenhauer sought ways to mitigate it, if not to refuse it entirely. Confronted with a Will that ceaselessly impels everything that exists, to exist, what can one do? Suicide is an option, of course, but Schopenhauer came down on the question of suicide – it merely solves the problem for you, an attitude that puts one back in the self-same world of wants, hopes, and desires. Only a "Willlessness" that is as stark and enigmatic as the Will itself will do. Schopenhauer mentions the practices of ascetics, mystics, quietists, hermits, those who practice refusal. But in the end this is still conciliatory. And, truthfully, few of us are up to the task. How can we live in the world, and yet refuse the tiring drama of striving and boredom? How can one live against life, while continuing to live? How should one adopt practices against life, in life? These are the questions with which Schopenhauer's philosophy closes – darkly, awkwardly, faltering. It is unclear – dubious, even – whether his own life was the reply.

~ * ~

As a Professor, Schopenhauer never tired of railing against academic philosophy. "Through the universities philosophy has become a livelihood and this has been its ruin"; "The philosophy-professors might possibly be of some use if they were content to teach sincerely what genuine philosophers have thought... they offer for sale the most preposterous stuff, as has been done in Germany for fifty years." Ever the pragmatist, he offers a solution: "It is very clear... that for philosophy nothing better could be done from outside and from above than for professorships in it to be abolished." But Schopenhauer concedes, noting that "only logic and at most a general and clearly presented history of philosophy should be permitted to lecturers..."

~ * ~

In spite of his attempts to provoke Hegel and his colleagues, Schopenhauer would indeed teach philosophy at the University of Berlin. However, he was not done with his attacks on academic philosophy. For the time of his seminar, Schopenhauer explicitly chose the same time as that of Hegel's. The ambition of the proposed course, and the fact that Schopenhauer had explicitly requested the same time slot as that of Hegel's lectures, could not but result in disappointment. The accounts of the particulars of the disappointment vary. When the first day of lecture came in the summer of 1820, it was said that only five students showed up to Schopenhauer's lecture, whereas Hegel's lecture next door was filled to capacity, as always. (Another account, which has to be fabricated, is that when Schopenhauer offered his seminar the following week, no one showed up at all – and Schopenhauer gave his lecture anyways.)

Schopenhauer's antagonism vis-à-vis the philosophical trends of his day brings to mind the cycles of trendy "theory" in academia and the art world today – lecture halls or galleries bursting at the seam with the disaffected and the eager, who clearly want to be there, but not too much. It is hard to imagine that the younger, more inexperienced, and less published Schopenhauer really believed that he could challenge the popularity of Hegel, much less the power-politics Hegel was known to play in the German intellectual scene. The futility of Schopenhauer's gesture is striking: better to ensure one's failure than to be uncertain of it.

~ * ~

Schopenhauer's time in Berlin was short, and filled with disappointment. His attempt to gain an audience for his work failed, his courses were under-attended, and his taunts to Hegel and his followers were largely ignored. His numerous attempts to see several translation projects through to publication all came to nothing (projects that included translating into German Baltasar Gracían's *Oráculo manual arte de prudencia* and Lawrence Sterne's *Tristam Shandy*). His on-and-off, decade-long affair with Caroline Richter, a Berlin chorus girl much younger than Schopenhauer, came to an end. He also suffered from a string of ailments: a nervous disorder in his hands, the loss of hearing in one ear, the early stages of arthritis, and chronic depression. And he was forced to deal with the ongoing lawsuit against him, for allegedly assaulting Caroline Marquet, a local seamstress that Schopenhauer repeatedly complains about in his letters – apparently the initial dispute was over Marquet's making too much noise in the stairwell of the building; Marquet accused Schopenhauer of verbal and physical assault. In a short essay Schopenhauer would later write: "We shall be quite civilized only when our ears are no longer outlawed, and it is no longer anyone's right to cut through the consciousness of every thinking being in its course of a thousand steps, by means of whistling, howling, bellowing, hammering, whip-cracking, letting dogs bark, and so on." In 1831, cholera arrived in Berlin, and with its arrival, Schopenhauer's departure.

Following these disappointments, Schopenhauer left academia completely and eventually settled in Frankfurt. In his biography, R.J. Hollingdale provides a summary of this final phase of his life:

From the age of forty-five until his death twenty-seven years later Schopenhauer lived in Frankfurt-am-Main. He lived alone, in "rooms," and every day for twenty-seven years he followed an identical routine. He rose every morning at seven and had a bath but no breakfast: he drank a cup of strong coffee before sitting down at his desk and writing until noon. At noon he ceased work for the day and spent half-an-hour practicing the flute, on which he became quite a skilled performer. Then he went out for lunch at the Englischer Hof. After lunch he returned home and read until four, when he left for his daily walk: he walked for two hours no matter what the weather. At six o'clock he visited the reading room of the library and read *The Times*. In the evening he attended the theatre or a concert, after which he had dinner at a hotel or restaurant. He got back home between nine and ten and went early to bed. He was willing to deviate from this routine in order to receive visitors: but with this exception he carried it through for twenty-seven years.

Other biographers provide a number of variations and supplements to this depiction. Schopenhauer wrote for no more than three hours in order to avoid becoming a "nonsense scribbler like Hegel." He not only played the flute, but collected flutes and other instruments as well, and when he played, his preferred music was Rossini (and not, as one might expect, Mahler or Wagner). In fact, when Wagner sent Schopenhauer a copy of the libretto from his opera *Der Ring des Nibelungen*, Schopenhauer sent back a short reply, noting that Wagner should stop writing music and focus on poetry instead.

~ * ~

Schopenhauer took his walks rain or shine. One can

imagine his curmudgeonly resentment as rain poured down on him. But, even when it was sunny, he was seen by the townspeople grumbling under his breath. Schoolboys would sometimes throw balls at him as he passed.

~ * ~

When he walked into a café or restaurant Schopenhauer would often place a coin down upon entering, offering it to anyone who displayed the least bit of intelligent conversation – he would even talk loudly about the prevention of venereal disease to make the wager easier (one would suppose). On his way out he collected his coin.

~ * ~

In the 1820s, Schopenhauer writes in one of his notebooks: "If it is said that life, from end to end, is nothing but a continuous lesson, whose results, moreover, are mostly negative, I might answer that, for this reason alone, I should have preferred to be left in a calm and self-sufficient nothingness, where I would have no need of lessons or anything else."

~ * ~

Schopenhauer is an example of an unconditional pessimist, and this is what makes his own brand of pessimism interesting – it is difficult to simply trace it to a key event in his life. From an early age, it seems to have been an intuition that formed a part of his character. Writing about his tour of Europe taken as a teenager some twenty-five years earlier, Schopenhauer compares his youthful discontent with that of the parable of the Buddha on first witnessing the world outside his palace:

> In my seventeenth year, without any learned school education, I was gripped by the *misery of life*, as Buddha was in his youth when he saw sickness, old age, pain, and death...my conclusion was that this world could not be the work of an all-loving Being, but rather that of a devil, who had brought creatures into existence in order to delight in the sight of their sufferings...

This almost gnostic-sounding sentiment recurs throughout Schopenhauer's pessimistic rants in *The World as Will and Representation* and *Parerga and Paralipomena*. But they are also not without a stark, embittered sense of humor. In *The World as Will and Representation* he notes: "The life of every individual, viewed as a whole and in general, and when only its most significant features are emphasized, is really a tragedy; but gone through in detail it has the character of a comedy."

According to one account, while living in Frankfurt Schopenhauer asked a colleague making a voyage to the far east to bring him back a statue of the Buddha. His colleague obliged, and once in his possession, Schopenhauer had the black-lacquered Buddha gilded. He cannot contain his excitement; the otherwise grumpy philosopher seems so pleased with the Buddha statue that he even considers showing it to a local Lutheran minister: "If only Reverend Kalb from Sachsenhausen showed up, he who panted from the pulpit 'that even Buddhism gets introduced in Christian lands'!... Reverend Kalb! Look over here! Hum, Mani, Padma, Oum!"

By one account, the statue was placed in the bedroom of Schopenhauer's apartment in Frankfurt, directly facing his bed. But Schopenhauer's own account has him placing the Buddha, with great pride, in his parlor room:

> It is totally genuine and presented entirely in the orthodox manner; I guess that it comes from the great foundry in Tibet; but it is already old. It will grace a console in the corner of my living room, and visitors – who at any rate enter the room with holy shivers and considerably dressed up – will immediately know where they are, in these hallowed halls.

Schopenhauer goes on to compare his leaner, more tranquil Tibetan Buddha with the "shorter, fatter" Chinese Buddha owned by a wealthy English merchant in Frankfurt. "Both," Schopenhauer notes, "have exactly the same orthodox, famous, gentle smile. The position, habit, hairdo, lotus: all are exactly the same!"

Another account has Schopenhauer placing the Buddha in such a way that it would be readily visible to a priest living in the building directly opposite his; in the morning the sun would illuminate the statue and indirectly flood the priest's apartment with light.

~ * ~

One of the unique aspects of Schopenhauer's philosophy is the way it is informed by Eastern thought. In the years immediately following his death, numerous philosophers took up Schopenhauer's "Eastern mysticism" in a variety of ways, some (like Nietzsche) quite critically. Traditionally, scholars have by and large tended to neglect this aspect of Schopenhauer's thought, sometimes dismissing it as a remnant of nineteenth-century Orientalism, at other times simply noting how Schopenhauer had misread or misunderstood the *Upanishads*. However, recent scholarship has re-visited Schopenhauer's engagement with Eastern thought in a more rigorous light, showing us a spiritual thinker deeply disenchanted with Western philosophy, and struggling to find a method for integrating concepts from vastly different traditions.

In one of his letters Schopenhauer remarks that he was introduced to classical Indian philosophy around 1813 or 1814 through the German Orientalist Friedrich Majer. The study of the ancient religions of the East was in fashion at the time, and the first translations of some of the key texts of Hinduism and Buddhism were being made available. Through painstaking translation, editing, and annotating of classical texts, the intellectual search was on for the religion of all religions, the origin of the religious impulse – the *Urreligion*. And, for a time, it was thought that the wisdom texts of ancient India constituted this primordial religion of all religions.

It is possible that Majer pointed the young Schopenhauer to Abraham Hyacinthe Anquetil-Duperon's

1801–1802 translation of the *Upanishads*, known then as the *Oupnek'hat* (a Latin translation of a Persian rendition of Sanskrit). While working on the book that he would become known for – *The World as Will and Representation* – Schopenhauer checked the book out from the Weimar library, along with a French edition of Antoine-Louis Polier's *Mythology of the Hindus*, published in 1809. Around the same time Schopenhauer had also checked out several issues of the *Asiatisches Magazin*. One of the volumes, from 1802, contained Majer's translation of the *Bhagavad-Gita*, a translation that Schopenhauer would use in writing *The World as Will and Representation*. Majer's prefatory notes to the *Gita* must have sounded like an invitation to Schopenhauer, just then formulating his own philosophy: "No interested reader will fail to see how these ideas and dreams, which are at least four thousand years old... stand in a marvelous connection with what a Plato, Spinoza, or Jacob Boehme believed and thought in very different times and regions of the globe..." Readings of the *Vedas* and secondary texts on Mahayana, Tibetan, and Chan Buddhism would follow. These and other works would be cited some thirty years later in Schopenhauer's article "Remarks on Sanskrit Literature."

In fact, Schopenhauer would, only half-jokingly, refer to his own copy of the *Upanishads* as "my Bible," noting later in life of the *Upanishads*: "it has been the consolation of my life and will be that of my death."

So central was Eastern thought to Schopenhauer that at one point he cites the *Upanishads* as one of the three beacons of his philosophy: "I confess, by the way, that I do not believe that my theory could have come about before the *Upanishads*, Plato, and Kant could cast their rays simultaneously…"

~ * ~

Schopenhauer was known for his fondness for his pet dog. When one died, it was replaced by another, each of them named Atma. The townspeople in Frankfurt tell of old Schopenhauer scolding his canine companion: "You are not a dog! You are a man! A man!"

~ * ~

Sometime around 1819, the mostly anti-social Schopenhauer noted to a friend, "Did you know that the three great pessimists were in Italy during a single year? Byron, Leopardi, and me. Yet none of us became acquainted with the other."

~ * ~

On a cold spring morning in 1805, Schopenhauer's father – Heinrich Floris – was found dead in a Hamburg canal nearby the family's home. The death was considered to be a suicide. Schopenhauer's father was also a long-time admirer of Voltaire.

~ * ~

Much is known of the standard biographical elements of Schopenhauer's life. His birth in Danzig, on the 22nd of February 1788, to Heinrich Floris Schopenhauer, a successful merchant, and Johanna Trosiener, who would later become well known as a popular novelist. A sister, Adele, was born a few years later. The young pessimist's relations with his parents were either strained (in the case of his mother) or estranged (in the case of his father). No doubt young Arthur was raised in a way that would prepare him to someday take over his father's business. Sensing discontentment on the part of their teenage son, Schopenhauer's parents offered him a deal: in exchange for his promise to continue his training as a merchant, they would take him on a European tour. They return a year later, at which time Arthur begins his apprenticeship in Hamburg. But tragedy strikes in April of 1805, as Heinrich Floris commits suicide. The death prompts Johanna to sell the family business and start a new life in the cultural capital of Weimar. Arthur ends his apprenticeship and prepares for university, throwing himself into his private studies of Greek and Latin. When he turns twenty-one, Arthur receives his share of his father's inheritance and enrolls as a student at the University of Göttingen before transferring to the University of Berlin.

By 1814 a series of significant changes are underway in Schopenhauer's life. He had just completed his doctoral dissertation, published as *On the Fourfold Root of the Principle of Sufficient Reason*, which, despite its academic-sounding title, remains a penetrating analysis of one of the pillars of Western philosophy, the so-called principle of sufficient reason – the notion that for every thing that exists, there is a reason for its existing. The work done in the *Fourfold Root* would allow him to take the next step and actually question the principle of sufficient reason in his later works, and even to attempt to move beyond it. That same year Schopenhauer began a life-long interest in Eastern philosophy, reading the *Upanishads* and the *Vedas*.

The year 1814 was also the year that Schopenhauer definitively split from his mother. Their relationship is, as biographers often note, a complicated one. While in Weimer, Johanna had been building a reputation for herself as a popular author, often holding literary salons ("tea parties") at her home – Goethe was a frequent visitor, and through this contact Goethe and Schopenhauer began an ongoing dialogue on aesthetics. But the relations between Schopenhauer and his mother had become more and more strained. The specter of his father's suicide, along with his own feelings of resentment, contributed to Schopenhauer's recurrent bouts of depression. The fact that Johanna had swiftly packed up and left for Weimar, leaving Schopenhauer behind, stuck in a business apprenticeship he neither wanted nor asked for, simply added to the already strained relationship. Schopenhauer repeatedly expresses misgivings about his mother's self-absorbed life in Weimer – though in all fairness she had mourned her husband's death and was now enjoying success in her own right. What remains of their correspondence reveals a real misunderstanding of temperaments. Schopenhauer was ever morose and critical of his mother's social-butterfly lifestyle, while holding a grudge over her abandonment of him (and, likely, of his father). Johanna's letters show her trying in all honesty to help her son out of his depression, though it took a toll on her patience. Schopenhauer accuses his mother of being more interested in her social status than the welfare of her own children; Johanna accuses Schopenhauer of being the victim of his own indecision, unable to take control of his own life. In November of 1806, feeling abandoned and stuck in a dead-end job, Schopenhauer wrote to her in the kind of tone that would later find its way into his philosophy:

> ...nothing is bound to hold fast in a transitory life; no unending pain, no eternal joy, no endur- ing sensation, no lasting enthusiasm, no higher decision that could hold good for life. Everything is annulled by the passage of time. The minutes, the countless atoms of small details into which every action decays, are the worms that consume everything great and bold. The monster, ordi- nary life, pushes down everything that strives upwards. There is nothing serious in life, because the dust is not worth the trouble.

Resentful about his past and uncertain about his future, the eighteen-year-old Schopenhauer's melancholy is both amusing and sincere, the sort of angst that has by now become the stuff of young adult fiction. Johanna's reply was as stark and morose as her son's letter, though more concise. She writes to Schopenhauer about "the melancholy brooding that you received as the inher- itance from your father." Exchanges like these set the stage for a final split. After a failed attempt to live with his family in Weimer, Johanna once again packed up and left for the country, writing a final note ("The door that you slammed so loudly yesterday, after you had conducted yourself extremely improperly toward your mother, closed forever between you and me"). After 1814 Schopenhauer would never see his mother again, absent even from her funeral in Bonn in 1838.

~ * ~

In 1831, a forty-one-year-old Schopenhauer intended to ask seventeen-year-old Flora Weiss for her hand in marriage. In her diary Weiss writes of feeling a "violent dislike" of Schopenhauer, which was "only intensified by his small presents." At a boat party in Berlin, Schopenhauer, attempting to court Weiss, offered her a bunch of fresh grapes. Weiss writes of her reaction: "I didn't want the grapes because old Schopenhauer had touched them, so I let them slide, quite gently into the water."

~ * ~

There is an anecdote told about Schopenhauer, who, in old age, actually became the grumpy old man depicted in his philosophical writings. One version of the story is that, while taking his daily walk, Schopenhauer came to one of the busier streets in Frankfurt. The disarray of carriages, carts, horses, dogs, and people produced a palpable irritation in the aging philosopher. Whether out of spite or resignation it is hard to say, but apparently Schopenhauer, tired of waiting for a clearing, simply closed his eyes and starting walking across the busy street. I like to imagine the flurry of thoughts that must have crossed his mind as he walked, slowly and steadily, across the street. Would he be run over by a rapidly-passing carriage, trampled by a team of horses, bowled over by a cart full of machinery or supplies, or simply tripped by mischievous children? Perhaps he was tempting fate or chance, or perhaps, for a brief moment, he sought to embody the futility and fragility of what it means to live a human life.

Whatever the case, in the end Schopenhauer crossed the street without any problem whatsoever. No doubt surprised, he apparently turned around and looked back, to see that everyone – horses included – had stopped to let him pass. They think he's blind.

~ * ~

Schopenhauer first met Goethe around the time the upstart philosopher had finished his dissertation. The meeting occurred through one of the many salons hosted by Schopenhauer's mother. Goethe then invited Schopenhauer to his home, where they discussed philosophy, poetry, and the arts. The encounter appears to have made an impression on the older, more established Goethe. In a letter to a friend Goethe writes of his discussions with "the *young Schopenhauer*," noting how, "with a certain astute obstinacy he is engaged in raising the stakes three- or sixfold in the card game of modern philosophy." Almost prophetically, Goethe comments: "It is to be seen whether *the people of his profession* will let him pass in their guild..."

~ * ~

Recognition came late for Schopenhauer, but it did come, in small doses. By 1850 Schopenhauer had managed to have further editions of his major works published, including a second, expanded edition of *The World as Will and Representation* in 1844, and a revised edition of his dissertation, *The Fourfold Root of the Principle of Sufficient Reason* in 1847. He had also just completed his last major work, a massive compendium of essays, aphorisms, and notes titled *Parerga and Paralipomena*, which would be published in 1851. Second editions of the minor works *On the Will in Nature* and *On Vision and Colors* would soon appear, both re-published in 1854. In April of 1853, a review article appeared in the *Westminster Review*, a radical philosophical journal founded by Jeremy Bentham, which featured contributions from the likes of Herbert Spencer, Mary Ann Evans (known by the pen name George Eliot), and John Stuart Mill. The article was titled "Iconoclasm in German Philosophy," and was written by the dramatist, critic, and translator John Oxenford. It helped introduce Schopenhauer's ideas to a broader audience. In the article, Oxenford "rediscovers" the philosophy of Schopenhauer, which he refers to as "a system of ultra-pessimism" that offers a sustained critique of Hegel's philosophy in particular, and of German Idealism in general.

Oxenford's article was translated into German a month after it appeared in English. It helped to spark a renewed interest in Schopenhauer's philosophy in Germany. Oxenford lauds Schopenhauer's philosophy not only for its rigor and critical acuity, but also for its antagonism against the self-aggrandizing romanticism and utopianism of Hegel and his followers. He applauds "the misanthropic sage of Frankfurt" for his persistence, for "working for something like forty years to subvert that whole system of German philosophy" that had become lost in petty academic debates and bloated speculation about "World Spirit." Along with Schopenhauer's eclectic references to Eastern thought, the desert Fathers, and literary figures like Calderón (all of which Oxenford's article makes mention), it was likely this stark pessimism that drew a new generation of readers to Schopenhauer near the end of his life, especially following the affirmative, heady romanticism of Hegel and his colleagues. With Schopenhauer, Oxenford notes, one gazes directly into the starkness of existence such as it is, a philosophy that sees not mythical "World-Historical actors" but instead a panoply of suffering, vanity, and hubris. British pragmatism, it seems, had discovered one of its own.

But how then to explain almost forty years of obscurity? Oxenford's answer sounds like it could've come from Schopenhauer's own essay "On Philosophy at the Universities":

But if there is really something remarkable about Schopenhauer, why this forty years' obscurity?... Because, he will tell you, he is not a professor of philosophy, is not a philosopher by trade, has no academical chair, and there has been an understanding among all the university professors to put down any man who is not one of their craft... As far as the promulgation of his views is concerned, he shall be doomed to solitary confinement, and every operation by which his opinion could find its way to the public shall be effectively stopped up.

This is, to be sure, one factor. But it is also likely that there is another factor, and that is the bleak outlook of Schopenhauer's world view. Pessimism is not the most consoling of philosophies – unless, perhaps, one is *already* a pessimist. Oxenford pushes Schopenhauer's pessimism to a moral extreme that Schopenhauer himself would have likely been weary of: "The world of phenomena is a delusion – a mockery; and the fact of being born into such a world is in itself an evil… The freedom of the will is, in a word, annihilation, and this is the greatest boon that can be desired."

~ * ~

Schopenhauer collected musical instruments more than he played them.

~ * ~

Near the end of his life, Schopenhauer would write, somewhat immodestly, in one of his notebooks: "Buddha, Eckhart and I teach essentially the same thing; Eckhart is shackled by his Christian mythology. In Buddhism the same ideas are to be found but not stunted by such mythology and hence simple and clear, in so far as any religion can be clear. With me there is complete clearness."

~ * ~

Nietzsche possessed several copies of Schopenhauer's *The World as Will and Representation* throughout his life. An edition from 1873 – among the books in Nietzsche's library held in Weimar – contains copious notes and marginalia.

Yet, in spite of Schopenhauer's frequent allusions to Indian and Buddhist thought, only a handful of these references caught Nietzsche's eye. One is a statement by Schopenhauer: "The creators of the *Vedas* and *Upanishads* were scarcely human" – which Nietzsche underlines. Another phrase of Schopenhauer's is singled out: "Nirvana alone makes it possible to willingly surrender the will to live" – to which Nietzsche has replied with a marginal note: "false."

~ * ~

Re-issues of Schopenhauer's books – including a third edition of *The World as Will and Representation* in 1859 – led to his works being taught, here and there, in the classroom. In 1855 the philosophy faculty at the University of Leipzig – in the city where a young Friedrich Nietzsche would first discover Schopenhauer's books – held a contest for the best essay on the work of Schopenhauer. Students made the pilgrimage to Frankfurt to have the opportunity to visit the misanthrope and his dog.

And gradually, one sees here and there Schopenhauer-esque books being published, mostly in German. Julius Frauenstadt, a former student of Schopenhauer and an enthusiastic follower, began writing articles on Schopenhauer's philosophy in the 1850s and 1860s, when the latter was still largely ignored (his book *Rays of Light from Schopenhauer's Works* was published in 1862, and the almost fawning *Schopenhauer: From Him and Through Him* was published in 1863; in his will Schopenhauer named Frauenstadt his literary executor...). In 1874 the poet and philosopher Philipp Mainländer begins work on *The Philosophy of Redemption*, which argues that a pervasive "Will-to-Death" must be the result of the knowledge that non-being is better than being. Mainländer's book would go unpublished at the time of his suicide on April 1st, 1875. Around the same time the German-British writer and translator Helen Zimmern published one of the earliest intellectual biographies of Schopenhauer, *Arthur Schopenhauer: His Life and His Philosophy* (1876). A few years after that Julius Bahnsen would publish *The Contradiction in the Knowledge and Being of the World* (1880), attempting what one could only call a blasphemous synthesis of Schopenhauer and Hegel. By the turn of the century there was a small but significant secondary bibliography on Schopenhauer, evidenced, for instance, by Johannes Volkeit's temptingly controversial *Arthur Schopenhauer: His Personality, His Teaching, His Faith* (1900).

But the most popular Schopenhauer book to be published during the era was Karl Eduard Robert von Hartmann's massive tome, *Philosophy of the Unconscious* (1869). It was at the time the most ambitious attempt to extend Schopenhauer's philosophy, combining as it does variants of pessimism, pantheism, Darwinian evolution, and the clinical psychology of the day. Next to Nietzsche, Hartmann did more than any other thinker to promulgate the gospel of Schopenhauer, though of course his Schopenhauer was of a particular type, a more "scientific" Schopenhauer, coldly revealing the indifference of the natural world, the organism, and the brain. For his part, Nietzsche never ceased grappling with the pessimistic endgame posed by Schopenhauer. When Nietzsche's first book, *The Birth of Tragedy*, was re-issued in 1886, he gave it the subtitle *Hellenism and Pessimism*. Schopenhauer's pessimism also reached beyond Germany, though in small and obscure doses, influencing French decadent authors such as J.K. Huysmans, who has the protagonist of his novel *À Rebours*, turn to Schopenhauer "to sooth his wounded spirit." Schopenhauerian pessimism also made its way further west, being introduced to American readers via Edgar Saltus' *The Philosophy of Disenchantment* (1885). By the first decades of the new century, an official Schopenhauer Society was founded by the Orientalist and Sanskrit scholar Paul Deussen, and one could readily detect the impact on Nietzsche, as well as on a string of twentieth-century authors (Jorge Luis Borges, Carl Jung, Thomas Mann, Ludwig Wittgenstein... And though he took great care to distance his work from Schopenhauer, Freud did own a copy of Hartmann's *Philosophy of the Unconscious*, and likely learned what he did of Schopenhauer from this book).

~ * ~

I like to think that, nearer the end of his life, Schopenhauer really began to appreciate the impossible ambition that is misanthropy. He had, after all, written pages on pages indicting nearly every instantiation of suffering – and human suffering in particular. It does not make for pleasant reading. His essay on what he called the "metaphysics of the sexes" reduces all sexual and erotic activity, inclusive of the entire culture of romantic love, to nothing more than tactical ploys for an impersonal and blind Will-to-Life, whose only aim is simply more life, at any cost, by whatever means, and for no reason. His notorious comments on women are still difficult to read to this day, and his hatred for the world of male philosophy professors inspired him to write an entire treatise on the topic. Added to this are vitriolic essays not only on philosophers, but also on priests, poets, and politicians, not to mention caustic commentary on artists, children, the elderly, students, "the public," and noisy neighbors. Even his pet dog didn't escape unscathed (especially when it was acting more like a human being than a dog). What was left for Schopenhauer to do, at the end of his life, but turn this vitriol against himself? The end of misanthropy is auto-misanthropy. Hatred of others leading to hatred of oneself. Some arrive at this, others begin in it.

In one of his last notebook entries, Schopenhauer writes: "When one has spent such a long life in insignificance, neglect, and disdain, they then come at the end with the beating of drums and the blowing of trumpets, and imagine that there is something."

~ * ~

Perhaps the most telling anecdote concerning Schopenhauer's posthumous "fame" has to do with Wilhelm von Gwinner, a jurist and civil servant who was to become the executor of Schopenhauer's will. After Schopenhauer's death, Gwinner proceeded to destroy nearly all of Schopenhauer's autobiographical papers. He then proceeded to write and publish not one, but three Schopenhauer biographies: *Arthur Schopenhauer as Seen at First Hand* (1862), *Schopenhauer and His Friends* (1863), and *Schopenhauer's Life* (1878). Not that this will help the grumpy old philosopher win any more admirers. But it is likely he would have preferred it that way.

~ * ~

An entry from Schopenhauer's last notebook: "The reason for growing old and dying is not physical but metaphysical."

~ * ~

Miguel de Unamuno

22 October 1936

~ * ~

The Basque philosopher Miguel de Unamuno is difficult to classify: he was a philosopher equally at home
in the genres of fiction, poetry, theater, and journalism.
His writing is at once deeply engaged with the problems – political and otherwise – of his time, and yet it
is also unnervingly unmoored from all attachments. He
shares a great deal intellectually with other existentialist thinkers of his generation who relentlessly examined
religion in the modern age – most notably Lev Shestov
and Karl Jaspers – but he was as weary of the mystic as
he was of the scientist. Like Camus, he was concerned
with the status of the human being in an increasingly
de-humanized world, but he held out no hope for a
renewed humanism. And like Theodor Adorno, he held
fast to the idea of philosophy as critique, but saw everywhere only contradiction and antinomy. Arguably, it
was Unamuno who allowed his fundamental doubts to
encompass everything, from religion to politics to science... to doubt itself. In one of his books he writes: "It
is not usually our ideas that make us optimists or pessimists, but our optimism or pessimism – of perhaps
physiological or pathological origin, the one as well as
the other – that makes our ideas."

~ * ~

The book for which Unamuno is most known – *Del sentimiento trágico de la vida* (*The Tragic Sense of Life*, 1912) – actually began as a secret diary he had been keeping for several years. By some accounts, this diary – which details a period of intense existential and religious uncertainty – was the only thing that prevented Unamuno from suicide.

In 1924 Unamuno was forcibly removed from his post at the University of Salamanca by the nationalist government. In 1930, following the fall of the dictatorship, he was reinstated. On his first day back, he began his lecture with: "As I was saying…"

~ * ~

Unamuno's sense of the tragic is a decidedly modern one – the result, simply, of too much thought. Consciousness is nothing more, he writes, than "a flash of lightning between two eternities of darkness." Furthermore, "if it is painful to have to cease to be one day, perhaps it would be even more painful to be oneself for all time and no more than oneself." In this ephemeral double-bind, we dimly intuit questions without answers and clumsily formulate problems without solutions. It all leads to "something which, for want of a better name, we shall call the tragic sense of life, and it carries along with it an entire conception of the Universe and of life itself…"

The crux of the problem is not just our awareness of mortality, finitude, and death – but our *concern* over these things (our concern to understand them, to make meaning of them, even to "fix" or at least deter them). "The human being, because he is a human being, because he possesses consciousness, is already, in comparison to the jackass or the crab, a sick animal." Unamuno puts it even more bluntly a few sentences later: "Consciousness is a disease." The only apparent conclusion from such a sentiment is that, as Unamuno puts it, "there is nothing more execrable than existence." Thought, stuck with itself.

~ * ~

Though he was critical of scientific rationalism, Unamuno was also fascinated by the demystifying capacity of scientific reason. In earlier eras, he notes, "efforts to make consciousness a substance and make it independent of extension – Descartes, remember, placed thought in opposition to extension – are only sophistical subtleties aimed at establishing the rationality of faith in the immortality of the soul." On the other hand, rationalism, taken to its extreme, dispenses with the last vestiges of theology. For instance, "scientific psychology – the only rational psychology – considers the unity of consciousness no more than a phenomenal unity." Thus a tension develops between consciousness and the life of consciousness. Unamuno continues: "it always appears that reason confronts our longing for personal immortality and contradicts us. And the truth is that reason is the enemy of life."

And yet, even here science doubles back. "Even those rationalists who do not fall prey to anti-theological rage still will insist on convincing humankind that there actually are good reasons for living and a consolation for having been born – even though a time will come, in some tens or hundreds of millions of centuries, when all human consciousness will have disappeared." A rift emerges between reason and life. "Sentiment cannot turn consolation into truth, and reason cannot turn truth into consolation."

This is the case whether consciousness is turned outwards, towards the world and the cosmos, or whether it turns inwards, towards the mind itself. Though a disease, consciousness for Unamuno also leads to its own annihilation. In a strangely poetic passage, Unamuno asks the reader to undertake a kind of meditation:

> Withdraw, reader, into yourself, and begin to imagine a slow dissolution of yourself: the light growing dim, things becoming dumb and soundless, silence enveloping you; the objects you handle crumbling between your fingers, the ground slipping from under your feet, your very memory vanishing as if in a swoon, everything melting away into nothingness and you yourself disappearing, not even the consciousness of nothingness remaining by way of grotesque handhold.

This is what Unamuno, in an evocative turn of phrase, calls "the rational dissolution."

~ * ~

Unamuno, the Basque philosopher who famously noted

"consciousness is a disease," was also an avid practitioner of origami, particularly of the *pajarita* (little bird). It was said he would often be found at his favorite café, not writing but folding *pajaritas* instead.

~ * ~

To ridicule. To be ridiculous. These are, for Unamuno, the only responses to the "tragic sense of life." The philosophy of ridicule, and also a ridiculous philosophy. "Don Quixote," Unamuno writes, "made himself ridiculous – but was he aware of the most tragic ridicule of all, the ridicule reflected in oneself, the ridiculousness of the human being in his own eyes?" A Quixotic philosophy.

~ * ~

Repeater Books

Repeater Books is dedicated to the creation of a new reality. The landscape of twenty-first-century arts and letters is faded and inert, riven by fashionable cynicism, egotistical self-reference and a nostalgia for the recent past. Repeater intends to add its voice to those movements that wish to enter history and assert control over its currents, gathering together scattered and isolated voices with those who have already called for an escape from Capitalist Realism. Our desire is to publish in every sphere and genre, combining vigorous dissent and a pragmatic willingness to succeed where messianic abstraction and quiescent co-option have stalled: abstention is not an option: we are alive and we don't agree.